"THE PAUSE THAT REFRESHES"

DAILY MEDITATIONS FOR SPIRITUAL RECOVERY

BY

REV. DR. EARL S JOHNSON
"PJ"

Acknowledgements:

For Marge Sanders and Kristi McFarland who lovingly and sometimes painfully typed this, and for Sherry Mattson who proofread and edited this! Thank you! Thank you! Thank you!

About the author:

Earl was born in Batavia, Illinois, on March 5, 1930. The son and nephew of several loving and funny alcoholics, Earl was raised in a world of heavy drinkers. He began drinking in college, seminary and while serving in the military. He began his road to recovery in the 1960's as he also began his second career as one of the leading experts in addiction and counselors of addicts. Over the next four decades, Earl earned both his Masters Degree and Doctorate in the field of drug and alcohol addiction and recovery. He taught many college courses on addiction and taught DUI (Driving Under the Influence) classes. He started several addiction treatment programs, including one for the homeless in Washington, DC, where he lived at Luther Place Shelter for eighteen months. During these decade, Earl, continued to serve his congregations as a dedicated pastor, and his family as a beloved husband, father of five, grandfather of fifteen and great-grandfather of three and counting...

Earl was a prophet, poet, political activist, philatelist, preacher and peacemaker! He loved jazz, camping, impressionist' art, theology, dramatic literature, haiku, bird watching and most of all, he loved baseball, first his Cubs, later his A's! He was creative, strong, smart, funny, thoughtful, forgiving, courageous, empathic, and kind.

The world lost a great soul when he died on June 30, 2003.

He continues to be remembered and missed by all who knew him.

dkj

JANUARY 1

A NEW YEAR

THE INSPIRATION:

"Sing a new song to the Lord;
Sing to the Lord, all men on earth.
Sing to the Lord, and bless his name,
Proclaim his triumph day by day." —Psalm 96: 1-2*

THE MEDITATION:

A new year calls for a new song! A song of thanksgiving; for the new day and the new year ahead with all of its possibilities; for God's grace which has brought us to this day through many trial and much suffering; for salvation made known to us through Jesus Christ; for sobriety without which nothing makes any sense.

Of the 365 (6) days in this new year, only one day, today, is of importance to us. We can live only day-to-day. Today is the only reality. Let us not dwell on the mistakes and miseries of days gone by, nor miss today by rehearsing for our tomorrows. Let us learn from our past mistakes and ask for and accept God's forgiveness. And with an eye to the future, let us live today, making the most of its possibilities; meeting its challenges, singing the new song that God has put in our hearts.

THE NEGOTIATION:

What is the new song we will be singing today?

THE PRAYER:

O Lord, thank you for this new day, this new year, and the new song in our hearts; give us strength to sing this new song to your glory today. Amen.

THE READING:

Psalm 96: 1-13

*Unless otherwise designated, all Scripture passages quoted are from The New English Bible, Oxford and Cambridge University Press, 1961.

JANUARY 2

DISOWNMENT

THE INSPIRATION:

"There are plenty to follow our Lord half-way, but not the other half.
They will give up possessions, friends, and honours, but it touches them
too closely to disown themselves." –Meister Eckhart

THE MEDITATION:

Disowning ourselves is no easy task. And yet this apparently is the task to which we are called. Jesus calls us to lose our lives for his sake in order to find life. This paradox of the Christian faith will never make any sense unless we step out in faith and experience finding life by disowning ourselves. The key to losing our lives is found in Jesus' words "for my sake." This means identifying with his life, his message, his mission. It means praying with him "...not as I will, but as though wilt" (Matthew 26:39).

Thousands of persons recovering from alcoholism have discovered the necessity of self-disownment. Sobriety and serenity are dependent upon a decision to turn our wills and our lives over to God. Because the task of disowning ourselves is so difficult, it can only be done a day at a time.

THE NEGOTIATION:

Is disownment possible for us today?

THE PRAYER:

Take my life, and let it me.
Consecrated, Lord, to thee;
Take my moments and my days;
Let them flow in ceaseless praise.
                    ---- Frances Ridley Havergal

THE READING:

Matthew 16:24-28

JANUARY 3

GRIEF

THE INSPIRATION:

"... you should not grieve like the rest of men, who have no hope."
--1 Thessalonians 4:14

THE MEDITATION:

Grief is what we experience when we lose someone or something important to us. The degree of grief is in proportion to the importance of the loss. Persons who are addicted to or dependent on alcohol, experience deep grief when they decide to give it up. Alcohol may very well have been the most important thing in one's life. Abstinence thrusts such a one into a grief situation.

Paul does not advise the Thessalonians not to grieve. He admonishes them not to grieve as others who have no hope. The Christian Gospel recognizes the importance and necessity of grief as a natural part of human experience. Grief may include many different stages: shock, denial, depression, loneliness, physical distress, panic, guilt, hostility, resentment, to mention a few. We need to understand that these stages are natural and allow ourselves to grieve. By accepting God's gift of hope, we work through our grief stage by stage as we readjust to reality. It is hope that enables us to emerge from our grief-work stronger, healthier, more productive and authentic persons.

THE NEGOTIATION:

Have we worked through our alcohol-loss-grief?

THE PRAYER:

Lord, when we experience loss, give us hope that we may grieve productively.
Be with us in our struggle to readjust to the realities of life.
Help us to emerge from our grief with a new zest for living.

THE READING:

Romans 8:1-39.

JANUARY 4

DEVOTIONS

THE INSPIRATION:

"He (God) plucks the world out of our hearts, loosening the claims of attachment. And he hurls
the world into our hearts where we and he together carry it in infinitely tender love."
--Thomas R. Kelly

THE MEDITATION:

The purpose of our daily devotion is twofold. (1) We provide ourselves a quiet time with God. It
is a time to be alone with and at one with God. The world is plucked out of our hearts; we are attached
to God alone, there is no other claim upon our lives. During this period we experience communion and
union with our Maker, our Redeemer, our Friend. It is in this unified attachment that (2) God hurls the
world back into our hearts. It is as if he says, "Now it is time to get back into the world where there is
work to be done—it is our work, yours and mine. There are people in need; there is pain, suffering,
injustice, oppression. Through your suffering, you have been given a special gift. Together let us use
your gift of sobriety and serenity in the loving service of others."

THE NEGOTIATION:

Does our withdrawing from the world result in a deeper concern for the world?

THE PRAYER:

We thank you Lord, for these quiet and peaceful moments with you.
Refresh and inspire us to walk with you this day that together we may express your love
and concern where there is need. Amen.

THE READING:

Matthew 11:25-30

QUESTIONS

THE INSPIRATION:

"Be patient toward all that is unsolved in your heart and try to love the questions themselves like locked rooms and like books that are written in a very foreign tongue. Do not now seek answers, which cannot be given you because you would not be able to live them. Live the questions now. Perhaps you will then gradually, without noticing it, live along some distant day into the answer."

--Rainer Maria Rilke

THE MEDITATION:

There are many questions to which we have no answers. "Why me?" "Why can't I drink like other people" "How did I get into this mess?" There are times when "why" and "how" questions are out of order. Times for "what" questions: "What is happening?": When the barn is burning down it is senseless to ask "How did the fire start?" At these times we need only ask, "What is happening?" and then put the fire out. Perhaps a day will come when the "why" and "how" can be answered, and perhaps not.

More important than getting the right answers is asking the right questions and living the questions now. "What can I do about my situation now?" Or better, "What would God have me do in this situation?"

We need patience with unsolved questions. It's all right for us not to have all the answers. Sometimes we're like the man who said, "Those people who think they have all the answers are very annoying to us who do." Let us learn to love the questions.

THE NEGOTIATION:

Are we asking the right questions?

THE PRAYER:

Lord, I believe; help my unbelief! Amen.

THE READING:

Mark 9:14-29

JANUARY 6

EPIPHANY

THE INSPIRATION:

"Jesus was born at Bethlehem in Judea during the reign of Herod. After his birth, astrologers from the east arrived in Jerusalem asking, 'Where is the child who is born to be king of the Jews? We observed the rising of his star, and we have come to pay him homage.'" – Matthew 2:1-2

THE MEDITATION:

Epiphany is a Greek word which means manifestation or showing forth. Epiphany, the twelfth day of Christmas, is when the Church celebrates the visit of the wise men to the Christ Child. The Child shows forth his glory to these foreign visitors. The manifestation of Christ's glory to all the world is the continued emphasis throughout the Epiphany season.

Astronomers have done no little speculating about that star which the wise men followed and many theories have been offered. The important questions for us are: "What star are we following?" "What vision directs our life?" "Where and to whom does it lead?" We have visions of sobriety, serenity, productivity, purpose and meaning in our existence. These and all worth visions come to rest in the majesty of Christ. As we behold his glory and embrace his life and message we too shall "rejoice exceedingly with great joy" and open up our treasures of love and service.

THE NEGOTIATION:

Are we open to God's manifestations of himself?

THE PRAYER:

O God, who in this day by the leading of a star didst reveal thine only begotten Son to the Gentiles; Mercifully grant, that we, who know Thee now by faith, may be brought to contemplate the beauty of thy Majesty; through the same thy Son, Jesus Christ, our Lord. Amen.
                                                              ---Collect for Epiphany

THE READING:

Matthew 2:1-12

JANUARY 7

ALCOHOLICS ANONYMOUS

THE INSPIRATION:

"Alcoholics Anonymous is a fellowship of men and women who share their experience, strength and hope with each other that they may solve their common problems and help others recover from alcoholism.

"The only requirement for membership is a desire to stop drinking. There are no dues for AA membership; we are self-supporting through our own contributions. AA is not allied with any sect, denomination, politics, organization or institution; does not wish to engage in any controversy, neither endorses not opposes any causes. Our primary purpose is to stay sober and help other alcoholics to achieve sobriety." -- AA Grapevine

THE MEDITATION:

AA is a program for recovering alcoholics whose primary aim is spiritual in nature. The AA program is very careful, however, to point out that it is not applied with any sect, denomination, or religious institution. This stance is necessary in order to provide a welcoming and accepting environment for any and all persons suffering from alcoholism. The Church, as a fellowship of the concerned and a healing community, and AA support and strengthen one another. The Christian truth found in the AA program will become obvious as we begin a series of meditations on the Twelve Steps.

THE NEGOTIATION:

Is there a difference between a religious and a spiritual program?

THE PRAYER:

God grant me the serenity to accept the things I cannot change, courage to change the things I can, and wisdom to know the difference. Amen.

THE READING:

AA Twelve Steps

JANUARY 8

THE FIRST STEP

THE INSPIRATION:

"We admitted we were powerless over alcohol—that our lives had become unmanageable."
---Alcoholics Anonymous

THE MEDITATION:

No one wants to admit defeat, powerlessness, or being unable to manage life. And yet it is this admission which is the very first step toward power and liberation. Becoming aware of our powerlessness and acknowledging it is the beginning of the truth that sets us free.

The paradox of power through powerlessness and freedom through captivity is seen in the words of George Matheson:

"Make me a captive, Lord, and then I shall be free; Force me to render up my sword, and I shall conqueror be. I sink in life's alarms when by myself I stand; Imprison me within thine arms, and strong shall be my hand.

Freedom is a decision more than a state of being. It is a decision to be a captive to God. When we make that decision, no problem is too great and no obstacle too high. It is then that miracles begin to take place. Indeed, life itself is a miracle. When we stand powerless before God, we are filled with his power. When we truly pray, "Thine is . . . the power," the power becomes ours.

THE NEGOTIATION:

Can we accept the paradox of power through powerlessness?

THE PRAYER:

We give up Lord. We surrender. We are powerless. Our lives are indeed unmanageable. Full us with your power as we stand empty before you. Guide us to make and live out the decision to be your captives that we may be free to do your will this day. Amen.

THE READING:

Romans 7:13-20

THE SECOND STEP

THE INSPIRATION:

"Came to believe that a power greater than ourselves could restore us to sanity."
--Alcoholics Anonymous

THE MEDITATION:

Having admitted powerlessness we look for a power greater than ourselves. That power is "God, the Father, Almighty, Maker of heaven and earth, and of all things visible and invisible." That power is not an impersonal, vague, indefinite blur but rather a personal, almighty Father. It is power revealed to us by Jesus as a loving, caring Person. One to whom he could say, "Father, into thy hands I commit my spirit!" (Luke 23:46)

God did not create the world and walk away from it. He began the creative process and is concerned about and involved in its continuation and development. The Creator loves His creation. He allows us to share in the creative process as we share his love and thereby bring new love to his world. The mystery of all mysteries is that this Almighty Power is available to restore us to sanity.

THE NEGOTIATION:

Doesn't being restored to sanity imply we were insane?

THE PRAYER:

Almighty God, Creator of all that exists: pour your power out upon us, and in your bountiful goodness keep us from all things that may harm us, that restored to sanity, we may cheerfully love and serve you in creation. Amen.

THE READING:

Psalm 8:1-9

JANUARY 10

THE THIRD STEP

THE INSPIRATION:

"Made a decision to turn our will and our lives over to the care of God as we understood Him."
--Alcoholics Anonymous

THE MEDITATION:

In the first step we admitted we couldn't handle alcohol. In the second step we professed faith that God could help us. Now, in the third step, we decide to let him do it. A word for turning our will and our lives over to the care of God is surrender.

A man, while climbing a mountain, lost his footing and fell off a steep cliff. He caught himself on a branch and hung on for dear life over a thousand-foot drop. It was then he called, "Lord, help me!" The Lord answered, "I'll help you if you trust me." "I trust you," cried the man. "Then," said the Lord, "let go of that branch."

Surrender means "let go—let God." When this happens we are open to reality, receptive to life, and sense feelings of relatedness and at-one-ment which becomes a source of inner peace and serenity, the possession of which frees us from the compulsion to drink.

Surrender is a process—a continuing and daily need.

THE NEGOTIATION:

Are we ready for unconditional surrender?

THE PRAYER:

O God, forasmuch as without thee we are not able to please thee: Mercifully grant, that thy Holy Spirit may in all things direct and rule our hearts; through your son, Jesus Christ our Lord. Amen.

THE READING:

Matthew 26:36-46

JANUARY 11

THE FOURTH STEP

THE INSPIRATION:

"Made a searching and fearless moral inventory of ourselves."
--Alcoholics Anonymous

THE MEDITATION:

A searching and fearless moral inventory is a very difficult and trying exercise. And yet such an exercise is necessary and can be a very rewarding experience. Let us pray with the Psalmist:

"Examine me, Oh God, and know my thoughts,
Trust me, and understand my misgivings.
Watch lest I follow any path that grieves thee;
Guide me in the ancient ways." Psalm 139:23-24

We truly search ourselves when we come to a deeper knowledge of our defects, earnestly long for the grace of God, and are led by God to a loving spirit toward others. A radical honesty is required to discover our defects. The more radical the honesty the greater the reward.

An honest inventory will be a ledger with two sides. Our moral inventory will show a positive side as well as the negative. The Fourth Step enables us to get a two dimensional picture of ourselves so that we may go to work eliminating our defects and nurturing our strengths.

THE NEGOTIATION:

Are we aware of any dishonesty in ourselves?

THE PRAYER:

Lord, we are self-adoring egomaniacs who despise the objects of our affection. Help us to know ourselves as you know us; full of defects and objects of our affection. Amen.

THE READING:

Psalm 139:1-24

JANUARY 12

THE FIFTH STEP

THE INSPIRATION:

"Admitted to God, to ourselves, and to another human being, the exact nature of our wrongs."
--Alcoholics Anonymous

THE MEDITATION:

There may be things we discover about ourselves in our "searching and fearless moral inventory" that we have difficulty believing God can forgive. It is when we question God's willingness to forgive and accept us that we need "another human being" to declare God's grace to us. James admonishes the Church to "confess your sins to one another" (James 5:16). Jesus recognized the importance of this form of confession and absolution when he said, "If you forgive the sins of any, they are forgiven." (John 20:23). Confession and absolution is a gift that Jesus has given to his Church.

We are not speaking here of simply "getting something off our chest," as valuable as that may be. Nor are we referring to "pouring out our hearts" as to a psychiatrist, which also has value. It is Christ's gift to his Church of confession and absolution of which we speak. The confessee acknowledges his or her sinful plight to God in the presence of a trusted Christian confessor who in turn declares God's forgiveness. The power of utilizing this gift of Christ must never be underestimated.

THE NEGOTIATION:

Can we trust ourselves to trust others?

THE PRAYER:

O God, our heavenly Father, I confess unto Thee that I have grievously sinned against thee in many ways; not only by outward transgressions, but also by secret thoughts and desires which I cannot fully understand, but which are all known unto thee. Amen. –Order for Public Confession.

THE READING:

John 20:19-23

JANUARY 13

THE SIXTH STEP

THE INSPIRATION:

"Were entirely ready to have God remove all these defects of character."
--Alcoholics Anonymous

THE MEDITATION:

We have been assured that "if we confess our sins, he (God) is faithful and just, and will forgive our sins and cleanse us from all unrighteousness" (1 John 1:9). Confession means more than listing or naming our sins; it means real, genuine, heartfelt repentance followed by a sincere desire, with God's help, to amend our lives and be renewed in the Spirit. It is in this sense of confession that the Psalmist rejoices:
"Happy the man whose disobedience is forgiven, whose sin is put away!"

God is by nature loving and forgiving. Let us allow him to express his nature and accept his acceptance of us. The slate is clean; we are pure and righteous in God's eyes. Being willing to allow God to remove our defects of character, we are now ready to be strengthened in our fellowship with God and with one another, and ready to receive the assurance and power of all that is implied in "the new life in Christ."

THE NEGOTIATION:

Are we ready to give up destructive thinking and behavior?

THE PRAYER:

Almighty and merciful God, grant unto us, being penitent, pardon and remission of all of our sins, time for amendment of life, and the grace and comfort of your Holy Spirit. Amen. –The Absolution

THE READING:

1 John 1:5-10

THE SEVENTH STEP

THE INSPIRATION:

"Humbly asked Him to remove our shortcomings."
--Alcoholics Anonymous

THE MEDITATION:

Humility is the road which leads to serenity. Humility must not be mistaken for the absence of self-love, which is essential for serenity. Without a love of one's self we would be incapable of loving others. Humility is, rather, the absence of self-adoration. It denotes an honest evaluation of one's self.

Among the work for which Christ's gospel came into the world was not less than to put down the mighty from their thrones, and to exalt the humble (Luke 1:52). When discussing with his disciples who is the greatest in the Kingdom of Heaven Jesus pointed to a child and said, "let a man humble himself till he is like this child, and he will be the greatest . . . " (Matthew 18:4).

A whole life-time geared to self-centeredness is not easily and abruptly reversed. Humility, as a process, is the product of the Holy Spirit in the yielding believer. The gift of humility is recognized by Paul when he says, "Don't cherish exaggerated ideas of yourself . . . but try to have a sane estimate of your capacities by . . . the faith that God has given you" (Romans 12:3 Phillips).

THE NEGOTIATION:

They gave me a medal for humility and when I wore it they took it away.

THE PRAYER:

O God, who opposes the proud, but gives grace to the humble; enable us to be so overwhelmed with your glory that we may humbly walk with you this day. Amen.

THE READING:

Romans 12:3-8

JANUARY 15

THE EIGHTH STEP

THE INSPIRATION:

"Made a list of all persons we had harmed, and became willing to make amends to them all.
--Alcoholics Anonymous

THE MEDITATION:

Serenity is dependent upon our relationships: with God, with ourselves, with others. Our vertical relationship with God is automatically expanded into a horizontal relationship with others. If we are right with God we are compelled to get right with others. "We love because he loved us first. But if a man says, 'I love God', while hating his brother, he is a liar." (1 John 4:19-20).

The task of making amends to persons we may have harmed through alcohol abuse is a tedious one. And yet, this is a necessary task. It is primarily our need. We may discover that the exercise of making amends is more valuable for us than those we have harmed. It is a risky task, for our overtures toward reconciliation may be rejected. If this be the case we must leave the matter in God's hands. When our acknowledgements of fault are accepted, we will experience the beauty of reconciliation.

There may be persons whom we have harmed beyond our awareness. Again, we can only leave our unknown victims in God's hands.

THE NEGOTIATION:

Making amends: whose need is it?

THE PRAYER:

As we make our peace with you, O Lord, give us the strength and courage to be reconciled with our brothers and sisters. Help us this day to seek out and make amends with someone we may have harmed. Amen.

THE READING: 1 John 4:13-21

JANUARY 16

THE NINTH STEP

THE INSPIRATION:

"Made direct amends to such people wherever possible, except when to do so would injure them or others." --Alcoholics Anonymous

THE MEDITATION:

Among the most difficult of all words to learn to say are, "I'm sorry – I was wrong!" Perhaps our reluctance to say these words is due to our unwillingness to admit to ourselves the truth. We can be wrong, we can make mistakes, we can behave foolishly and badly. A mature person is one who assumes responsibility for his or her behavior. It is the immature person who refuses to take responsibility and blames his or her behavior on "being brought up on the wrong side of the tracks" or on "being potty-trained wrong" or whatever. Adam blames Eve, Eve blames the serpent, "The devil made me do it." David resisted assuming responsibility until he was confronted by Nathan: "You are the Man!" (2 Samuel 12:7).

God has given each of us free will. We are responsible for the decisions we make and the manner in which we behave. Accepting this fact makes it easier to learn to say, "I'm sorry—I was wrong!" The more we say it, and mean it, the easier it becomes.

THE NEGOTIATION:

Does saying, "I'm sorry," do us any good?

THE PRAYER:

O Lord, we give thanks to you for the greatest of all your gifts to us: freedom of our wills. Keep us from abusing this gift, and give us strength to live as free men and women assuming responsibility for our actions. Amen.

THE READING:

2 Samuel 12:1-15

JANUARY 17

THE TENTH STEP

THE INSPIRATION:

"Continued to take personal inventory and when we were wrong promptly admitted it."
---Alcoholics Anonymous

THE MEDITATION:

Our personal inventory should include two categories: wrong which we have done _and_ good which we have left undone. Too often we dwell on the first and neglect the second. There are sins of commission _and_ sins of omission. In Jesus' story of the Jericho Road (Luke 10:30-37) those who beat up, rob, and leave the man half-dead are condemned but so are the priest and the Levite who "pass by on the other side." Ours is a double ledger inventory. It's not only, "Who have I harmed today?" but also, "Who haven't I helped?—What human need have I passed by?"

Personal inventory is not an activity we engage in once in a life time or even from time to time, but rather an ongoing process. Continuing personal inventory enables us to keep right with others and with God.

"By baptism we were buried with him, and lay dead, in order that, as Christ was raised from the dead in the splendor of the Father, so also we might set our feet upon the new path of life" (Romans 6:4). Dying daily to sin means rising daily to new life.

THE NEGOTIATION:

What human need will we respond to today?

THE PRAYER:

Dear Lord, we confess to you that we have sinned both in our actions and in our failure to act. Being forgiven and accepted by you, enable us to be reconciled with others. Amen.

THE READING: Romans 6:1-11

THE ELEVENTH STEP

THE INSPIRATION:

"Sought through prayer and meditation to improve our conscious contact with God as we understand Him, praying only for knowledge of His will for us and the power to carry that out.
--Alcoholics Anonymous

THE MEDITATION:

Devotion, for many people, is limited to a daily schedule of religious exercises. Others think of it more in terms of faithfulness to a task one has assumed. Again, there are those who emphasize the emotional or mystical dimensions of devotion, describing it as expressing a feeling of attraction. All of these are too narrow to express the essence of the Christian life. Devotion is understood as the total framework of one's existence as a Christian: one's point of view, one's perspective, one's center and circumference, one's spirit, and one's work. It is not a description of something one does, but of what one is and how it informs every dimension of one's life.

The religious exercise in which we are now engaged is that activity which concerns itself with ourselves and with God in which "he plucks the world out of our hearts and puts the world into our hearts." This limited, but not restricted activity is confined to certain periods of time, but related to everything we do each day. It is in this sense that we do our daily devotions.

THE NEGOTIATION:

Can this exercise have an effect on me today?

THE PRAYER:

We thank you Lord, for these precious moments when we may negotiate with ourselves and with you. Speak to us now: "be still, and know that I am God." We are listening, Lord. Speak your will for us and give us the power to carry it out. Amen.

THE READING: Psalm 46:1-11

JANUARY 19

THE TWELFTH STEP

THE INSPIRATION:

"Having had a spiritual awakening as the result of these steps, we tried to carry the message to alcoholics, and to practice these principles in all of our affairs." –Alcoholics Anonymous

THE MEDITATION:

There are many persons who are recovering from alcoholism who will say they are glad they are alcoholics. Not glad about the suffering endured or the pain caused others, but glad that the result of the total experience has been a spiritual awakening. Were it not for the misery of alcohol abuse in the past, we may not have found the spiritual insight we enjoy today. We have experienced the truth of Paul's statement: " . . . in everything God works for good with those who love him" (Romans 8:28). Everything that happens is not good in and of itself, but good can come out of everything when we love God. Many of us have come to know and love him in the abyss.

Having survived the abyss of alcoholism and come to a spiritual awakening, we have been given a special and rare gift. A gift we are called to pass on to others. The paradox of this gift is that the more we share it, the more precious it becomes to us. We have been given the message for a purpose. That purpose lies not only in us but also in carrying the message to others.

THE NEGOTIATION:

Have we experienced a spiritual awakening?

THE PRAYER:

We thank you Lord, for the great and precious gift that you have given to us. Having had a spiritual awakening, help us to share this gift with others. Amen.

THE READING: Romans 8:26-30

JANUARY 20

FAITH

THE INSPIRATION:

"And what is faith? Faith gives substance to our hopes, and makes us certain of realities we do not see. —Hebrew 11:1

THE MEDITATION:

Faith is not, as the Sunday School boy said, "Believing what you know ain't true." Faith is assurance and conviction. Faith is not proof or fact in the scientific sense. As Tennyson put it:

"Strong son of God, immortal Love,
Whom we, that have not seen thy face,
By faith, and faith alone, embrace,
Believing where we cannot prove."

We speak only of the Christian faith, not the Christian proof. The Christian faith means betting our lives that God is as Jesus says he is. The fact of this faith is God's power in our lives, power where we were powerless. No recovered alcoholic can deny miracles—we are miracles! Faith makes miracles of our lives; faith makes us laugh at powerlessness; faith gives us hope in hopelessness; faith gives us peace in turmoil; faith gives us love in lovelessness. Faith is betting our lives on God and daring to live as if he is as Jesus says he is. That's assurance! That's conviction.

THE NEGOTIATION:

Are we ready to bet our lives on God?

THE PRAYER:

Almighty and everlasting God, who hast given to them that believe great and previous promises; Grant us so perfectly, and without all doubt, to believe in thy Son Jesus Christ, that our faith in thy sight may never be reproved. Amen. —Collect for Faith

THE READING: Matthew 17:14-21

JANUARY 21

LIGHT

THE INSPIRATION:

"The real light which enlightens every man was even then coming into the world."
        --John 1:9
"I am the light of the world." --John 8:12
"You are the light for all the world." --Matthew 5:14

THE MEDITATION:

A recurring theme throughout the Epiphany Season is light which is one of the more popular and meaningful symbols in the Bible. It begins in the first chapter of Genesis: "God said, 'Let there be light;' and there was light. And God saw the light was good" (:3-4). But humans didn't think so—the light was too bright for them—they preferred to live in darkness. Yet God doesn't become discouraged, he sends "the true light" into the world. "I am the light of the world," he says. And he doesn't stop there, but continues, "You are the light of the world." As the Father sends Jesus into the world so Jesus sends us into the world.

Consider how much of our drinking was done in the dark—quite literally in dingy places which the world calls atmosphere. How many precious hours have we sat in the dark of alcohol influence? "The People who sat in darkness have seen a great light" (Isaiah 9:2). He is the light of the world, who sends us, into the world to be light.

THE NEGOTIATION:

What things would we rather do in the dark? Why?

THE PRAYER:

O God, who has revealed to us the brightness of the true Light, we give thanks to you that we no longer must sit in darkness. And we pray that as we come to know the mysteries of that Light, that we may joyfully bring your Light to others. Amen.

THE READING: John 1:1-12

JANUARY 22

THE BIBLE AND ALCOHOL

THE INSPIRATION:

"Shame on you! You who rise early in the morning to go in pursuit of liquor and draw out the evening inflamed with wine." --Isaiah 5:11

THE MEDITATION:

The Bible, both Old Testament and New, is consistent in its condemnation of drunkenness and alcohol abuse. At the same time, the entire Bible is consistent in its position on the use of alcohol. The Psalmist thanks God for the gift of wine "to gladden the heart of man" (105:15), and Paul advises Timothy to "use a little wine for the sake of your stomach and for your frequent ailments" (1 Timothy 6:23). The use of alcohol, for medicinal or other purposes, is a debatable issue which is not of primary concern for us. It is the abuse of alcohol, and particularly our own, that is our main concern. Becoming involved in the Wet-Dry debate may very well dissuade us from our first and foremost concern: sobriety and serenity for ourselves and others who still suffer from alcohol abuse.

We have learned, and perhaps are still learning, that without sobriety serenity is impossible. First things must come first. Many of us have learned that without sobriety we have nothing and run the risk of losing everything.

THE NEGOTIATION:

Can we allow others to use alcohol without jealousy or judgment.

THE PRAYER:

O God, continue to give us the strength to maintain sobriety, that by your grace we may grow in serenity and so become increasingly useful and productive in your Kingdom which we seek first. Amen.

THE READING: Matthew 6:25-33

TRUST IN US

THE INSPIRATION:

"We ask you, Lord, for nothing but what you have given us, the chance to prove ourselves. We will not fail. Trust in us." –Paul Gallico

THE MEDITATION:

In Paul Gallico's, "The Poseidon Adventure," Frank Scott utters the prayer above. Need we ask for anything more than the chance to prove ourselves? Has God not already given us the resources we need to cope with any problems that confront us? God has created us "in his image." We have within us the freedom and strength to deal with any dependence or addiction. God's power is in us. These resources are ours. We need nothing more than to utilize the power and resources which are even now at our disposal. Asking for more power implies we are now without resources. Asking that we may utilize the power that we indeed have within us is giving ourselves a chance to prove ourselves. There is no more sitting back and waiting for God to do something. God has already done something. Let us do something with what he has done. We will not fail.

To ask God to "trust in us" is a switch from our usual prayer that we might trust in him. It is recognizing that our relationship with God is one of interdependence: we need God—God needs us. If we truly trust in him, we can ask him to trust in us.

THE NEGOTIATION:

Can God put his trust in us?

THE PRAYER:

Lord, we thank you for the powers we have within us to deal with the hardships with which we are confronted. You can trust in us, Lord, to utilize the resources you have given us. We will not fail. Amen.

THE READING: Genesis 1:26-31

JANUARY 24

STEADFASTNESS

THE INSPIRATION:

"Mayor: Turn back, turn back!
                You belong to the calm waters of this village.
Brand: Forward! Forward! Victory lies ahead.
                Forget your village, Forget that you were beasts.
                Now you are men of the Lord. Climb onward. Climb!" –Henrik Ibsen

THE MEDITATION:

There is a call to turn back. It is a very inviting call at times. The calm waters of this village beckon us. The good times we had drinking, the rewards we received from intoxication, call us to turn back. Our minds are selective and seductive. We tend to remember the fun we had in the "good old days" and forget the pain we endured and caused others. We remember when we could buy a double-dip ice cream cone for a nickel in the "good old days." But what we forget is how scarce nickels were in those days.

In addition to the voice calling us back to the calm waters, there is the voice of reality calling us forward to victory. We are no longer beasts. We need no longer live by our animal instincts. We are now men and women of the Lord. We need to hear both voices in us: the subtle voice promising us the rewards of calm waters and the voice calling us to climb onward. Let us not "make believe" that there is no call to turn back, and when we hear it let us listen anew to the exciting and challenging call to climb onward.

THE NEGOTIATION:

Do we still hear the voice calling us to turn back?

THE PRAYER:

Give me, O Lord, a steadfast heart, which no unworthy affection may drag downward; give me an unconquered heart, which no tribulation can wear out; give me an upright heart, which no unworthy purpose may tempt aside. Bestow on me also, O Lord, understanding to know Thee, diligence to seek Thee, wisdom to find Thee, and a faithfulness that may finally embrace Thee. Amen. –Thomas Aquinas

THE READING: 1 Corinthians 15:51-58

THE CONVERSION OF ST. PAUL

THE INSPIRATION:

Meanwhile Saul was still breathing murderous threats against the disciples of the Lord. He went to the High Priest and applied for letters to the synagogues at Damascus authorizing him to arrest anyone he found, men and women, who followed the new way, and bring them to Jerusalem. While he was still on the road and nearing Damascus, suddenly a light flashed from the sky all around him. He fell to the ground and heard a voice saying, 'Saul, Saul, why do you persecute me?' "Tell me Lord,' he said, 'who you are.' The voice answered, 'I am Jesus, whom you are persecuting.'" – Acts 9:1-5

THE MEDITATION:

The observance of this festival, commemorating the conversion of St. Paul, began in the sixth century Church. Paul experienced a sudden and spectacular conversion experience. While this is sometimes the case, most conversions are gradual experiences as the Holy Spirit nurtures us from day to day. Whether sudden or gradual, conversion is necessary in order to find purpose in our lives and meaning in our existence.

There are at least three kinds of conversion. 1) Restricted conversion is when a person experiences a divine-human encounter, however he or she is restricted to a legalistic, rigid set of rules which disallows Christian freedom. 2) Limited conversion is when a person expresses a need for God's help and turns to him, however, it is on the intellectual level and does not include personal commitment. 3) Full Christian conversion means an experience that is transforming, releasing, transcendent, and genuine. It emphasizes the central focus of life around the revelation of God in Jesus Christ. As an experience it is holistic and breaks the power of alcohol, guilt, legalism, and pride.

THE NEGOTIATION:

What kind of a conversion have we experienced?

THE PRAYER:

Lord God, you taught the whole world through the preaching of your apostle, Paul. We celebrate his conversion and pray that we may follow his example and be witness to your truth in this world. –Collect for the Conversion of St. Paul Contemporary Worship

THE READING: Acts 9:1-22

THE PURPOSE OF THE BIBLE

THE INSPIRATION:

"It is for truth, not for literary excellence, that we go to Holy Scripture. Every passage of it ought to be read in the light of that inspiration which produced it, with an eye to the soul's profit, not to cleverness of argument. A simple book of devotion ought to be as welcome to you as any profound and learned treatise." --Thomas Kempis

THE MEDITATION:

As we regard the Bible primarily as a book of devotion, we begin to reap the benefits for which it was written. The Bible is perhaps the most misused and abused book ever written. The Bible contains various types of literature: prose, poetry, drama, prophecy, letters, sermons, apocalyptic, etc. Yet it is basically a book of devotion. The Bible deals with historical and scientific matters, and yet is not a history book or a science book. The questions of "where," "when," and "how" are not of primary importance. The Bible is concerned with "who" and "why" questions.

The Bible begins with the words, "In the beginning, God . . . " (Genesis 1:1). No attempt is made to prove God's existence or explain where he came from. The Bible is a book of faith! Its purpose is to inspire faith as we read it devotionally. Through the Bible, God's love for us, and will for us is revealed. No other use of the Bible should dissuade us from this central purpose.

THE NEGOTIATION:

Do we misuse the Bible by making it a book of history, science, magic, fortune-telling?

THE PRAYER:

O Lord, we thank you for your most holy and precious Scriptures. May your will for us give us inspiration in our struggle against alcohol abuse and for sobriety and serenity as we turn to your word each day. Amen.

THE READING: 2 Timothy 3:14-17

JANUARY 27

ADVOCACY

THE INSPIRATION:

"When he (Paul) reached Jerusalem he tried to join the body of disciples there; but they were all afraid of him, because they did not believe that he was really a convert. Barnabas, however, took him by the hand and introduced him to the apostles." –Acts 9:26-27

THE MEDITATION:

We can understand the reluctance of the disciples to accept Paul into their fellowship. After all Paul had been a violent enemy of the Church. Were it not for Barnabas, Paul may have never been accepted. Barnabas, "the Son of Encouragement," served as an advocate for Paul. An Advocate is one who pleads the cause of another.

We have had a host of advocates pleading our cause. Persons who have fought and are fighting against the stigma that alcoholics are "hopeless cases," "moral degenerates," "skid row bums," etc. These advocates have helped create a climate where our recovery can better take place.

Most of us have discovered that there are several personal advocates who have contributed to our achieving sobriety. None of us can make it entirely on our own. We need other people in our search for serenity. And other people need us. As we have been blessed with advocates pleading our cause, so we have responsibility to become advocates for others.

THE NEGOTIATION:

How many people have served as our advocates?

THE PRAYER:

We thank you, God, for the many persons, known and unknown, who have contributed to the serenity which we enjoy this day. Help us be alert this day to opportunities to serve as advocates for others. Amen.

THE READING: Acts 9:20-31

JANUARY 28

A BRIDGE OVER TROUBLED WATERS

THE INSPIRATION:

"Only life can satisfy the demands of life. And this hunger of mine can be satisfied for the simple reason that the nature of life is such that I can realize my individuality by becoming a bridge for others, a stone in the temple of righteousness.

Don't be afraid of yourself; live individually to the full—but for the good of others.

To be free and responsible. For this alone was man created." –Dag Hammarskjold

THE MEDITATION:

However we articulate it, the purpose of our lives, meaning of our existence, can find satisfaction only outside of ourselves. Our individuality is related to our relationship with others. Our potential can only be seen and realized by becoming bridges for others. Jesus expressed this same purpose for his life in many different ways. His purpose is basically no different than ours: he came to serve and sends us to serve.

To be free and responsible! That is the essence of life. We can only be responsible for ourselves. We alone are responsible for our behavior i.e. what we drink. No one else is responsible for us. We are responsible for no one else. However, we are responsible to others. To discover our individuality is to become a bridge for others. The only way we can live for the good of ourselves is to live for the good of others.

THE NEGOTIATION:

How do we articulate our purpose for being?

THE PRAYER:

O Lord, who has bridged the gap between ourselves and you by sending your Son into the world; help us to take up the task of being bridges for others as we go out into this day in your name and in your presence. Amen.

THE READING: John 13:1-16

JANUAR 29

THE FATHER'S HOUSE

THE INSPIRATION:

" 'What made you search?' he said. 'Did you not know that I was bound to be in my Father's house?' As Jesus grew up he advanced in wisdom and in favour with God and men." --Luke 2:49-52

THE MEDITATION:

This well-known text from the Epiphany Season gives us the only glimpse we have of Jesus during "the hidden years," from infancy until about age thirty. The twelve year old Jesus had separated from his parents for several days in the big city of Jerusalem. We can hardly blame them for being anxious. They didn't realize he was so zealous for his Father's house.

It is often the case that persons who abuse alcohol lose their zeal for the Father's house. Alcohol abuse does not prompt favor with God and other people. Separations need to be restored. Reconciliation with God and others is a prerequisite for sobriety and serenity.

Some find it difficult to return to the Father's house. Shame is a factor for some; pride for others. The Church of Christ is a community of the concerned, a fellowship of reconciliation. Our deepest needs are met in our Father's house: our need to give thanks, to be nurtured, to find favor with God and others.

THE NEGOTIATION:

Are we open to our Father's call to his house?

THE PRAYER:

O come, let us worship and bow down, Let us kneel before the Lord, our Maker.
For he is our God, and we are the people of his pasture, and the sheep of his hand.
O that today we would hearken to his voice! Amen. –Psalm 95:6-7

THE READING: Luke 2:41-52

JANUARY 30

THE SEARCH FOR MEANING

THE INSPIRATION:

"Man's search for meaning is a primary force in his life, not a 'secondary rationalization' of instinctual drives. . . The meaning of our existence is not invented by ourselves, but rather detected.

Man's will to meaning can be frustrated . . . The existential vacuum is a widespread phenomenon . . . . (which) manifests itself mainly in a state of boredom . . . Suicide . . . alcoholism and juvenile delinquency are not understandable unless we recognize the existential vacuum underlying them."

--Victor E. Frankl

THE MEDITATION:

Our search for meaning is indeed a primary force in our lives and is not indirectly related to our alcoholism. Will-to-meaning is a more basic pursuit than Freud's will-to-pleasure or Adler's will-to-power. Our most basic questions are, "Who am I?" "Why am I here?" "Where am I going?" When these questions are unanswered or frustrated we live in an existential anxiety. We have learned that the boredom of this vacuum and the pain of this anxiety can be temporarily and artificially relieved by alcohol. We also know that this relief results in expanded boredom and intensified pain.

Our search for meaning must lead us in other directions. There are perhaps no substitutes for the relief we experience from alcohol. Nothing else does exactly what alcohol does to us. While there are no substitutes, there are alternatives. There are other ways and means of pursuing meaning.

THE NEGOTIATION:

What alternatives to find meaning are open to us?

THE PRAYER:

O Lord, give us the common sense to cease trying to invent meaning in our existence, and help us to detect the meaning you have for us. Amen.

THE READING: Psalm 144:1-15

JANUARY 31

THE SHAKING OF THE FOUNDATIONS

THE INSPIRATION:

"There is something immovable, unchangeable, unshakeable, eternal, which becomes manifest in the crumbling of our world. On the boundaries of the finite the infinite becomes visible; in the light of the Eternal, the transitoriness of the temporal appears . . . It is the only way to look at the shaking without recoiling from it . . . If the foundations . . . begin to crumble . . . only two alternatives remain – despair, which is the certainty of eternal destruction, or faith, which is the certainty of eternal salvation." --Paul Tillich

THE MEDITATION:

We have experienced the shaking of our foundations and the foundation of the world around us. We know the fears and feelings of helplessness that are experienced in an earthquake. We also know that it is in the midst of the crumbling that we meet the Eternal. God is so often discovered and experienced in the abyss. We would never say that God can only be found in the abyss. This has been our experience. Others discover the Eternal in other ways. Let us never allow our experience to become the norm which we impose upon others.

For us it was the crumbling of the foundations that brought us to the awareness of the two alternatives open for us; despair or faith. We chose the take the "leap of faith" and as we continue in that faith our awareness of the eternal becomes more real.

THE NEGOTIATION:

Would we have come to the Eternal without the shaking of our foundations?

THE PRAYER:

We thank you, Lord, for all of the experiences that have brought us to our present relationship with you. Continue to shake us, Lord, that we might grow in this relationship. Amen.

THE READING: Job 14:1-22

FEBRUARY 1

THE STEWARDSHIP OF TIME

THE INSPIRATION:

"I would rather be ashes than dust.
I would rather my spark should burn out in a brilliant blaze
        Than it should be stifled by dry rot.
I would rather be a superb meteor,
        Every atom of me in magnificent glow
                Than a sleepy and permanent planet.
Man's chief purpose is to live, not to exist.
        I shall use my time." --Jack London

THE MEDITATION:

We are entrusted with a stewardship. The word steward comes from two words, "sty" and "ward". Literally a steward is a "ward of the sty," or "a keeper of the pigs." The pigs belong to someone else, but the ward is in charge of things that belong to someone else—to God. These things are our possessions, our talents, and out time.

This is a gift to us from God. We do not own time, yet we may use it any way we wish. We have wasted, misused, and abused much time in the past. We have squandered hours and hours while drinking. That time is no longer ours—we can never regain it. We can, however, use the present time, learn from past misuse of time, and plan to use future time as stewards in God's Kingdom. When we merely exist we are abusing God's gift of time. It is when we live that we use the gift.

THE NEGOTIATION:

What is our definition of the word "time?"

THE PRAYER:

We thank you, Lord, for this wonderful and indefinable gift of time. Forgive us for the time we have wasted by merely existing in days gone by. Help us to know that time is your gift to us. Give us motivation to use "our" time by living as your stewards. Amen.

THE READING:

Ephesians 5:15-20

THE PRESENTATION

THE INSPIRATION:

"This way, Master, thou givest they servant his discharge
  In peace; now thy promise is fulfilled.
For I have seen with my own eyes the deliverance which thou
  Hast made ready in full view of all the nations:
A light that will be a revelation to the heathen,
  And glory to thy people Israel." --Luke 2:29-32

THE MEDITATION:

February 2 is observed as the Presentation of our Lord by some and as the Purification of the Virgin Mary by others. Still others know it only as Ground Hog's Day! It was the fortieth day after his birth that Mary and Joseph brought the infant Jesus to the temple according to the tradition. The old man Simeon takes the Christ Child in his arms and uttered the words which we call the "Nunc Dimittis."

Simeon's words stress the universalism of the Christian Gospel. Here in his arms he recognizes God's spiritual treasures which are meant for all people. The same peace, the same salvation, the same light which is offered to use is offered to all. We who are recovering from alcohol abuse have special needs in our struggle. But basically our need is the human need. While we have a unique struggle and consequently have unique opportunities, we share basically the same hopes and fears of all people. We need to be loved, we need to love. This need makes all humanity our brothers and sisters to whom we are responsible.

THE NEGOTIATION:

Are we basically any different from other people?

THE PRAYER:

Blessed are you, O Lord out God, for you have sent us your salvation. Inspire us by your Holy Spirit to see with our own eyes, to the glory of Israel who is the light of all nations, your son, Jesus Christ our Lord. Amen. –Collect for the Presentation of Our Lord

THE READING: Luke 2:22-40

LIVING IN THE NOW

THE INSPIRATION:

"Look to this day
for it is life.
The very life of life.
In its brief course lies all
the realities and verities of existence.
The bliss of growth
The splendor of action,
The glory of power—

For yesterday is but a dream
And tomorrow is only a vision
But today, well lived,
Makes every yesterday a dream of happiness
And every tomorrow a vision of hope. —Sanskrit Proverb

THE MEDITATION:

Now is the only reality. Last year, last week, yesterday, five minutes ago, do not exist. Next year, next week, tomorrow, five minutes from now, are not real. The only time we can live in is the present. If we are reliving the past or rehearsing for the future, we are cheating ourselves from living the only true reality which is now.

"Behold, now is the acceptable time; behold now is the day of salvation" (2 Corinthians 6:2). The past, with its joys and sorrows is gone—let us learn from it. The future with its hopes and fears, is not here—let us keep an eye on it. Now is ours—let us live it.

THE NEGOTIATION: How much of this day will we live in the now?

THE PRAYER:

We know at this moment, O Lord, that we need not succumb to temptations and computations that plague us. Keep us from chasing phantoms which do not exist. Teach us, O Lord, to live in the now. Amen.

THE READING:

2 Corinthians 6:1-10

FEBRUARY 4

PAYING GOD HIS DUE

THE INSPIRATION:

" 'Are we or are we not permitted to pay taxes . . ?' . . . Jesus said, 'Show me the money in which the tax is paid.' They handed him a silver piece. Jesus asked, 'Whose head is this, and those inscription?' "Caesar's,' they replied. He said to them, "Then pay Caesar what is due to Caesar, and pay God what is due to God.' This answer took them by surprise. —Matthew 22:17-22

THE MEDITATION:

We too may be taken by surprise when confronted with the question, "What is due God?" The surprising answer to the question is: all, all life, all creation, and above all our conscience. To Jesus, obedience to Caesar is not necessarily obedience to God. Jesus says to give Caesar his due, but do not give Caesar what belongs to God. It is our conscience which is due to God.

As we give God his due we also serve our own best interests. A clear conscience is an important part of maintaining sobriety and experiencing serenity. When our conscience is captive to the Gospel we experience freedom. It is then that we have an individual allegiance. It is when our allegiance is divided, when we try to serve God and Mammon that we are vulnerable to alcohol abuse.

THE NEGOTIATION:

Can we know serenity while holding a divided allegiance?

THE PRAYER:

My will is not my own
Till Thou has made it Thine;
If it would reach a monarch's throne
It must its crown resign;
Amid the clashing strife;
When on Thy Bosom it has leant
And found in Thee its life. Amen. —George Matheson

THE READING:

Matthew 22:15-22

FEBRUARY 5

THE WAY OF COUAGE AND FAITH

THE INSPIRATION:

"There is another way, if you have the courage.
The first I could describe in familiar terms
Because you have seen it, as we all have seen it,
Illustrated, more or less, in lives of those about us.
The second is unknown, and so requires faith—
The destination cannot be described;
You will know very little until you get there;
You will journey blind. But the way leads to possession
Of what you have sought for in the wrong place. "   --T.S. Eliot

THE MEDITATION:

We, who have tried the way of alcohol to reach our destination, are encouraged when we discover that there may be another way. Since our first way failed, we desperately try to find and hang onto another. But the other way requires courage and faith. It requires guts and God! The second way is not easy. We seek immediate satisfaction and relief. We don't want to travel blind. And yet with faith and courage, courage and faith we journey on. Then one day it comes to us and we suddenly are aware of possessing that for which we have been seeking in the wrong place. We have learned that we cannot find God in a bottle!

THE NEGOTIATION:

Have we really tried the way of courage and faith?

THE PRAYER:

Lord, what is my confidence which I have in this life? Or what is the greatest comfort I can derive from anything under heaven? Is it not Thou, O Lord, whose mercies are without number? Where hath it ever been well with me without Thee? I rather choose to be a pilgrim on earth with Thee than without Thee to possess heaven. Where Thou art there is heaven, and where Thou art there is death and hell . . . In Thee, therefore, O Lord God, I place my whole hope and refuge. Amen.   --Thomas A. Kempis

THE READING: Matthew 17:19-20

FEBRUARY 6

GOD IN A BOTTLE?

THE INSPIRATION:

"In all the earth there was no other like him, no other fitted so sublimely and magnificently drunken. . . Why, when it was possible to buy God in a bottle . . . and become a God oneself, were not men forever drunken?" --Thomas Wolfe

THE MEDITATION:

Perhaps we can identify with Eugene's question in <u>Look Homeward, Angel</u>. It appears that there are a minority of us, at least, for whom alcohol does something very special. Alcohol does, indeed, make some of us feel like we are God. If this be the case, then why would we ever want to give up our divinity by drawing a sober breath?

We have learned, however, that these feelings of omnipotence are only temporary and artificial. And yet they are real for us at the time. We do have within us a desire to play God. We find this desire temporarily and artificially satisfied by alcohol. Alcohol gives us fleeting opportunities to be what we truly want to be. We find ourselves striving to satisfy our religious needs by non-religious means. Our highest and most noble calling is not to be God, but rather children of God.

THE NEGOTIATION:

How is alcohol involved in our search for God?

THE PRAYER:

Let my soul cleave unto You, now that You have freed it from the sticky birdlime of death. How wretched it was! And You irritated the pain of its wound, so that forsaking all else, my heart might be converted unto You, who art above all, and without whom all things would be nothing.

You have made us for yourself, O Lord, and our hearts are restless until they find rest in You. Amen. --St. Augustine

THE READING: Psalm 105:1-45

FEBRUARY 7

FAULTFINDING

THE INSPIRATION:

'Don't criticize people, and you will not be criticized. For you will be judged by the way you criticize others . . . Why do you look at the speck of sawdust in your brother's eye and fail to notice the plank in your own? . . . Take the plank out of your own eye first, and then you will see clearly enough to remove your brother's speck of dust." --Matthew 7:1-3,5 (Phillips)

THE MEDITATION:

When Jesus was using the metaphors of a speck of sawdust and a plank, he demonstrated his deep insight into human nature. He is speaking about what modern psychologists call projection. One of the ways we defend ourselves from seeing the truth about ourselves is to project our faults upon someone else. The reality of the situation is often that our faults are much worse than the fault we find in someone else.

Projection is a rather common ploy used by alcohol abusers. We cannot face the painful truth of our own defects, weaknesses, and powerlessness, so we project it upon others. With such a striking exaggeration that it is humorous Jesus tells us to take the planks out of our own eyes, before we can see clearly enough to be concerned about the speck of dust in someone else's eye.

THE MEDITATION:

What planks are we carrying around in our eyes?

THE PRAYER:

O Lord, open our eyes that we might be aware of the planks that blind us of our own defects. When we see specks in the eyes of others, help us first to look to ourselves, and then with love, patience, and understanding seek to help, not judge, our brothers and sisters. Amen.

THE READING:

Matthew 7:1-5

FEBRUARY 8

PRAYER

THE INSPIRATION:

"We pray to God because we believe in him through Jesus Christ; that is to say, our prayer can never be an entreaty to God, for we have no need to come before him in that way. We are privileged to know that he knows our needs before we ask him. This is what gives Christian prayer its boundless confidence and its joyous certainty. It matters little what form of prayer we adopt or how many words we use, what matters is the faith which lays hold on God and touches the heart of the Father who knew us long before we came to him." --Dietrich Bonhoeffer

THE MEDITATION:

Prayer is not talking to God, and certainly not talking at God, and not necessarily talking with God. Prayer may not be talking at all. It is communion with God. It is living in an awareness of God's presence. This may include talking but above all it means listening. When we meet Almighty God in all his glory it is far more important to listen to what he wants than tell him what we want.

Paul advises us to "pray constantly" (1 Thessalonians 5:17). This certainly does not mean that we walk around all day with our hands folded and our heads bowed. Prayer implies far more than what happens between "Dear Lord" and "Amen." To pray constantly means to practice God's presence while we go about out daily living.

THE NEGOTIATION:

Do we agree that prayer doesn't change things, but rather changes people and people change things?

THE PRAYER:

O Lord, thank you for the joyous privilege of prayer. You know our needs, our hurts, our compulsions, our good intentions, and our evil desires. "Speak, Lord, for thy servant hears" (1 Samuel 3:19). Amen.

THE READING:

Matthew 6:5-8

FEBRUARY 9

THE LOD"S PRAYER - INTRODUCTION

THE INSPIRATION:

"Our Father, who art is heaven."

THE MEDITATION:

While Jesus was praying in a certain place, his disciples came upon him. They were impressed by the power of prayer that they witnessed in his life, and so they asked, "Lord, teach us to pray." Jesus responded, not with a lot of rules to follow but simply by offering an example of prayer which we have come to know as the "Lord's Prayer" or the "Our Father." This brief prayer has served as a model for all Christian prayer. These few words embrace the totality of prayer.

Jesus' favorite name for God was "Father." He taught us to use that word. By so doing we are encouraged to accept God as our Father—as one who truly cares for us and is concerned about our sobriety and serenity and all our needs. A personal, loving, caring Father is concerned about the total well-being of his children. Furthermore he is out Father; the father of all his children whether he is acknowledged as personal God or not. Just as he cares personally for us, so he cares for all his children.

"Who art in heaven" reminds us that this personal Father is also the Almighty God, full of power and glory, who can so far more than that which we ask or think. This Almighty, Omnipotent, God is our Father.

Because we know the Lord's Prayer so well, it is extremely difficult for us to truly pray it being conscious of each phrase.

THE NEGOTIATION: Can we pray the Lord's Prayer being fully aware of each petition?

THE PRAYER:

Our Father, who art in Heaven, Hallowed be Thy Name. Thy Kingdom come, Thy will be done, on earth as it is in heaven. Give us this day our daily bread; and forgive us our trespasses, As we forgive those who trespass against us. And lead us not into temptation, but deliver us from evil. For thine is the Kingdom, and the power, and the glory, forever and ever. Amen.

THE READING: Luke 11:1-13

FEBRUARY 10

THE LORD'S PRAYER – FIRST PETITION

THE INSPIRATION:

"Hallowed by Thy Name."

THE MEDITATION:

Literally we are asking the God's name will be hold or honored. We have no right to tell God to have a holy and honorable name. His name is holy and honorable in and of itself. What we pray for in this petition is that we may honor God's name and live in such a way that his holiness is reflected in our lives.

The word "holy" denotes that which is majestic, great, wonderful, exalted, unsearchable, incomprehensible, incomparable, and, in its most practical sense, what which is set apart for God.

God's name is set apart for him, and him only. We call the Bible holy because it is set apart from all other books as a revelation of God's will and love for us. We call the altar holy because it is set apart for the worship of God. We call the Church holy because we have been set apart by the call of the Gospel of Jesus Christ. When God's name is holy to us, we become holy, set apart for him.

Alcohol abuse robs us from recognizing the holiness of God's name and makes it impossible for us to live holy lives. We cannot live lives set apart from the Holy God if another god (alcohol) is vying for our allegiance.

THE NEGOTIATION:

De we see ourselves as set apart for God?

THE PRAYER:

Holy, holy, holy! Though the darkness hide Thee,
Through the eye of sinful man Thy glory may not see.
Only Thou art holy, there is none beside Thee.
Perfect in power, in love, and purity.   --Reginald Heber

THE READING:

Isaiah 6:1-5

THE LORD'S PRAYER - SECOND PETITION

THE INSPIRATION:

"Thy Kingdom come."

THE MEDITATION:

God's Kingdom comes when and where he chooses. We could pray for His Kingdom to come from here to eternity and still be unaware of its presence. In this petition we pray that God's Kingdom may come to us—that we may be aware of and involved in his rule. The Kingdom of God is wherever and whenever God rules in the hearts and lives of people. Jesus said the Kingdom of God is among us. (--Luke 17:20)

God's Kingdom, then, is not located on a map or a calendar. The only geography connected with the Kingdom is where the people happen to be whom he rules. God's Kingdom comes to fulfillment in the future but its only reality is the present as we live under his rule now.

Jesus came to proclaim the reality of God's Kingdom among us and available to us today. We live in that Kingdom so long as God rules our hearts and lives. As we seek first that Kingdom we are enabled to live in a productive and serene manner today. Our desire to serve other gods diminishes with the awareness and reality of God's Kingdom among us.

THE NEGOTIATION:

Do we desire God to rule our hearts this day?

THE PRAYER:

Your Kingdom come, O God. Hear our prayer. Help us this day to walk in the light, life, and joy of Your Kingdom. May Your rule so penetrate us that we may willingly share the love we feel with others. Your Kingdom come! Amen.

THE READING:

Luke 17:20-21

THE LORD'S PRAYER – THIRD PETITION

THE INSPIRATION:

"Thy will be done, on earth as it is in heaven."

THE MEDITATION:

God's will is done without out praying about it. In this petition we pray that God's will may be done by us. We are praying for strength to know and do God's will. In this petition we are putting ourselves at God's disposal. We are opening up our lives to him so that his will can be done in and through us. It takes a courageous act of faith to truly utter this petition for we are putting ourselves in the attitude of willingness to do whatever God wills.

Before we can make a commitment to do God's will, we must first have some understanding of what God's will for us is. Specifically, this is not always an easy task. It is often difficult for us to be certain what God would have us do in certain situations. However, we do know, in general, what God's will is for us this day. He wills that we keep from anesthetizing ourselves with alcohol. He wills that we forgive, love, accept, and help other people with whom we will come in contact. He wills a positive and cheerful attitude. He wills that we celebrate life. Beginning with the general and obvious often enables us to determine God's will in specifics.

THE NEGOTIATION:

Are we willing to put ourselves at God's disposal?

THE PRAYER:

Take, O Lord, and receive, all my liberty, my memory, my understanding, and all my will, all that I have and possess. Thou hast given them to me; to Thee, O Lord, I restore them; all things are Thine, dispose of them according to Thy will. Give me Thy love and Thy grace, for this is enough for me.
--Ignatius Loyola

THE READING:

Luke 22:39-44

FEBRUARY 13

THE LORD's PRAYER – FOURTH PETITION

THE INSPIRATION:

"Give us this day our daily bread."

THE MEDITATION:

The first three petitions are the "Thy" petitions. Now, quite appropriately, we turn to the "us" petitions. The plural (us) is significant. We are not only praying for ourselves but for all people. We ask nothing for ourselves than we ask for all others.

Daily bread, of course, implies far more than the stuff on which we spread butter. Daily bread means everything that is necessary to sustain our physical needs.

God gives daily bread to us even when we don't pray for it. In this petition we pray that we might acknowledge our daily bread as his gift and to receive it with thanksgiving.

We also know that there are others of "us" who are literally starving for lack of daily bread. Gratitude, if it is sincere, compels us to share.

We are mindful that we do not "live by bread alone" (Matthew 4:4). We live by other gifts outside of the realm of physical need. Spiritual, social, psychological gifts. Lest we forget, there are the gifts of sobriety and serenity. Gratitude, again, compels us to share. One stands among us who says, "I am the bread of life, whoever comes to me shall never be hungry" (John 6:35).

THE NEGOTIATION:

What is the daily bread God gives to us?

THE PRAYER:

We give Thee but Thine own,
Whate're the gift may be;
All that we have is Thine alone.
A trust, O Lord, from Thee. Amen. –William W. How

THE READING: John 6:35-30

THE LORD'S PRAYER – FIFTH PETITION

THE INSPIRATION:

"And forgive us our trespasses, we w forgive those who trespass against us."

THE MEDITATION:

If only Jesus had left the last part off, we would have no difficulty praying this petition. It's the "as we forgive . . ." that gets to us. Do we dare ask God to forgive us as we forgive others? Do we want God to deal with us as we deal with others? This petition puts us on the spot.

Is forgiving others a prerequisite to being forgiven? Or is being forgiven a prerequisite for forgiving others? "Be generous to one another, tender-hearted, forgiving one another as God in Christ forgave me" (Ephesians 4:32). Paul, using the past tense (forgave) suggests that our ability and willingness to forgive others is based upon our being forgiven. We begin with our experience or being forgiven, accepted, loved by God.

Heaven knows, we have much for which to be forgiven; not only the harm and suffering we caused others, but also the wasted time and energy in fruitless squandering of our lives. "If we forgive our sins and cleanse us from every kind of wrong" (1 John 1:9). Being forgiven and cleansed of our many wrongs, gives us the motivation to forgive others and be generous and tender-hearted toward them.

THE NEGOTIATION:

Are there any whom we are unwilling to forgive?

THE PRAYER:

As we experience Your love, acceptance and forgiveness, O Lord, enable us to love, accept and forgive those who may injure or offend us. Amen.

THE READING:

Matthew 5:21-26

FEBRUARY 15

THE LORD'S PRAYER – SIXTH PETITION

THE INSPIRATION:

"And lead us not into temptation."

THE MEDITATION:

God does not tempt us to do evil. Yet there is a source of temptation which we have all experienced. That source is within and without. The Bible calls the source the devil, the world and our own flesh. Whether we believe in the devil as a personified source of temptation or not, none of us can dispute the reality of temptation and our yielding to its power.

There are temptations within and outside of us which make the consumption of alcohol very inviting. This is certainly not our only temptation, but we know that if we lose out on this one we will be powerless against many others.

There are two things we can do about temptation. The first is to be faithful to ourselves by avoiding exposure to temptation insofar as we have control over the situation. In the early stages of recovery from alcohol abuse, many people find that avoiding the environments where alcohol is readily available is a wise course of action. As we grow in serenity this avoidance becomes less important. The second thing we can do is, when we are tempted, turn to God and seek his strength.

THE NEGOTIATION:

What conscious efforts can we make to avoid temptation?

THE PRAYER:

Grant us, O Lord, to pass this day in gladness and peace, without stumbling and without strain; that, reaching the eventide victorious over all temptation, we may praise Thee, the eternal God, who art blesses, and dost govern all things, world without end. Amen. –Hozorabic Sacramentary

THE READING:

Matthew 26:36-46

THE LORD'S PRAYER – SEVENTH PETITION

THE INSPIRATION:

"But deliver us from evil."

THE MEDITATION:

We pray in this petition that God would deliver us from all evil, whether it affects body, mind, spirit, possessions, or reputation. In the face of evil we pray that God would give us the strength to endure it with patience and finally gain the victory.

The Gospel proclaims a God whose suffering love shares the world's pain and, at the same time, gives a victorious joy and peace which the world cannot give. The reality of evil in the world is not to be ignored, but it is seen through the eyes of faith which believes that God can bring good out of evil.

Paul reminds us, "All things work together for good for those who love God" (Romans 8:28). That good comes out of evil is obvious at times; the good in our lives today may be the result of abusing alcohol in the past. At other times the good is not so obvious. Perhaps there are examples of evil in the world out of which we will never see any good. But maybe someone else will. We never know how people are touched by evil. The key to what Paul says is "for those who love God." It is a love and trust in God which allows him to bring all things to his goal in his time.

THE NEGOTIATION:

Can good come out of evil without our recognizing it?

THE PRAYER:

O God, we know that You desire nothing but good for your children. We pray that when we are confronted with the reality of evil we may patiently endure and You would bring good out of it. Fill us with your love that our love for You may grow. Amen.

THE READING:

Romans 8:26-30

FEBRUARY 17

THE LORD'S PRAYER - CONCLUSION

THE INSPIRATION:

"For thine is the Kingdom, and the power, and the glory, forever and ever. Amen."

"A humble man is not disturbed by praise. Since he is no longer concerned with himself, and since he knows where the good in him comes from, he does not refuse praise, because it belongs to the God he loves, and in receiving it he keeps nothing for himself, but gives it all, with great joy, to his God."
--Thomas Merton

THE MEDITATION:

The conclusion to the Lord's Prayer, not found in the Scripture accounts, was added later by the Church as a fitting and proper termination to the prayer Jesus taught us. It is not a petition; it is a profession, an acclamation of faith. We have prayed for "the Kingdom come," "Thy will be done," "Hallowed be Thy name." We petitioned for his power and goodness in asking for daily bread, forgiveness of sins, and the strength to resist temptation and overcome evil. Now we remind ourselves that the glory of his Kingdom and power belong solely to him. With joy, we give all glory to him; "All honor and glory are Yours, Almighty God, now and forever."

We conclude with an old and beautiful Hebrew word, "Amen." Amen is an exclamation meaning "truly," "surely," "it shall be so."

THE NEGOTIATION:

Can we accept praise?

THE PRAYER:

Holy art Thou, Almighty and Merciful God. Holy art Thou, and great is the Majesty of Thy glory . . . Unto Thee, O God, Father, Son and Holy Spirit, be all honor and glory in Thy holy Church, world without end. Amen. —The Prayer of Thanksgiving

THE READING:
Deuteronomy 8:11-17

FEBRUARY 18

THE GIFT OF THE HOLY SPIRIT

THE INSPIRATION:

"I Believe that I cannot by my own reason of strength believe in Jesus Christ, my Lord, or come to him, but the Holy Spirit has called me through the Gospel, enlightens me with His gifts, and sanctified the whole Christian Church on earth, and preserves it in union with Jesus Christ in the one true faith."
--Martin Luther

THE MEDITATION:

The work of the Holy Spirit in and through us leaves little room for us to be proud of our faith, our sobriety, serenity, or any other so called accomplishments in our lives. The most important prayer that we can, therefore utter is a prayer for the gift of the Holy Spirit. This gift results in faith and any other attributes which we have. It is only when we are guided by the Holy Spirit that we can please God. It is under the guidance of the Holy Spirit that we can become truly human, as God intends us to be. TO pray for this gift and accept Him when He comes is the essence of the whole business of being human.

Jesus said, "If you, then, bad as you are, know how to give your children that is good for them, how much more will the heavenly Father give the Holy Spirit to those who ask him!" (Luke 11:12-13). Let us ask and accept the Gift.

THE NEGOTIATION:

Can we take pride in our faith or accomplishments?

THE PRAYER:

Come Holy Spirit, God and Lord;
Be all Thy gifts in plenty poured
To save, to strengthen and make whole
Each ready mind, each waiting soul.
Oh by the brightness of Thy light
In holy faith all men unite,
And to Thy praise by every tongue,
In every land our hymn be sung.
Alleluia! Alleluia!   --Martin Luther

THE READING:
Luke 11:5-13

FEBRUARY 19

THE MYSTERY AND POWER OF ALCOHOL

THE INSPIRATION:

"Remember that we deal with alcohol—cunning, baffling, powerful! Without help it is too much for us. But here is One who has all power—that One is God. May you find Him now!

Half measures availed us nothing. We stood at the turning point. We asked His protection and care with complete abandon." Alcoholics Anonymous

THE MEDITATION:

"Cunning, baffling, powerful," this is only the beginning of a long list of adjectives that could be applied to the noun alcohol. Perhaps we will never understand or be able to describe the subtle, mysterious power of ethyl alcohol (C_2H_5OH) over some of us. So power is this substance in the lives of some of us that only "One who has all power" can give us the strength to get out from under its grips.

Half-hearted attempts to overcome this cunning and baffling power will not bring lasting and satisfying results. Total commitment is required. We must seek God's help with "complete abandon." Many of us have learned that without sobriety we can have nothing else that is meaningful. Sobriety must come before every other pursuit, for without it we lose all. May we find the One who has all power now.

THE NEGOTIATION:

Is it necessary to understand the power alcohol has over us?

THE PRAYER:

Almighty and all-powerful God, we are confronted with a power over us, which we cannot understand and which only can be overpowered with Your help and strength. Grant us that help and strength as we live under Your protection and care this day. Amen.

THE READING:

Isaiah 40:27-31

FEBRUARY 20

DEALING WITH BOREDOM

THE INSPIRATION:

"Liquor wasn't a crutch for Liz, it was an exit. A quick flight to a world of her own making. Liz could walk without crutches . . . but she couldn't wait to walk, she must fly. It wasn't that this world was too much for her; it was that it wasn't enough." --Elizabeth Burns

THE MEDITATION:

Alcohol is indeed used as an escape by many people. But escape drinking is not the only kind of abuse of alcohol. There is also the kind which seeks to flee to something that is missing in one's life. We abuse alcohol when we use it to escape from problems but also when we use it to try to find something missing. It may be that the world isn't enough for us; that we find our existence dull, mundane, boring.

When we find life boring, we often ask who or what is responsible for our boredom. We seek to find cause outside of ourselves. We look in the wrong direction. Each of us must assume responsibility for our own feelings—our own boredom. Other people or life's conditions do not bore us—we allow ourselves to be bored by them. We need to "own" our own boredom before we can deal with it. The new life in Christ is by far too exciting and challenging to allow boredom.

THE NEGOTIATION:

Where do we look for the cause and relief from boredom?

THE PRAYER:

Almighty God, give us a vision of Your purpose for us. Help us to see all of the exciting possibilities and challenges that are before us this day. May we celebrate the life which You gave us to Your glory. Amen.

THE READING:

Psalm 24:1-10

THE CHURCH'S ONE FOUNDATION

THE INSPIRATION:

"Built on a rock the Church doth stand
Even when steeples are falling;
Crumbled have spires in every land,
Bells still are chiming and calling;
Calling the young and old to rest,
Calling the souls of men distressed,
Longing for life everlasting."   --Nicolai Grundtvig

THE MEDITATION:

There was a time when the church steeples stood in the middle of every town; the center of village life. Even the word "parson" meant "the person." The institutional church has lost its influence. Not many today see the Church as something that makes "hell's foundations quiver." Few see the Church today as Jesus saw it when he commissioned a few disciples to go out and proclaim the Good News.

Part of the problem is that people are often idealists. The assumption is that the Church is a group of people without flaws and defects, completely Christ-like. Jesus was no so blind about human nature. He saw the Church as a group of people who were honest enough to confess their sins, who met together to find strength to grow, who were filled with gratitude for the ways God has helped them, and who founds God's power to share his love in the world. The Church is not for perfect people but for people willing to make progress. The Church still calls and ministers to the distressed.

THE NEGOTIATION:

What is the foundation on which the Church is built?

THE PRAYER:

We give thanks, O Lord, for your Church, instituted by and founded upon Your Son Jesus Christ. As we hear the call and become involved in the Body of Christ, we pray that we may be effective in this ministry of and to the distressed. Amen.

THE READING:
Matthew 16:13-19

FEBRUARY 22

THE PATH OF DETERMINATION

THE INSPIRATION:

"Tired
And Lonely,
So tired
The heart aches
Meltwater trickles
Down the rocks
The fingers are numb
The knees tremble
It is now;
Now that you must not give in.

On the path of the others
Are resting places
Places in the sun
Where they can meet,
But this
Is your path,
And it is now,
Now, that you must not fail."   --Dag Hammarskjold

THE MEDITATION:

There are times when we feel like giving in. Times when pain is so real and severe that we crave instant relief. Times when the pull to revert to our former way of dealing with distress is overwhelming. It is not, at the time, that we must not give in, that we must not fail. It is now, at this time, that God's power on the path of sobriety and serenity sustain us. Our dedication on the path of sobriety and serenity gives us no rest—unless we rest in God's strength.

THE NEGOTIATION: Are there times when we feel like giving in?

THE PRAYER:

Dear Lord, when the pain becomes overwhelming and our will and strength are exhausted, give us the insight to turn to You for Yours help that we may not fail on the path we have chosen. Amen.

THE READING:
                    Psalm 28:1-9

FEBRUARY 23

LENT

THE INSPIRATION:

"Jesus said, 'If anyone wishes to be a follower of mine, he must leave self behind; he must take up his cross and come with me. Whoever cares of his own safety is lost; but if a man will let himself be list for my sake, he will find his true self.'" --Matthew 16:24-25

THE MEDITATION:

It is at this time of the year that we begin the Lenten Season—the season when the Church places special emphasis on the Cross. During Lent we meditate on and contemplate the Cross of Christ and our own cross-bearing as we prepare for the celebration of Easter.

To follow Jesus means to bear a cross. In general usage we speak of cross-bearing as something that is imposed upon us and over which we have no control. And so we hear people say, "My weak heart is a cross I must bear," or "Alcoholism is a cross I must bear." These tragedies in life are not what Jesus means by cross-bearing. For Jesus our cross is something that we voluntarily give up. It is a choice we consciously made to deny ourselves comforts, luxuries, and selfish interests in order to follow in the steps of Jesus. These are glorious steps of joy which we discover only through sacrificial cross-bearing.

THE NEGOTIATION:

How does one find his or her true self?

THE PRAYER:

Dear Lord, Your Son chose the path of the Cross which led to joy and glory. We pray that we may follow him by taking up our cross of self-denial and sacrifice in the service of others, that we may share in his joy and glory. Amen.

THE READING:

Luke 14:25-33

FEBRUARY 24

ST. MATTHIAS

THE INSPIRATION:

"They prayed and said, 'Thou Lord, who knowest the hearts of all men, declare which of these two though hast chosen to receive this office of ministry and apostleship which Judas abandoned' . . . They drew lots and the lot fell on Mattias, who was then assigned a place among the twelve apostles." --Acts 1:24-25

THE MEDITATION:

Matthias was chosen by lot to fill the vacancy left when Judas Iscariot abandoned his apostleship by betraying Jesus. Although this is the only place in the Bible he is mentioned, the implication is that he was a follower of Jesus from the beginning of his ministry. Tradition located Matthias' missionary work in Ethiopia.

Is Matthias' call to ministry and apostleship any different than ours? Does not the lot also fall upon us? An apostle is one who is sent by the Lord. A minister is one who serves the Lord. Where and to whom does the Lord send us to serve? Perhaps our experience with alcoholism has equipped us for a very special ministry. It is in our understanding of our weakness and God's strength that the lot falls on us. We are sent to serve. May we never abandon our ministry and apostleship.

THE NEGOTIATION:

What is this lot that has fallen on us?

THE PRAYER:

Almighty God, who gave to Matthias a special ministry and apostleship. We pray for the guidance of your Holy Spirit that we may know the special ministry to which You call us. And give us strength to perform this service to Your Glory. Amen.

THE READING:

Acts 1:15-26

FEBRUARY 25

THE HECTIC PACE

THE INSPIRATION:

"Take time. Give God time to reveal Himself to you. Give yourself time to be silent and quiet before Him, waiting to receive through the Spirit the assurance of His presence with you, of His power working in you . . . To seek Him, to find Him, to tarry in His presence, to be assured . . . that He actually listens to what we say, and is working in us." --Andrew Murray

THE MEDITATION:

Our technocratic culture complicates the experience of God's presence. Modern society, for all the benefits it brings, depersonalizes. "Future Shock," the rapid pace of change, described by Alvin Toffler, is upon us. The result is that many of us have sought relief through alcohol, which plays an important role in the human attempt to deal with meaninglessness.

The hectic pace of modern life is a factor not only in alcohol problems, but also in drug addiction, heart disease, emotional break-down, and many other maladies. The physical and psychological apparatuses of many persons will not stand the stress of this reckless pace. Survival may depend upon taking time to develop a strong devotional life.

As Jesus withdrew to the hills, wilderness, or mountains for quiet times of prayer and meditation, so we need to withdraw daily from the hectic pace of life.

THE NEGOTIATION:

Do we take enough time with God?

THE PRAYER:

We thank You, Lord, for leading us to this time with You. Allow us now to find peace in this moment. Refresh us with your presence now. Abide with us this day as the hectic pace begins once again. Amen.

THE READING:

Psalm 37:1-7

FEBRUARY 26

BEARING FRUIT

THE INSPIRATION:

"A man had a fig tree growing in his vineyard; and he came looking for fruit on it, but found none. So he said to the vine-dresser, 'Look here! For the last three years I have come looking for fruit on this fig tree without finding any. Cut it down. Why should it go on using up the soil?' But he replied, "Leave it, sir, this one year while I dig around it and manure it. And if it bears next season, well and good; if not, you shall have it down.'" --Luke 13:6-9

THE MEDITATION:

Repentance is the point of Jesus' story. To repent means to face up to our failures, to turn around, to re-orient our lives, to bear fruit for which we are meant. The fig tree that doesn't bear fruit is cut down. This is not a very inviting story. We would rather hear about the still waters, green pastures, lilies of the field, and birds of the air. But we are not sheep, not flowers, not birds. We are human beings, created in God's image, and our purpose is to bear fruit. It could be that the parts of the Bible we least like to hear are those which will do us the most good.

To have a fruit-bearing function means that we are responsible-able to respond. The fig tree parable is a warning but also a promise that we count for something. What we do matters. Life is not "a tale told by an idiot." There is rhyme and reason in our existence. God expects us to bear fruit.

THE NEGOTIATION:

Have we faced up to the fruitlessness of alcohol abuse?

THE PRAYER:

Merciful God, we turn to you with repentant hearts for our many failures. Give us strength as we seek to reorient our lives. Nurture us with your Spirit that we may live productively, bearing fruit which pleases you. Amen.

THE READING:

Luke 13:1-9

FEBRUARY 27

CRUEL KINDNESS

THE INSPIRATION:

"It is a poor or false friendship that allows a friend to perish without help, that dare not lance an abscess to save his life." --Francis de Salas

THE MEDITATION:

We of all people ought to understand that not being helped or rescued is sometimes the best thing that can be done. It is when we run out of rescuers that we must face up to our true dilemma. We also ought to know that lancing our pride with open confrontation is a very kind deed. These deeds of cruel kindness—leaving us unrescued and stabbing us with truth—may have saved our very lives.

These lessons in cruel kindness are very valuable to us in helping others suffering from alcohol abuse. If we keep picking up, rescuing, covering up for an alcoholic friend we may very well be contributing to his or her condition. If we fail to confront an alcoholic friend about the reality of his or her situation, again we may be contributing. True friendship is willing to take the risk of confrontation. We may lose, we may be told to "go to hell." That's the risk of being so kind that we are cruel. Doing the "right" thing for an alcoholic is not necessarily the good thing.

THE NEGOTIATION:

How has cruel kindness helped save our lives?

THE PRAYER:

O Lord, we thank you for those people who loves us enough to leave us alone or confront us with the painful truth of our condition. Give us the courage and strength to do the same for others who suffer as we did. Amen.

THE READING:

Matthew 23:16-36

FEBRUARY 28

THE WOUNDED HEALER

THE INSPIRATION:

"In an old legend in the Talmud the Messiah is seen sitting among the poor, binding his wounds one at a time, while waiting for the moment that he will be needed. Jesus has added a new dimension of this story by making his own broken body the way to liberation and new life. This means that he who wants to announce liberation is not just called to care for his own wounds but even to make them into the main source of his healing power. But which are our wounds? Words such as alienation, isolation, and loneliness have been used to indicate our wounded condition." --Henri Nouwen

THE MEDITATION:

Those who have abused alcohol certainly can understand the wounds of alienation, separation, isolation and loneliness. Everyone, of course, has at times experienced these wounds. However, these wounds become a way of life for alcohol abusers. We also have experienced the deep and crying need for liberation from dependence and/or addiction. Having experienced the "new life," we have a special calling to announce liberation to others. As we care for our own wounds, we make them a source of healing power for others. We are called to be wounded healers.

Our experience with suffering, with our wounds, has equipped us with an understanding and empathy for the suffering of others. Other people whether they abuse alcohol or not, can benefit from our being wounded. The new life is ours to announce, and by so doing, that life becomes more meaningful and glorious.

THE NEGOTIATION:

Can we thank God for our wounds?

THE PRAYER:

Dear Lord, we thank You for the liberation and new life as have experienced through Your Son, Jesus. As his wounds become a source of healing power for us, enable us to carry on his mission of healing and reconciliation by utilizing our wounded condition in the service of others. Amen.

THE READING: Isaiah 53:1-12

FEBRUARY 29

THE GOD DEBATE

THE INSPIRATION:

"It's God that's worrying me . . . What if He doesn't exist? If He doesn't exist, man is the chief of the earth, of the universe. Magnificent! Only how is man going to be good without God? That's the question. For whom is man going to love then? To whom will he be thankful? To whom will he sign hymns?" --Feder Dostoevsky

THE MEDITATION:

Instead of professing to establish the reality of God by philosophical reasoning, the Bible from beginning to end takes the reality of God for granted. Immanuel Kent has said, "it is necessary that one should be convinced of God's existence, but not so necessary that one should prove it." God's existence need not be proved. The debate for and against God down through the ages is meaningless. What is meaningful is God's existence for us.

The fact that we have life now, that we are now meditating on God, that we are in communion with him, is enough, even though it proves nothing. Our sobriety, our search for serenity convinces us of God's presence.

THE NEGOTIATION:

Need we prove God's existence?

THE PRAYER:

O God, through whom all things are, which of themselves could have no being; God, from whom to go out is to waste away; to whom to return is to revive; in whom to dwell is to live; God, to whom faith excites, hope uplifts, love joins; God, through whom we overcame the enemy, O You do I supplicate . . . After You I am groping . . . Cause me, O Father, to seek You aright; let me not stray from the path. Amen. --Augustine

THE READING:

Romans 11:32-36

MARCH 1

SAYING AND LIVING A YES

THE INSPIRATION:

"For all that has been—Thanks!
To all that shall be—Yes!"

"To say Yes to life is at one and the same time to
say Yes to oneself."

"You dare your Yes—and experience meaning.
You repeat your Yes—and all things acquire a meaning.
When everything has a meaning, how can you live
anything but a Yes." --Dag Hammarskjold

THE MEDITATION:

It is only when we can say thanks for all that has been that we can say yes to all that shall be. Can we thank God for our total life and experience what has brought us to this point in time? Can we, while deeply regretting the suffering and pain we endured and caused others, thank God for what has been? If so, we are now ready to say Yes to all that shall be.

Saying Yes is surrendering our lives to God's will for us as we know it through the Gospel. Yes to God is Yes to life, Yes to ourselves. God promises that we might have life in all its abundance if we respond affirmatively to Christ's Gospel.

Saying Yes, of course, if only the beginning. It is living that Yes where we meet the exciting and challenging possibilities God has in store for us. Paul says that Jesus "is the Yes pronounced upon God's promises" (2 Corinthians 1:20). Herein is meaning!

THE NEGOTIATION:

Do we dare to say Yes?

THE PRAYER:

Dear Lord, for all that has been—Thanks!
O Lord, to all that shall be—Yes! Amen.

THE READING: 2 Corinthians 1:15-22

MARCH 2

OPINIONS AND FAITH

THE INSPIRATION:

"A string of opinions no more constitutes faith,
than a string of beads constitutes holiness."   --John Wesley

THE MEDITATION:

We have opinions about many things; about things that have great significance and about things that make very little difference to anyone. We have theological and philosophical opinions, we have opinions about alcohol, alcohol abuse, alcohol abusers, and recovery from alcohol abuse. These opinions are valuable to us, and we have every right to them.

Other people do not necessarily find our opinions as valuable as we do. We cannot impose our opinions on others. If we try we only alienate others. Still, we have a responsibility to express our opinions, to tell others what and how we view things. If others agree with us, all well and good; if they disagree, we must allow them that right. Rejecting the opinions of one another does not mean rejecting one another.

Let us not get locked into our opinions. Opinions do not equal faith. Faith is living, active, and growing. As the living faith grows our opinions may change. Opinions take on different values as we are nurtured in the faith.

THE NEGOTIATION:

Have our opinions changed in the last few years?

THE PRAYER:

Forth in Thy Name, O Lord, I go.
My daily labor to pursue,
Thee, only Thee, resolved to know
In all I think, or speak, or do. Amen.   --Charles Wesley

THE READING: Matthew 22:41-46

MARCH 3

OUR NEED FOR THE DRAMA

THE INSPIRATION:

"We ought to see how each of us may best arouse others to love and active goodness, not staying away from our meetings, as some do, but rather encouraging one another." --Hebrews 10:24-5

THE MEDITATION:

The meetings referred to are of course public worship. We need to be aroused by God and by other Christians. At the same time we are needed to arouse others. Worship is a vertical and horizontal drama. Both worship and drama have elements of presence, empathy, imagination (faith), and creativity. When worship and drama are not creative, one is ritual and the other is show business. Theatre starts with the ultimate and brings it down to the particular. Liturgy means the work of the people; God's people working together, being aroused by God, encouraging one another in love and active goodness. The work of God's people, obviously, is not confined to an hour on Sunday morning.

Many persons who have messed their lives up with alcohol are reluctant to go to church. They feel that they will not be accepted. Where there is worship there is acceptance. We need to worship both privately and corporately. Others need us in their worship.

THE NEGOTIATION:

How can our worship become more liturgy and less ritual?

THE PRAYER:

O worship the King, all glorious above,
O gratefully sing his wonderful love.
Our shield and defender, the Ancient of Days,
Pavilioned in splendor and girded in praise. Amen.   --Robert Grant

THE READING: Psalm 104:1-35

MARCH 4

WORKAHOLISM

THE INSPIRATION:

"Happy people work, sometimes very hard, in the fulfillment of their duties. But others work as a drug to keep their thoughts of their own conscience, their own inner misery. When work is done for its own delight, or to provide the economic necessities, it is normal; but when it is a compulsion to escape from inner guilt, it ceases to be work and becomes an addiction." --Fulton Sheen

THE MEDITATION:

Most of us who have been dependent upon and/or addicted to alcohol have learned from our own experience or that of others the futility of substituting one addiction for another. Work can become an escape from guilt and inner misery. It can become a means of trying to prove something to others or ourselves that is untrue. Work can become mere business, which goes nowhere, repeats itself, and goes around in circles. Constructive work is behavior, which goes somewhere, has purpose, has a goal, leads to an end. Our work is not our purpose for living. But our work ought to fit into our purpose for living. Work does not provide us meaning, but rather our meaning is carried out in part in our work. Our main work, says Jesus, is not to work for perishable food, but rather for the imperishable food he gives (John 6:27). Our work is to do God's will—it is this we must fit into our vocation.

THE NEGOTIATION:

How do we see the purpose of our work?

THE PRAYER:

O God, help us to perform our duties with laughter and kind faces; and let cheerfulness abound with industry. Give us to go blithely on our business all this day, and bring us to our resting beds weary and content and undishonored; for Jesus Christ's sake. Amen. – Robert Louis Stevenson

THE READING: John 6:22-29

MARCH 5

A KINGDOM NOT OF THIS WORLD

THE INSPIRATION:

"Pilate. . . summoned Jesus, 'Are you the King of the Jews?' he asked. Jesus said, "Is it your own idea, or have others suggested it to you?' 'What! Am I a Jew?' said Pilate. 'Your own nation and their chief priests have brought you before me. What have you done?' Jesus replied, 'My Kingdom does not belong to this world. If it did, my followers would be fighting to save me from arrest.'" --John 18:33-35

THE MEDITATION:

It would have been so easy for Jesus to satisfy Pontius Pilate during his trial. Pilate was asking Jesus for his credentials. Was he a King or not? And, if he was, what kind of a King? Jesus' answers do not satisfy Pilate. Jesus says his "Kingdom does not belong to this world." That is his Kingdom is not derived from, grounded in, nor determined by this world. If that were the case Jesus' followers would resort to violence to save him. Jesus' Kingdom is derived from, grounded in, and determined by Another.

Jesus calls us to citizenship in his Kingdom, which is of God. There are other Kings and other Kingdoms calling for our allegiance. In Sweden, Jack London's book "John Barleycorn" goes by the title "King Alcohol." Of all the Kings calling for our devotion, only one does not belong to this world. And that is the only Kingdom which enables us to live meaningfully in this world.

THE NEGOTIATION:

Can we serve more than one King?

THE PRAYER:

We thank You, O Lord, that through Your Son You revealed to us a Kingdom which is derived from, grounded in, and determined by You. Give us the strength to live under Your authority in all that we do and say and think. Amen.

THE READING: John 18:33-40

MARCH 6

VALUES CLARIFICATION

THE INSPIRATION:

"The world, as we live in it, is like a shop window into which some mischievous person has for overnight, gone and shifted all the price-labels so that the cheap things have the high price-labels on them, and the really precious things are priced low. We let ourselves be taken in. Repentance means getting those price-labels back in the right places." --William Temple

THE MEDITATION:

One of the necessary tasks in the recovery process from alcohol abuse is the clarification of our values. One way to help do this is to make a list of twenty things we like to do. Then rank them; and ask ourselves are they giving or receiving activities, would we prefer doing them alone or with someone(s), how much money is involved in each, would they have been on our list five years ago? Such questions will tell us a great deal about our values.

Having clarified what our values actually are, we need to ask ourselves, how they fit with God's will for us. While doing thus we must remember, "The Lord does not see as many see; men judge by appearances but the Lord judges by the heart" (1 Samuel 16:7), and again, Jesus said, "God sees through you" (Luke 16:15).]

THE NEGOTIATION:

How can we rearrange our values?

THE PRAYER:

Almighty God, unto whom all hearts are open, all desires know, and from whom no secrets are hid: Cleanse the thoughts of our hearts by the inspiration of Thy Holy Spirit, that we may perfectly love Thee, and worthily magnify Thy Holy Name; through Jesus Christ, Thy Son, our Lord. Amen. –Order of Public Confession

THE READING: Luke 16:10-15

MARCH 7

DOING OUR DUTY

THE INSPIRATION:

"Is he (the master) grateful to the servant for carrying out his orders? So with you: when you have carried out all your orders, you should say, 'We are servants and deserve no credit; we have only done our duty.'" – Luke 17:9-10

THE MEDITATION:

How often we become elated by success, forgetting that doing good is our duty. How often we take pride in accomplishments, forgetting that we are only following the orders of Another. There is no reason in our becoming puffed up when we are aware of God's task for us.

Our duty from God is to do good and refrain from doing evil. Our orders from God are simply to love God, others and ourselves. God may have unique ways for us to express love, but, however we do it, we deserve no credit.

Our duty is to live sober lives by refraining from all of the squandering that goes with alcohol abuse. Our orders call for a productive and serving life style. When sobriety and serenity are achieved, we know what Paul means when he says, "I have strength for anything through him who gives me power" (Philippians 4:13).

THE NEGOTIATION:

Can we take credit for our sobriety?

THE PRAYER:

Most merciful God, let me not be elated by success nor cast down by failure, neither puffed up by the former nor depressed by the later. I want only to take pleasure in what draws me to You, only to grieve for what displeases You. Grant me, O Lord, a mind to know You, a heart to seek You, wisdom to find You. Amen. – Thomas Aquinas

THE READING: Luke 17:7-10

MARCH 8

THE REAL TREASURE

THE INSPIRATION:

"Do not store up for yourselves treasures on earth, where it grows rusty and moth-eaten, and thieves break in to steal it. Store up treasures in heaven, where there is no moth and no rust to spoil it, no thieves to break in and steal. For where your wealth is, there will your heart be also." --Matthew 6:19-21

THE MEDITATION:

Jesus does not advocate that we take vows of poverty. Nor does he say that we should make no plans for the future. Jesus pleads for an ordering of priorities. No one can abuse alcohol and keep his or her priorities in order. As we begin that long task of reordering priorities we asked to make daily deposits of kind words, good works, and courageous witness of our faith. These are the intangibles which are real and become visible in times of crisis. These are treasures which are rust-proof, moth-proof and thief-proof. Those treasures do not depreciate in value and are not subject to the whims of Wall Street.

However Christians articulate the meaning and purpose of their lives; the Gospel of Jesus Christ is at the heart of it. It is the life and message of Jesus that gives meaning and purpose to our lives. This Gospel is our priceless treasure.

THE NEGOTIATION:

Do our priorities need reordering?

THE PRAYER:

Jesus, priceless Treasure
Source of purest pleasure
Truest friend to me;
Long my heart hath panted
Till it well-night fainted,
Thirsting after Thee.
Thine I am, O spotless Lamb,
I will suffer nought to hide Thee
Ask for nought besides Thee.   --Johann Franck

THE READING: Matthew 6:19-24

MARCH 9

GOD'S TASK AND OURS

THE INSPIRATION:

"Do we want to help people because we feel sorry for them, or because we genuinely love them? The world needs something deeper than pity, it needs love... But in our love of people are we to be excitedly hurried, sweeping all men and tasks into our loving concern? No, that is God's function. But He, working within us, portions out His vast concern into bundles, and lays on each of us our portion. These become our tasks." --Thomas Kelly

THE MEDITATION:

Our task is not to save the world and alleviate all of the suffering in it. That is God's task. Ours is to respond to the needs where we are and when we can. When we try to take on God's task we can only end up frustrated and harried. These are feelings which can be threatening to serenity and sobriety.

In a parable Jesus has the King say, "Anything you did for me or my Brothers here, however humble, you did for me" (Matthew 25:40). Jesus tells us that only by responding in service to human need can our loving gratitude to God find an outlet in action. People in need are God's proxies. The only way we can serve God is by serving the needs of his children. The needs which we meet each day, are the portions or tasks God lay on us.

THE NEGOTIATION:

What tasks will God lay on us this day?

THE PRAYER:

O Lord, we pray for all Your children everywhere, that all suffering may cease. Help us, Dear Lord, to translate this prayer into the specific needs to which we may respond this day. Amen.

THE READING: Matthew 25:31-46

MARCH 10

SELF-INDULGENCE

THE INSPIRATION:

"As we grow spiritually, we find that our old attitudes toward our instinctual drives need to undergo drastic revisions. Our demands for emotional security and wealth, for personal prestige and power all have to be tempered and redirected.

We learn that the full satisfaction of these demands cannot be the sole end and aim of our lives... When we are willing to place spiritual growth first—then and only then do we have a real chance to grow in healthy awareness and mature love." --Bill W.

THE MEDITATION:

Our instincts are that part of us that seek after physical pleasures and avoidance of physical pain. Our instincts tell us, "If it feels good, do it!" Having a low frustration tolerance, we often turned to alcohol to feel good or to avoid feeling bad. Alcohol works! It works in a temporary and artificial sense. We will never understand alcohol as a problem unless we first see it as a solution.

God created us to be far more than a bundle of instincts. We thank God for our instincts—they are essential for our survival. But we thank him above all that we are created in his image. This means we have the potential for fellowship with our Creator. Growth toward this potential allows us to view and react to our instincts in constructive and abundant living.

THE NEGOTIATION:

Have we revised our attitudes toward our instincts?

THE PRAYER:

O Lord, there are times when we feel like reverting back to the days when we were dominated by our instincts. At these times, O Lord, strengthen us with the assurance of Your presence that we may grow in the awareness of who You have created us to be. Amen.

THE READING: 1 Thessalonians 4:2-8

THE SERENITY PRAYER

THE INSPIRATION:

"God grant me the serenity
To accept the things I cannot change,
Courage to change the things I can,
And wisdom to know the difference."   -- Reinhold Neibuhr

THE MEDITATION:

Serenity means peace with God, with one's self, and with other people. In order to find and experience this peace we must learn to accept the things we cannot change. Serenity does not mean that everything goes our way and that we have no problems. It means being able to live and cope with unsolved problems. There is much about the world we cannot change. One of the main "things" we cannot change is other people. We can ask them to change. We can motivate, stimulate, and encourage them to change, but we cannot change them.

One of the main "things" we can change is ourselves. This often requires courage for we would rather follow the line of least resistance and remain the way we are. But we can change ourselves. We are responsible for ourselves, our behavior, our thoughts, our feelings. These we can change, if we have the courage and the will to ask for God's help.

THE NEGOTIATION:

What changes can we make in our lives?

THE PRAYER:

Dear Lord, give us the wisdom to know that we are responsible for ourselves and that with Your help and guidance we can change. We pray also, O Lord, for the wisdom to know and accept those things and persons we cannot change. Give us, Lord, a deep sense of responsibility for ourselves and to others. Amen.

THE READING: Romans 12:17-21

MARCH 12

ARE WE INVOLVED?

THE INSPIRATION:

"Were you there when they crucified my Lord?
Were you there when they crucified my Lord?
O, sometimes it causes me to tremble, tremble, tremble.
Were you there when they crucified my Lord?" -- Negro Spiritual

THE MEDITATION:

It is a question with which we are confronted each Lenten Season. It's more than a question of presence—it's a question of involvement. But how can we be involved in an unjust crucifixion that took place so long ago and far away? We forget that Jesus' death was a legal execution. It was with the consent of the religious establishment that Jesus was put to death by the authority and democracy of the Roman government. In a profound sense, that Crucifixion points an accusing finger at all of us.

The question for us today is, "How are we involved in the crucifixions taking place in our time, in our world?" Are we involved in the suffering of the oppressed, the persecuted, the starving, the diseased? Of course not! Not directly perhaps, but does our inactivity implicate us? By doing nothing are we contributing to the injustice?

Sometimes we feel like we have enough to do just to stay sober ourselves. That task is so great we don't have the time or energy to get involved in other people's problems. And yet we will discover sooner or later that it is only through our involvement in other people's problems that we can find serenity.

THE NEGOTIATION:

Are we involved in the injustice and oppression and suffering in today's world?

THE PRAYER:

Forgive us Lord for our insensitivity to human need and suffering. May the Crucified One lead us to know, that like him, we are not here to be served, but to serve. Amen.

THE READING: Luke 23:32-48

MARCH 13

THOSE DANGEROUS RESENTMENTS

THE INSPIRATION:

"Slander drives a wise man crazy and breaks a strong man's spirit. Better the end of anything than its beginning; better patience than pride. Do not be quick to show resentment; for resentment is nursed by fools. Do not ask why the old days were better than these; for that is a foolish question."
--Ecclesiastes 7:7-10

THE MEDITATION:

Resentments are the dubious luxury of normal people, but for we alcohol abusers they are poison. We cannot grow in our quest for sobriety and serenity if we continue to harbor resentments. There is nothing like resentments to drive us crazy and break our spirits.

What or whom do we resent? Do we resent that we cannot drink with the rest of them like we did in the old days? That is indeed a foolish question. Whom do we resent? What can be done about this most unhealthy of emotions?

Jesus suggests that we pray for those whom we resent. Indeed he goes even further and tells us to pray for our persecutors (Matthew 5:44). Jesus does not promise that prayer will cause them to stop persecuting us but it will change our attitude toward them. It is our attitude that is dangerous and destructive. We will discover that we cannot hold resentments toward those for whom we pray.

THE NEGOTIATION:

What resentment can we eliminate through prayer today?

THE PRAYER:

O Lord, who does forgive us and accept us. We pray for those who have harmed us. Take away all bitterness in our hearts. Give us the courage to initiate reconciliation; and if rejected help us love our rejectors as You love them and us. Amen.

THE READING: Ecclesiastes 7:1-12

THE VALUE OF DOUBT

THE INSPIRATION:

"Mysticism makes men sane; mere logic drives them mad. Leave a little fallow corner in your heart for the seed of mystery to grow. Leave an alter to the unknown God." -- G. K. Chesterton

THE MEDITATION:

There are tides of the spirit just like the sea. Faith and doubt came in upon us at various times. Both are necessary for us. Doubt is the readjustment of our lives to the requirements of new experience. A new experience of sobriety will bring with it many doubts. A growing, living faith brings doubts. Without these doubts we would never grow. The seed of mystery keeps our faith alive. As we learn to know God more and more, the more we learn he is always unknowable.

Let us not despair over doubt. It is a symptom of life not death. A theological student once dropped out of the seminary stating to the officials that he no longer believes in God. That same student later in his life wrote the inspiring hymn, "O Love that wilt not let me go." Doubt has meaning and value. It is a highway to a more mature faith.

God's promise to us is not certainties but faith, not mere logic but peace which passes all understanding.

THE NEGOTIATION:

Have we experiences the difference between certainty and doubt?

THE PRAYER:

O love that wilt not let me go,
I rest my weary soul in Thee;
I give Thee back the life I owe,
That in Thine ocean depths its flow
May richer, fuller be. Amen. – George Matheson

THE READING: Ephesians 3:1-13

THE LORD NEEDS IT

THE INSPIRATION:

"When they were approaching Jerusalem . . . he (Jesus) sent off two of his disciples with these instructions. 'Go into the village just ahead of you and . . . you will find a tethered colt on which no one has yet ridden. Untie it, and bring it here. If anyone asks you, 'why are you doing this?' just say, 'The Lord needs it.'" -- Mark 11:1-3 (Phillips)

THE MEDITATION:

"The Lord needs it" was enough explanation. No one disputed the disciples' action when they borrowed the colt. Are we as willing to do the same with our possessions when the Lord has need of them? Jesus never implied that to possess things was a sin. However, if we have possessions which interfere with our relationship with God, we are asked to give them up.

What do we have that the Lord needs? Our time, our special abilities, our possessions? Often times the things that mean the most to us are the very things the Lord needs. If our most cherished possessions are a hindrance to us in our spiritual growth, we need to give them up.

We know how important alcohol was to us and how it interfered with our relationship to God and others. Now we know we needed to give that up. What more do we need to give up? What do we have that the Lord needs?

THE NEGOTIATION:

What are our real needs?

THE PRAYER:

O Lord, You know our deepest needs and our hearts desires. Lead us to a willingness to give up those things that hinder our relationship with You as well as those things for which you have need. Help us to be willing and cheerful stewards of all that we have and all that we are. Amen.

THE READING: Mark 11:1-10

MARCH 16

PRACTICING PURITY

THE INSPIRATION:

"Who may go up the mountain of the Lord?
And who may stand in his holy place?
He who has clean hands and a pure heart . . .
He shall receive a blessing from the Lord,
And justice from God our Savior." – Psalm 24:3-5

THE MEDITATION:

Our immediate response may be that we will never make it to the mountain of the Lord. Our dirty hands and impure hearts will never allow us to stand in the Lord's holy place. And that's true, we'll never make it on our own. But God is our Savior and by his grace his mountain is available to us.

There is much dirt and impurity in our past. But God cleanses and purifies us if we come to him in repentance. He can and does create in us clean hearts and renew his Spirit within us.

The way of Purity is that road that leads to sobriety and serenity. We will never achieve absolute purity. That is, however, the direction we travel. While we never reach perfect purity, we are expected to make progress in purity. We can, with God's help, become more pure it our thoughts, words and deeds. This progress is an impossibility while abusing alcohol. Happy and healthy is the person who grows in purity.

THE NEGOTIATION:

What can we do to practice purity today?

THE PRAYER:

Create a pure heart in me, O God,
And give me a new and steadfast spirit;
Do not drive me from Thy presence
Or take Thy Holy Spirit from me;
Revive in me the joy of Thy deliverance
And grant me a willing spirit to uphold me. Amen. --Psalm 51:10-12

THE READING: Psalm 24:1-10

PATIENCE

THE INSPIRATION:

"We have need of patience with ourselves and with others; with those below, and those above us, and with our equals; with those who love us and those who love us not; for the greatest things and for the least; against sudden inroads of trouble, and under daily burdens; disappointments as to the weather, or the breaking of the heart; in weariness of the body, or the wearing of the soul. . .   In all these things . . . patience is the grace of God, whereby we endure evil for the love of God." – E. B. Pusey

THE MEDITATION:

The Bible calls us to run with patience the race that is set before us with our eyes fixed on Jesus (Hebrews 12:1-2). We might expect that energy or zeal might be the word, but it is patience.

Too often we are like the man who prayed, "Lord, give me patience; and I want it right now!" We want to get over our alcoholic past right now. We want our compulsion and all of the problems it caused to leave us right now.

Patience is its own reward. It preoccupies the soul with a sort of serenity which suppresses compulsion, vain endeavor, and rebellious desire. The key to patience is that our eyes are fixed on Jesus.

THE NEGOTIATION:

A test of patience is "How long can we wait for it?"

THE PRAYER:

In all things, dear Lord, may we find patience with our eyes fixed on Jesus. In our little pet peeves and our life and death struggles inspire us through Your Son to persevere. Amen.

THE READING: Hebrews 12:1-11

MARCH 18

HABITS

THE INSPIRATION:

"We are spinning our own fates, good and evil, never to be undone. Every smallest stroke of virtue or vice leaves its ever-so-little scar. The drunken Rip Van Winkle, in Jefferson's play, excuses himself for every fresh dereliction by saying, "It won't count this time!" Well he may not count it, and a Kind Heaven may not count it, but it is being counted nonetheless. Down among his nerve-cells and fibers the molecules are counting it, registering it and storing it up to be used against him when the next temptation comes. Nothing we ever do, in strict scientific literalness, is wiped out." -- William James

THE MEDITATION:

How often have we told ourselves, "It won't count this time" or "Only one more time, then I'll quit"? Every time counts and the most important time is the next time. How often have we been like the man who was told all he has to do is avoid the first drink—so he walked into a bar an ordered two drinks and drank the second one?

Our behavior conditions us. If we put our hand in hot water, the pain will cause us to remove it quickly. But if our hand is in water that is gradually heated to that same temperature it will cause us little discomfort. Each time we abuse alcohol it matters.

The more we practice the presence of God the more habitual that Presence becomes.

THE NEGOTIATION:

What good habits can help us break bad habits?

THE PRAYER:

Help us, O Lord, to recognize the power of goodness and love; and with the recognition give us the will to practice that power in our life today. Amen.

THE READING: Luke 4:14-16

MARCH 19

PRACTICING THE PRESENCE OF GOD

THE INSPIRATION:

"Although I have been a minister and a missionary for fifteen years, I have not lived the entire day of every day . . . to follow the will of God. Two years ago a profound dissatisfaction led me to begin trying to line up my actions with the will of God . . . about every half hour. But this year I have started out to live all my waking moments in conscious listening to the inner voice, asking . . . 'What Father, do you desire . . . this minute! It is clear that this is exactly what Jesus was doing all day every day."
　　　　　--Frank Laubach

THE MEDITATION:

The general reaction to Laubach's intention is either "It's impossible!" or "He's crazy!" But these reactions come from people who have never really considered or attempted to practice the presence of God. The consideration and attempt come only after a profound dissatisfaction with the way things are. To become aware of that dissatisfaction is a rare gift which those of us who have habitually abused alcohol can appreciate. In order to want something better, we must first come to grips with how bad things are.

Practicing the presence of God is no easy discipline. We learn only by stages; beginning with hours, and working down through minutes, we come to this moment. The most important moment in our lives is the one that is ours now.

THE NEGOTIATION:

What does God desire this moment?

THE PRAYER:

Dear Lord, You have led us to desire a more constant contact with You. Increase in us the will to grow in conscious awareness of Your presence with us that Your desire may be ours. Amen.

THE READING: John 10:22-30

MARCH 20

SURVEYING THE CROSS

THE INSPIRATION:

> "When I survey the wondrous Cross
> On which the Prince of Glory died,
> My richest gain I count but loss
> And pour contempt on all my pride."   -- Isaac Watts

THE MEDITATION:

During the Lenten Season we are called to survey the Cross. As we do, our values and priorities are clarified and reoriented. As we ponder that Cross things which we thought were so important take on less significance and the real values of life are seen in their proper perspective.

Contemplating the mystery of the Cross brings a blow to our pride which plays an important role in alcohol abuse. Pride is dangerous for us because it means that we are trusting in ourselves rather than in God. Pride furthermore means an expression of superiority rather than compassion for others. Pride is, therefore, a flagrant denial of love for God and others. Surveying the Cross pours contempt on all our pride.

Paul states it quite strongly: "God forbid that I should boast of anything but the cross of our Lord Jesus Christ" (Galatians 6:14).

THE NEGOTIATION:

What does pride have to do with our sobriety and serenity?

THE PRAYER:

Dear God, we thank You for the great expression of Your Love for us through the Cross of Your Son Jesus Christ. May we respond to this amazing love by surrendering all our pride and rededicating our lives to You. Amen.

THE READING: Galatians 6:11-16

MARCH 21

SPRING!

THE INSPIRATION:

"Green now is on the larches;
Springtime in triumph marches.
And every day uncloses
A host of new primroses;
Then daffodils and marybuds let us in garlands bring,
For Christ has come again to greet the spring."   -- Jan Struther

THE MEDITATION:

As we come to the vernal equinox we become aware of the evidence of new life all around us. New life brings us to remembrance of the Resurrection of Jesus Christ and the possibilities of new life for us. The old English word for Spring is "Lent" and the Saxon goddess of spring was "Eastra."

Those of us who have experienced the hell of alcohol abuse are in a unique position to perceive the wonder of resurrection in our own lives.

A man who had been sober for a few weeks after years of alcohol abuse once said, "You know I have walked through a park on my way to work for twenty years, and this morning I discovered something I never realized before: there are birds and flowers in that park!" Let us keep our eyes and ears open to the evidences of new life about us and be reminded of the power of Christ's Resurrection within us.

THE NEGOTIATION:

What evidence of new life will we see and hear today?

THE PRAYER:

"Dear Lord, we thank You for the Spring and all of the evidences of new life which it brings. Help us to be aware of the power of the Resurrection of Your Son in our lives, and live that new life in its abundance and glory. Amen.

THE READING: Song of Songs 2:11-12

SELF-KNOWLEDGE

THE INSPIRATION:

"He came to his senses." -- Luke 15:17

"Let us look to our own consciences as we do to our own hands, to see if they be dirty."
-Florence Nightingale

"The highest and most profitable reading is the true knowledge and consideration of ourselves."
-Thomas A Kempis

THE MEDITATION:

The Prodigal Son never gave much thought to himself. All he wanted was his share of his inheritance so he could go to the far country and have a good time. After squandering his inheritance in reckless living he ended up in a pig pen. It was then that he came to his senses.

Self-knowledge doesn't come easy. Few of us look to our own conscious and seek to read ourselves—until we get into trouble. Each of us has ended up in a pig pen of our own making. We know the loneliness and desperation of the far country. It is there that we come to our senses. It is in the helplessness and hopelessness of alcoholic defeat that we begin to look at and know ourselves. And knowing ourselves and our place in life brings us to a decision to go home to the Father who is patiently waiting to embrace us with his love.

THE NEGOTIATION:

What good has come out of our journey to the far country?

THE PRAYER:

We praise You, O Lord, that You have brought us home from the far country. We thank You that out of our experience in the pig pen, You brought us to a deeper understanding and experience of who we are and who You are. Amen.

THE READING: Luke: 15:11-24

PROCRASTINATION

THE INSPIRATION:

"The best intentions to lead a serviceable life may evaporate for no other reason than the habitual substitution of well-wishing for well-doing. . . Many are congenially sailing on a zoneless, shoreless sea of well-wishing. The breeze of a mild good will fills their sails . . . But they never land. They mean well but they mean well feebly. They never come to . . . a practical assumption of responsibility, to a costly and efficient expenditure of time, thought, energy, and money in useful work."
--Harry Emerson Fosdick

THE MEDITATION:

Good intentions come easy to us. We are aware of many things that we can be doing to live useful lives. We are also aware of some things we ought not do for a meaningful existence. How often have our good intentions led is to say, "I'll quit tomorrow" or make some other well-meaning promise to ourselves or others?

Procrastination has been and is our enemy. The good intentions of yesterday bring us pain today when they are unfulfilled. This pain of failure can be eliminated, we have learned, temporarily and artificially by alcohol.

Even when sobriety is found procrastination is a dangerous enemy. We need to realistically ask ourselves what good and useful service can we render today and do it remembering that all problems cannot be solved in any one day.

THE NEGOTIATION:

What good intentions will we accomplish today?

THE PRAYER:

"Most merciful God, let us ardently desire what pleases You, prudently seek, truly learn, and faithfully fulfill all to the praise and glory of Your name. Order my day so that I may know what You want me to do, and for my soul's good, help me to do it. Amen." –Thomas Aquinas

THE READING: Matthew 21:28-32

LET GO—LET GOD

THE INSPIRATION:

"Profound immersion in the Divine Love is a shaking experience. But it is not an unsettling experience; one becomes at last truly settled, a coordinated, integrated personality. This is the life beyond earnestness, beyond anxiety, beyond strain. Its strength sets in when we let go . . . Active as never before, one lives in the passive voice, alert to be used, fearful of nothing, patient to stand and wait." – Thomas Kelly

THE MEDITATION:

Letting go, turning our lives and wills over to the power of God, does not mean we sit back and do nothing. Nor does surrender mean we are giving up the freedom of our will. On the contrary, surrender means increased action and freedom on our part; only now are we aware of the action of God in us.

A fish going down-stream might feel totally passive in the powerful current that sweeps it into the sea. Yet the fish must do the steering if the destination is to be reached.

As we acknowledge our powerlessness over alcohol and let go—let God, that letting is itself an action which places great demands on us. It is an active and passive cooperation with God as we steer through life by his power.

THE NEGOTIATION:

Must we sacrifice our freedom when we turn our will over to God?

THE PRAYER:

Dear Lord, as we surrender our lives and wills over to Your power, we pray that we would so direct our course that we will be actively involved in service to others. Amen.

THE READING: Psalm 59:1-17

MARCH 25

THE ANNUNCIATION

THE INSPIRATION:

"The angel said to her, 'Do not be afraid, Mary, for God has been gracious to you; you shall conceive and bear a son, and you shall give him the name Jesus. He will be great; he will bear the title of 'Son of the Most High'; the Lord God will give him the throne of his ancestor David' . . . 'Here am I,' said Mary; 'I am the Lord's servant; as you have spoken so be it." -- Luke 1:30-32, 38

THE MEDITATION:

The Annunciation has been observed by the Church since the fifth century. It is not by coincidence that today is exactly nine months until Christmas, for it is Jesus' birth that is announced. God indeed was gracious to Mary and she accepted his grace by her willingness to service him even though she was mystified by the announcement.

God announces his will for us in mysterious and sometimes troubling ways. Through our own unique background and experience God announces his special plan for us. That plan may trouble and mystify us. When it would make more sense to us to escape from our problems, God tells us to live out the solutions. When we would rather take the easy way out, God troubles us with his plan which involves discipline and self-surrender. Most mysterious and troubling is God's announcement that he wants us to carry on the mission of the "Son of the Most High."

THE NEGOTIATION:

What is God's unique announcement for us today?

THE PRAYER:

Almighty God, You announce Your will for us in mysterious and troubling ways. We pray that as Mary once heard and accepted the angel's message of your will, we too may hear Your call and respond with full faith and willingness to serve; through Your Son, Jesus Christ our Lord. Amen.

THE READING: Luke 1:26-38

MARCH 26

RELATEDNESS

THE INSPIRATION:

"Imagine men awakening at last . . . to a sense of universal solidarity on their profound community . . . It is a new kind of love, not yet experienced by man, which we must learn to look for . . .

For men . . . to learn to love one another, it is not enough that they should know themselves to be members of one and the same 'thing'; . . . they must acquire the consciousness, without losing themselves, of becoming one and the same 'person'. (That is) what I have called Omega Point."
-- Pierre Teilhard de Chardin

THE MEDITATION:

In a very real sense our relationships define who we are. One of our basic needs is a feeling or deep trust and relatedness to life. A part of the charm of alcohol is its ability to provide a temporary sense of unit within oneself, with others, with the universe, with God. When our need to feel at one with ourselves and all else is frustrated we experience an existential anxiety which can be temporarily and artificially tranquilized by alcohol.

Becoming aware of God's love for us helps us realize our uniqueness in God's creation. We are not isolated phenomena existing by a chance of nature. We belong! God's love for us individually proclaims our importance. Each of us should know that we are related to all else and that God has a purpose for us in his scheme for all things. Without each of us the universe is incomplete.

THE NEGOTIATION:

What is our relationship to the universe?

THE PRAYER:

Dear Lord, we thank You for Your love and concern for us. Give us a love and concern for Your whole creation and help us to assume responsibility for our part in your infinite plan. Amen.

THE READING: Hebrews 2:5-9

MARCH 27

THE CREATIVE VALUE OF SUFFERING

THE INSPIRATION:

"When did it first dawn on you that we men don't live unto ourselves? In suffering. When did the blessedness of compassion bring comfort to you? In suffering. When did your heart come close to those who were so distant and cold to you? In suffering. Where did you catch a glimpse of the higher destiny of your life? In suffering. Where did you feel God was near to you? In suffering. Where did you first realize the blessedness of having a Father in heaven? In suffering." – Albert Schweitzer

THE MEDITATION:

When we seriously ponder the questions above we become convinced of the creative value of suffering. The suffering we brought upon ourselves and caused other people through our alcohol abuse is not counted for nothing. We can, of course, ignore the lessons of suffering as we can disregard any of our teachers.

Questions concerning the why of suffering have been asked by people since they have had reasoning powers. The Book of Job deals with these questions. Job finds no satisfactory answers in his why questions. The message of the Book of Job is that in the midst of suffering Job could say, "I know that my vindicator lives" (John 19:25).

Suffering does not mean that God is punishing us or disciplining us or that he has rejected us. Suffering means that we have the opportunity to grow in communion with our living Vindicator.

THE NEGOTIATION:

Are we thankful for the opportunities that suffering brings?

THE PRAYER:

Help us merciful Father to nestle confidently in Your arms when we face suffering; and through it, O Lord, may we learn the lessons that You would teach us. Amen.

THE READING: Job 19:21-29

MARCH 28

SELF-RIGHTEOUSNESS

THE INSPIRATION:

"You know how I have slaved for you all these years. I never once disobeyed your orders; and you never gave me so much as a kid, for a feast with my friends. But now that this son of yours turns up, after running through your money, with his women, you kill the fatted calf for him." -- Luke 15:29-30

THE MEDITATION:

The story of the Prodigal Son is not simply about a bad boy who left home and a good boy who stayed home. It's the story of a self-indulgent son and a self-righteous son and a loving father. The reason that Jesus told this story is because he was accused of welcoming sinners. The loving father goes down the lane to meet the younger brother and he goes out into the field to meet the older brother. It is in the father's house that the alienated brothers meet. The older brother has no business taking his brother's inventory and confessing his sins. Nor has the younger brother any business confessing his brother's self-righteousness.

Those of us who have "reformed" from the self-indulgence of alcohol need to be on guard lest we develop a self-righteousness. Our reformation is through the grace of the Father. It is in the Father's House that all self-righteousness and self-indulgence is forgiven and brothers and sisters who were alienated are reconciled.

THE NEGOTIATION:

Can we identify with both the younger and older brother?

THE PRAYER:

"Our loving God, you know our frailties and failings. Give us your grace to overcome these. Keep us from those things that harm us, and guide us in the way of salvation and service; through your Son, Jesus Christ our Lord. Amen." – Collect for Nineteenth Sunday after Pentecost

THE READING: Luke 15:25-32

MARCH 29

SIN AND ALCOHOL ABUSE

THE INSPIRATION:

"Sin is anything that comes between us and God, or between us and other people.

The contagion of the world's slow stain." -- Percy B. Shelley

THE MEDITATION:

Alcohol abuse is looked upon in some circles as sin. In other circles, it is regarded as an illness in that outside help is needed to effect its arrest. Alcohol abuse is more than sin, more than illness; it is an emotional, physical, social and spiritual disorder. Suffering persons need help and treatment, not condemnation—hope, not recrimination.

Our behavior when drinking was often anti-social and destructive. Consequently we are branded as wicked sinners. Such branding falls prey to the concept of sin as the abridgement of the law rather than as a state of being—of separation and alienation from God and from our fellow human beings.

When we abuse ourselves with alcohol we are living in sin if we understand sin as a state of separation from God and other human beings. We know we do not have to physically die to go to Hell—we know Hell as a living reality. Our basic need is Resurrection, new hope, and new life.

THE NEGOTIATION:

How is sin involved in alcohol abuse?

THE PRAYER:

Dear Lord, we thank You that You have revealed Yourself to us through your Son as a loving, waiting Father who is always willing to accept, receive, and forgive us when we separate and alienate ourselves from You. Give us Your peace in this moment. Amen.

THE READING: Psalm 32:1-22

MARCH 30

ASSUMPTION

THE INSPIRATION:

"Who is aware of his unwitting sins?
Cleanse me of any secret fault.
Hold back Thy servant also from sins of self-will,
        lest they get the better of me.
Than I shall be blameless
        and innocent of any great transgressions."
            --Psalm 19:12-13

THE MEDITATION:

We all have unwitting sins and secret faults which we assume are not there. To assume is to suppose or take for granted. If we look closely at the word "assume" we will see a hidden truth; it makes an "ass" out of "u" and "me".

We assume that others see things the way they do. What others see as stubbornness the assumer sees as conviction. What others see as selfishness the assumer sees as rewards from God. What others see as hypocrisy the assumer sees as faithful duty.

In our struggle against alcohol abuse we assume that other people understand us, or we assume that no one understands us. Let us not assume that we know the burdens of others or that others know our burdens. Assumption keeps us from establishing the relationships we need. Assumption is a subtle sin. Let us open our hearts to God's claim upon our lives now. Let us not assume that God means "some other time" when he says "now".

THE NEGOTIATION:

What assumptions about ourselves and others do we need to get rid of?

THE PRAYER:

"May all that I say and think be acceptable to Thee, O Lord, my rock and my redeemer. Amen."
            -Psalm 19:14

THE READING: Psalm 19:1-14

MARCH 31

THE PIG'S ADVANTAGE

THE INSPIRATION:

"All mankind is of one Author, and is one volume, when one man dies, one chapter is not torn out of the book, but translated into a better language; and every chapter must be so translated.
--John Doone

THE MEDITATION:

In Tennessee Williams' play "Cat on a Hot Tin Roof" Big Daddy speaks of the pig's advantage is ignorance of mortality and avoidance of existential questions. The pig doesn't ask questions concerning the meaning of existence. The pig eats slop, lies down in the mud, takes a nap, and doesn't ask: "Who am I? Why am I here? Where am I going? What does it all mean?" Herein lies the pig's advantage over human beings. We humans ask existential questions and are aware of our mortality.

As a chapter in the Author's book, each one of us has meaning and purpose. The volume is incomplete without us. Even though alcohol abuse may have brought us to a pig's existence, we never acquire the pig's advantage. We can never forget that we will die and we can never completely avoid questions about the meaning of our existence.

Our purpose and meaning can only be seen through the eyes of the Author. God created us and invites us to share in his plan for all creation by bringing new love to the world.

THE NEGOTIATION:

Not having the pig's advantage, what are our alternatives?

THE PRAYER:

We thank You, O Lord, for the advantages of freedom and reason and responsibility that You have given to us. May we use these advantages in such a way that our lives may be translated into Your language of love. Amen.

THE READING: Matthew 10:29-31

APRIL 1

APRIL FOOLS

THE INSPIRATION:

"We are fools for Christ's sake." -- 1 Corinthians 4:10

THE MEDITATION:

On April Fool's Day we might well be reminded of the many times while abusing alcohol that we made fools out of ourselves. We could like to forget these episodes but we cannot. They are permanently on our records. What we have done, we have done and cannot redo it or forget it. Rather than trying to forget our past foolishness let us learn from it and allow it to strengthen us in the present and future.

Since forgetting is an impossible way of coping with past foolishness, we must turn to another word—that word is forgiveness. As we repent of our foolishness and seek with God's help to amend our lives, he forgives us. Perhaps others will never forgive us—that is beyond our control. But God forgives us and consequently we can forgive ourselves.

While we are forgiven and called from our past foolishness, we are at the same time called to be fools for Christ's sake. This means that, regardless of what other people say and think, we are to order our lives after the life and message of Jesus. If we seriously do this, we will be regarded by the world as fools.

THE NEGOTIATION:

What are the positive and negative aspects of being called a fool?

THE PRAYER:

Dear Lord and Father of mankind,
Forgive our foolish ways.
Reclothe us in our rightful mind.
In purer lives Thy service find.
In deeper reverence, praise. Amen.
                    --John Greenleaf Whittier

THE READING: 1 Corinthians 4:8-13

APRIL 2

TRANSCENDENCE

THE INSPIRATION:

"The sway of alcohol over mankind is unquestionably due to its power to stimulate the mystical faculties of human nature . . . sobriety diminishes, discriminates, and says not; drunkenness expands, unites, and says yes . . . It makes him for the moment one with truth. Not through mere perversity do men run after it . . . The drunken consciousness is one bit of the mystic consciousness." --William James

THE MEDITATION:

One of our basic human needs is transcendence. We need to be lifted above ourselves. We need to get out of touch with our horizontal earth-boundness and in touch with a vertical dimension of life. When we become dependent upon or addicted to alcohol, alcohol was not just a symbol of the vertical dimension of life. It was the vertical dimension. We substituted the symbol—the very nature of which is to point beyond itself—for that which was symbolized. Alcohol was not a symbol of our experience of God, it was God.

Our basic need for transcendence is always with us. We never outgrow our need to get "high". Alcohol and other drugs can temporarily and artificially supply that need. There are no substitutes to the particular "high" we experience with alcohol, but there are alternatives. The most viable of which is getting "high" on God.

THE NEGOTIATION:

How do we deal with our need for transcendence?

THE PRAYER:

"Oh! That thou wouldst enter into my heart and inebriate it. Amen."　--Augustine

THE READING:　Psalm 25:1-22

APRIL 3

LOYALTY

THE INSPIRATION:

"I am not bound to win, but I am bound to be true. I am not bound to succeed, but I am bound to live by the light that I have. I must stand with anybody that stands right, stand with him while he is right, and part with him when he goes wrong." – Abraham Lincoln

THE MEDITATION:

Is it an oversimplification and generalization to say that most of our troubles, including troubles with alcohol, have to do with a lack of loyalty? The lack of loyalty to God, and consequently to the Church and other relationships, is at the heart of most of our problems. Loyalty to God implies turning our life and will over to God's power.

There is no "if" in our loyalty to God. Jacob failed when he tried it that way: "If God will be with me, if he will protect me . . . and give me food to eat and clothes to wear . . . then the Lord will be my God" (Genesis 28:20-21). Loyalty to God means surrender.

It was loyalty that brought Jesus to Jerusalem. It was loyalty that brought him to the cross. Jesus was loyal to the vision of peace and love. Our loyalty to God and His vision for us results in loyalty to ourselves, to the Church, to other people to whom we are responsible. Loyalty means we forgive the short-comings of others as God forgives us.

THE NEGOTIATION:

Are there any "ifs" in our loyalty to God and others?

THE PRAYER:

O Lord, like the crowds who sang Hosannas to Jesus, we often praise You with our lips and reject You with our hearts. Take away all disloyalty and unfaithfulness from us that we may be totally committed to Your vision of peace and love. Amen.

THE READING: Matthew 21:1-11

APRIL 4

VISIONS OF GREATNESS

THE INSPIRATION:

"We've got some difficult days ahead. But it really doesn't matter with me now. Because I've been to the mountaintop . . . Like anybody, I would like to live a long life . . . But I'm not concerned about that now. I just want to do God's will. And He's allowed me to go up to the mountain. And I've looked over, and I've seen the promised land . . . My eyes have seen the glory of the coming of the Lord." -- Martin Luther King, Jr. April 3, 1960

THE MEDITATION:

There are some people, few in number, who have seen and responded to a vision which encompasses a cause which is larger than life itself. While most of us believe in the Fatherhood of God and Brother-Sister-hood of all people, there are few who are willing to live and die for that cause. And yet the mountaintop is there before us beckoning us to ascent, to come and peek over into the promised land.

We know that alcohol abuse allows us little time and energy for the great causes of life. Our own dependence or addiction narrows our vision until it focuses only on our own needs. As we find release by God's strength our vision broadens, and God's will for us as well as for the whole creation becomes increasingly important.

We cannot all achieve greatness in the relative sense, but each of us can achieve a greatness in becoming what God intended us to be. Realizing our human potential is all that God asks of us.

THE NEGOTIATION:

To what larger-than-life cause is God calling us?

THE PRAYER:

Dear Lord, release us from our selfishness and petty concerns that we might dream dreams and see visions of Your will for Your whole creation. Amen.

THE READING: Joel 2:28-32

APRIL 5

AMAZEMENT

THE INSPIRATION:

"It is amazement (astonishment, wonder) that the reader of the New Testament continually encounters in its accounts of the men and women who have ears hearing or having eyes see the bursting life, the sudden power, the sharp judgment and surprising liberty of which Jesus spoke . . . Astonishment pulsates in the Gospels, a psychic resonance of power in all the modes it touches man's hearts." -- Richard Niebuhr

THE MEDITATION:

It is often said that there is nothing new under the sun. Emerson admitted that "all literature is quotation." Most of the teachings of Jesus are paralleled elsewhere: in the Prophets, the Psalms and rabbis of his day. What is the uniqueness of the Gospel of Jesus Christ? Why the amazement, the astonishment, the wonder that prompted his bearers to say, "No man ever spoke as this man speaks" (John 7:46)?

The uniqueness of Jesus is that his message cannot be separated from the person. The Gospel is the life and message of Jesus Christ. Here is the incarnate love of God in action. The amazing thing is that his message and life (the Gospel) still touches people's hearts today.

The word "Gospel" literally means good news. It is always good and always new and we wonder in astonishment as the Gospel speaks to our deepest needs.

THE NEGOTIATION:

Are we open to the wonder of the Gospel in our lives?

THE PRAYER:

"Were the whole realm of nature mine,
That were an offering far too small;
Love so amazing, so divine,
Demands my soul, my life, my all. Amen."   -- Isaac Watts

THE READING: Luke 5:17-26

APRIL 6

THEOLOGY

THE INSPIRATION:

"We are only operating a spiritual kindergarten in which people are enabled to get over drinking and find the grace to go on living to better effect. Each man's theology has to be his own quest, his own affair." –Bill W.

THE MEDITATION:

Theology is simply the study of God. We live by theology. Our sobriety and serenity are dependent upon it. Let us now get stuck in kindergarten in our theological development. Let us not be afraid of theology. Let us not be intimidated by theologians.

Theology deals with existence and is anchored in reality. It has no other purpose than to interpret life and help us to be sensitive to its meaning. To do theology is not to talk about spiritual things; it is to talk about things spiritually. The aim of theology is meaning, devotion and action. It seeks to extend our vision of things, letting us sense the depth dimensions of life. Theology sensitizes our ears and hearts that we may hear the winds of the Spirit blow through the many landscapes of our existence.

Theology results in action. Our concept of God determines who we are and how we speak and feel and act. Sobriety and serenity are, therefore, dependent upon our theology. The Church is a fellowship of people who seek to do theology.

THE NEGOTIATION:

Can we articulate our theology?

THE PRAYER:

O Lord, You reveal Yourself to us in many ways and yet always remain mysterious. We pray that we might grow in our understanding and experience of You that we might come to a deeper knowledge of Your purpose for our lives. Amen.

THE READING: Psalm 145:1-21

CHEAP GRACE

THE INSPIRATION:

"Cheap grace is the preaching of forgiveness without requiring repentance, baptism without church discipline, communion without confession, absolution without personal confession. Cheap grace is grace without discipleship, grace without the cross, grace without Jesus Christ, living and incarnate.
--Dietrich Bonhoeffer

THE MEDITATION:

Anything that has value does not come cheaply. Our sobriety is of utmost value to us because without it we are vulnerable to the loss of everything. Sobriety and serenity are not the same thing; but serenity is only possible where there is sobriety. Sobriety does not come cheaply. It costs us a great deal. If we desire sobriety enough we will be willing to pay the high price.

Because sobriety and serenity can only be achieved by the power God gives us, they must be seen as coming to us by grace. Grace is God's free and undeserved love for us. We can never earn it, buy it, or in any way deserve it. But once we accept God's grace our grateful response will cost us something. If God's grace is worth anything to us we will respond in discipleship: Voluntarily and cheerfully taking up our cross daily in service to others in the name of Jesus Christ.

THE NEGOTIATION:

What does God's grace in our lives cost us?

THE PRAYER:

We thank You, O Lord, for Your love and care for us, which we do not deserve. We pray that Your Grace may be accepted by us that we willingly respond by service in Jesus' name not counting the cost. Amen.

THE READING: Romans 3:21-26

APRIL 8

GLORY BY!

THE INSPIRATION:

"In the Cross of Christ I glory,
Towering o'er the wrecks of time;
All the light of sacred story
Gathers round its head sublime.

When the woes of life o'er take me,
Hopes deceive and tears annoy,
Never shall the Cross forsake me;
Lo! It glows with peace and joy." --John Bowring

THE MEDITATION:

Just prior to his arrest, trial, and crucifixion Jesus said, "Now the Son of Man is glorified, and in him God is glorified" (John 13:31). In the Fourth Gospel the crucifixion is seen so strongly in the light of the Resurrection that the Cross itself is seen as glorification. In John's Gospel the verb "to lift up" is used of the Cross in three ways—the lifting up of Jesus on the Cross, the lifting up of Jesus in Resurrection, and the lifting up of Jesus in ascension to God's heavenly glory.

When Jesus spoke of what his love for God and people would cost him, he spoke of that cost in terms of glory. For Jesus the only real glory was the cost of love. God was glorified in Jesus when in obedient love he accepted the Cross. Christ is glorified in us when we accept the price of that same obedient love. Therein lies the source of our sobriety and serenity.

THE NEGOTIATION:

How can God be glorified in our lives?

THE PRAYER:

O Lord of all glory, we thank You that through the glorification of Your Son You have given us a glimpse of Your love for us. Enable us to glory in the Cross of Christ by responding in obedient love. Amen.

THE READING: John 13:31-35

APRIL 9

SELFISHNESS AND UNSELFISHNESS

THE INSPIRATION:

"We are most ourselves when we lose sight of ourselves." –J. H. Newman

"The love of our neighbor is the only door out of the dungeon of self," --George MacDonald

"Love your neighbor as yourself." --Mark 12:31

THE MEDITATION:

To love our neighbor as ourselves implies a love of oneself. In this sense there is such a thing as healthy, positive, and constructive selfishness. We must be very selfish in seeing that our needs are fulfilled in matters where our sobriety is at stake. Without sobriety we can do ourselves and anyone else no earthly good. Selfishness, in this sense, is a self concern for our welfare and consequently a concern for others.

While in a narrow sense selfishness is good, in its broader aspect it is unhealthy, negative, and destructive. The paradox of sobriety and serenity is that we must share them in order to keep them. The true conception of Christian living is not measured by our own achievements, but rather by the growth and quality of life that we stimulate in others.

Unless we love and show interest for ourselves, we cannot love and show interest for others. And any love for ourselves or others, is possible, only because God first loved us.

THE NEGOTIATION:

How much love can we give of ourselves to others today?

THE PRAYER:

O Lord, who has taught us through Your Son that true greatness is found in forgetting ourselves in the service of others, grant us grace to learn the hard lesson of unselfishness, that those around us may rise to their full potential and accomplish Your holy will. Amen.

THE READING: Mark 10:35-45

APRIL 10

EASTER IS NOT AN ISLAND

THE INSPIRATION:

"We knew that Christ, once raised from the dead, is never to die again: he is no longer under the dominion of death. For in dying as he died, he died to sin, once for all, and in living as he lives, he lives to God. In the same way you must regard yourselves as dead to sin and alive to God, in union with Christ Jesus." --Romans 6:9-11

THE MEDITATION:

There is an island in the South Pacific about 2,400 miles off the west coast of Chile. It was discovered in the Western world by the Dutch explorer Roggeveen on Easter Sunday 1722. Consequently it has been named Easter Island.

Easter, that event which we celebrate this time of the year, is however, not an island. The annual observance of Eastern Sunday cannot be isolated from the rest of our lives and observances. The Resurrection of Jesus Christ has relevance to us each day of our lives.

Paul makes the Resurrection central: "If Christ was not raised, then our gospel is null and void, and so is your faith" (1 Corinthians 15:14). We who have been raised to new life from the depths of alcohol abuse know how important that new life is for us each day. Easter is not an island, it is a way of life. We walk in newness of life seeking to know and do God's holy will. We do this not as a matter of grim obedience, but of living life as a doxology of triumphant praise.

THE NEGOTIATION:

What does the Easter Event mean for our daily living?

THE PRAYER:

Almighty God, as we joyfully celebrate the festival of the Resurrection of Christ, we pray for Your strength that Your love may show the power of Resurrection in what we thank and say and do. Amen.

THE READING: Romans 6:5-14

APRIL 11

RESPONSIBILTY

THE INSPIRATION:

"Evil has been represented in our time as something imposed upon (us) from without, not made by man from within. The dreadful conclusion follows inevitably that, as he is not responsible for evil, man cannot alter it; . . . there is no hope for you and me . . . The trouble is not outside us but inside us, and therefore, by the grace of God, we can do something to put it right." --Dorothy L. Sayers

THE MEDITATION:

We are responsible for ourselves. There is always something, by the grace of God that we can do when confronted by trouble. We are responsible for our behavior. Our actions are our actions. We are responsible to decide whether to drink or not to drink. Some of us may have been kicked out of bars but none of us were ever kicked into a bar.

We are also responsible for our thoughts. How and what we think is up to us. Other people and outside stimuli suggest things to us but what we do with them is our responsibility.

Furthermore we are responsible for our feelings. When we feel anger we sometimes cop out by telling someone, "You made me angry." If we are responsible for our feelings, we can only say, "I allowed myself to become angry because of something you said or did." We must own our feelings before we can begin to deal constructively with them by the grace of God.

THE NEGOTIATION:

Are we responsible for all our acts, thoughts and feelings?

THE PRAYER:

O Lord, we thank You for the freedom you have given us. We pray that by Your grace we may accept the responsibility which this great gift places upon us. Amen.

THE READING: Jeremiah 31:29-30

APRIL 12

SORROW

THE INSPIRATION:

> "To Sorrow I bade good morrow,
> And thought to leave her far away behind;
> But cheerily, cheerily
> She loves me dearly;
> She is so constant to me, and so kind."   --John Keats

THE MEDITATION:

We have tried to say good bye to sorrow many times. We would think that the sorrow we experienced through alcohol abuse would leave us once we begin living in sobriety. It's true drinking brought such sorrow to ourselves and others which is alleviated by sobriety and serenity. However sorrow itself seems to love us dearly and keeps coming back. Sobriety and serenity do not guarantee we will be free of sorrow. What they do guarantee is that we will be able to cope with and grow with sorrow.

Jesus does not promise those who follow him a life of ease and comfort without sorrow. On the contrast Jesus promises uneasiness and discomfort to those who deny themselves and take up their cross and follow him. Life has its inevitable sorrows. Jesus assures his followers that their sorrow will be turned into joy. Jesus promises a joy which cannot be taken away. In our sorrow God's presence is most deeply felt. That presence is the source of joy born out of sorrow which abides with us and cannot be taken away.

THE NEGOTIATION:

How have our past sorrows been turned into joy?

THE PRAYER:

> Abide with me, fast falls the eventide;
> The darkness deepens, Lord, with me abide.
> When other helpers fail and comforts flee,
> Help of the helpless, O abide with me. Amen.   -- Henry F. Lyte

THE READING: John 16:19-24

APRIL 13

THE SEARCH FOR GOD

THE INSPIRATION:

"Why stand so far off, Lord, hiding thyself in time of need?" -- Psalm 10:1

"How long, O Lord, wilt thou hide thyself from sight?" – Psalm 89:46

"If only I knew how to find him." -- Job 23:3

THE MEDITATION:

We hear anguish in the cries of the Psalmists and Job as they search for God. Perhaps we have experienced that same anguish. The intoxication of alcohol abuse often causes a person to get "religion." We call to God in anguish but he hides himself from us. If only we knew how to find him.

God cannot be found. God is the One who finds us. Rather than frantically searching for God, let us allow God to find us. Rather than seeking God in some distant "out there" let us experience the nearness of God's presence. Rather than looking for God in some spectacular signs in the heavens, let us behold the God in us.

God reveals himself to us in many mysterious ways. If we are open to God finding us we will experience his presence in unexpected times and places. The best way to come into contact with God is to be still and allow him to find us. And the best way to come to a greater knowledge of God is by doing his will. The God who finds us is not a god created in our image.

THE NEGOTIATION:

Are we willing to let God find us?

THE PRAYER:

Dear Lord, of Thee three things I pray,
To know Thee more clearly
Love Thee more deeply
Follow Thee more nearly
Day by day. Amen.   --Richard of Chichester

THE READING: Psalm 10:1-18

APRIL 14

RECONCILIATION

THE INSPIRATION:

"Forgiveness, wherever we find it, is the restoration of a relationship between two persons which has been broken by the disloyalty of one of them; and it can take place only in the light of truth. It is for this reason that repentance and forgiveness belong together. . . God's law is not destroyed by his grace but is rather confirmed." – John Knox

THE MEDITATION:

Reconciliation is the foundation upon which serenity is established. Reconciliation is the result of repentance and forgiveness between ourselves and others and between ourselves and God.

Alcohol abuse includes a loyalty to alcohol which results in disloyalty to others. Reconciliation comes through our repentance and the forgiveness of those to whom we were disloyal. Let us seek the joy of reconciliation by forgiving others even when they make no gestures toward repentance.

We also have a deep need to forgive others. Resentments and grudges are a hindrance to sobriety and make serenity an impossibility. Let us seek the joy of reconciliation by forgiving others even when they make no gestures toward repentance.

Paul says, "From first to last this has been the work of God. He has reconciled us . . . to himself through Christ, and has enlisted us in this service of reconciliation" (2 Corinthians 5:18). Being reconciled to God we become ambassadors of Christ in the ministry of reconciliation.

THE NEGOTIATION:

How can we practice our ministry of reconciliation today?

THE PRAYER:

Merciful Lord, we thank You that by Your grace we have experienced the joy of reconciliation with You. We pray that we may not let this grace go for nothing, but rather take seriously this service of reconciliation to which you have enlisted us.

THE READING: 2 Corinthians 5:18-6:1

APRIL 15

SELF-IMAGE

THE INSPIRATION:

"Man is the highest, the richest, the most significant object within the range of our investigations because it is in him that cosmic evolution is culminating at this moment before our eyes... But dare we think that it can and should extend further? . . . Man is momentarily a climax in the universe . . . But may he not also be the bud from which something more complicated and more centered than man himself is to emerge? Could there not be . . . a humanity which will be the sum of . . . persons?"
  --Pierre Teilhard de Chardi

THE MEDITATION:

As significant as we might be corporately in the universe, many of us nonetheless have problems with our self-image. Individually we often acquire an inflated or deflated self appraisal. Deflation of self-image is a common characteristic of alcohol abuse. We might be successful in putting up a front which will convince others we feel OK about ourselves, but deep down no alcohol abuser has a high opinion of him/herself.

The OKness of our self image begins with our awareness that as a part of humanity created in God's image we hold a special place in all creation. This brings us to the realization and experience of God's love for us individually. There is a uniqueness and dignity which the Creator reserves for each one of us. Through heredity and environment and our own personal experience God has brought us to a special place and has particular tasks for each of us. Herein lies the OKness.

THE NEGOTIATION:

How are we individually special to God?

THE PRAYER:

O Lord, we are so small and insignificant in Your whole creation; yet You have taught us through Your son that we are important to You and are loved by You. Help us to know and carry out Your plan for us. Amen.

THE READING: Jeremiah 9:23-4

APRIL 16

WINGS LIKE EAGLES

THE INSPIRATION:

"Those who look to the Lord will win new strength, they will grow wings like eagles."
--Isaiah 40:31

THE MEDITATION:

There is a story of a baby eagle who fell from his nest and was picked up by a farmer who nursed him back to health and raised him on his farm with the chickens. The eagle ate chicken food, acted like a chicken and indeed thought of himself as a chicken. When the eagle was full grown, the farmer, concerned that he was not living up to his potential to fly like the other eagles, took him to the top of a cliff and threw him off. The eagle crash landed and scampered back to the chickens. The farmer didn't give up and on the fifth try the eagle started to fly and soared up toward the mountains and was never seen again.

Easter, to which we give special attention at this time of the year, means Resurrection, new life, being born again. Easter makes eagles out of chickens. We are born to be eagles, but through alcohol abuse we have lived as chickens. We allow our environment, our attitudes, our prejudice to keep us from living up to our potential. We are created in God's image. He means for us to fly like eagles not live like chickens.

A man with a history of severe alcohol abuse had a tattoo on his arm which read "Born to Lose". After some time of sobriety he had the slogan removed at great expense. Easter is the good news that people can change, that losers can become winners, that chickens can become eagles.

THE NEGOTIATION:

Are we living up to God's potential for us?

THE PRAYER:

Dear Lord, help us to love what You will for us, and put to use the gifts that You give us. Amen.

THE READING: Isaiah 40:31

APRIL 17

RATIONALIZATION

THE INSPIRATION:

"The evil must be called by its right and ugly name when it is discovered; otherwise we shall excuse our lack of fortitude as an "inferiority complex" and our inordinate love of the flesh as a 'release of the libido." Judas missed salvation because he never called his avarice by its right name—he disguised it as a love of the poor." -- Fulton Sheen

THE MEDITATION:

Alcohol abusers are masters of rationalization. We felt compelled to rationalize our drinking behavior in order to deceive ourselves and others. The reasons we gave for our behavior were not always reasonable. They amounted to alibis or excuses. We told ourselves we used alcohol because we needed to relax from the pressures of our work, or because we were celebrating our birthday or Millard Fillmore's or someone else's. We would not cut through the rationalization to call the behavior by its right name—dependency or addiction to alcohol.

We do not have to rationalize our behavior unless there is an inner subtle, perhaps unconscious, voice telling us there is something wrong. No one feels compelled to give reasons for drinking a glass of water.

When we begin our sobriety and search for serenity we discover that rationalization is a habit-pattern which is not easy to change. This is one of the reasons we need these daily periods of devotion and meditation. As we practice God's presence he gives us a growing discretion to call things by their right name.

THE NEGOTIATION:

What behaviors are we still rationalizing?

THE PRAYER:

O Lord, we pray that the light of Your Word may so fill our hearts that we may be able to distinguish truth from falsehood; and enable us to live in your truth as we are drawn closer to You each day. Amen.

THE READING: Luke 14:15-24

APRIL 18

DISCOVERING GOD'S SURPRISES

THE INSPIRATION:

"Now to him who is able to do immeasurably more than all we can ask or conceive, by the power which is at work among us, to him be glory in the church and in Christ Jesus from generation to generation evermore!" --Ephesians 3:20-21

THE MEDITATION:

One of the amazing discoveries that comes to us when we turn our life and will over to God's power is that God is full of wonderful surprises. When we are willing to let go and let God we discover that he is able to do immeasurably more than all we can ask or conceive. By taking God seriously we discover that there are no limits to his surprises.

There was a time, perhaps not too far from the present, when we thought it absolutely impossible to exist without alcohol. By practicing God's presence we are surprised by the power he works in us. If we remain open to his presence we continue to be amazed by God's surprises.

No matter how impossible our problems may seem, we discover that God's power and strength is more than adequate. He appears with amazing power bringing victory to our defeated souls, hope to our despairing hearts, healing to our broken minds.

We respond to God's surprises by giving him glory in and with the Church. The Church is a fellowship of people who are constantly surprised by God.

THE NEGOTIATION:

What surprises does God have in store for us today?

THE PRAYER:

Almighty God, You constantly surprise us with Your power at work in and through us. Keep us always open to Your amazing revelations. Help us to live in a spirit of excitement and expectation as we anticipate the surprises that You have for us this day. Amen.

THE READING: Ephesians 3:14-21

APRIL 19

PRIDE

THE INSPIRATION:

"The Pharisee stood up and prayed thus: 'I Thank thee, O God, that I am not like the rest of men, greedy, dishonest, adulterous, or for that matter, like this tax-gatherer. I fast twice a week, I pay tithes on all I get."   --Luke 18:11-12

THE MEDITATION:

The attitude of pride was of great concern to Jesus. He spent a good deal of time warning people of the dangers of pride. Pride plays an important role in alcohol abuse and can be a destructive force in our search for sobriety and serenity. Pride is dangerous, according to Jesus, because it means we trust in ourselves rather than in God.

When our pride is threatened we often, like the Pharisee, resort to comparing ourselves with others. We seek to build ourselves up by contemplating how bad off others are. We point to the winos on skid row, the woman lying in the gutter, or the man across the street who comes home drunk and kicks his dog. When we parade our virtues before God and other people we look pretty good in comparison. We sometimes forget that God's expectations for us are based upon our potential.

When we become aware of those who are worse off than ourselves we can only, like Augustine when he saw the drunk lying in the street, say "There but for the grace of God lie I." The grace of God leaves no room for pride in our hearts.

THE NEGOTIATION:

Is there anything of the Pharisee in us?

THE PRAYER:

Deliver us, O Lord, from the destructive attitude of pride. Help us to see ourselves in the light of your will for us; and by your grace keep us dwelling on our virtues and not the faults of others. O God, be merciful to us, sinners that we are. Amen.

THE READING: Luke 18:9-14

APRIL 20

A DAY AT A TIME

THE INSPIRATION:

"The present moment is significant, not as the bridge between past and future, but by reason of its contents, contents which can fill our emptiness and become ours, if we are capable of receiving it. Here and now—only this is real." --Dag Hammarskjold

THE MEDITATION:

After major surgery a man asked the doctor, "How long will I have to lie here helpless?" "Oh, only one day at a time," was the answer. Many of us have learned the wisdom of that answer. We came to the realization that it was impossible for us to control our consumption of alcohol—that we must abstain. "How long will we have to live without alcohol?" we asked. "Oh, only one day at a time," was the answer we received. That answer removes a heavy load from our minds. To worry about tomorrow, or next week, or next month, or next year is a load with which we cannot cope. We discover that we can cope with this day, this hour, this moment. Here and now is the only reality; here and now is life.

Jesus says, "Do not be anxious about tomorrow, tomorrow will look after itself. Each day has troubles enough of its own" (Matthew 6:34). Let us deal with today's troubles, today's problems, today's temptations, today's compulsions when they are real—today. Today is significant because of its contents. The content of today, which can fill the emptiness we feel, is the grace of God. The presence of God's grace is all we need today to live abundantly.

THE NEGOTIATION:

Do we fully appreciate the significance of today?

THE PRAYER:

"Lord—Thine the day,
And I the day's. Amen." —Dag Hammarskjold

THE READING: Hebrew 3:7-14

PERFECTIONISM

THE INSPIRATION:

"A man should not be afraid of anything at all as long as his will is good, nor should he be at all depressed if he cannot achieve his aim in all his works. But he should not consider himself to be far from virtue when he finds real goodwill in himself, because virtue and everything good depend on goodwill. You can lack nothing if you have true goodwill, neither love not humility nor any other virtue ... If you do not lack the will, but only the power, to do some good thing, you have really done it in the sight of God." -- Meister Eckhart

THE MEDITATION:

Many of us who have gotten ourselves into trouble with alcohol are perfectionists. So impressed are we with our own omnipotence that we expect everything we do to be perfect. And yet we are repeatedly struck by the blows of the reality that we are imperfect. Imperfection causes the perfectionist a great deal of pain and depression. We learned through experience that this pain and depression could be temporarily relieved by alcohol. We also learned that the "relief" intensified the pain and depression.

We need to consciously and unconsciously, intellectually and emotionally, accept the reality that we are not perfect, nor does God require perfection of us. Perfection is not an achievable goal but rather a direction in which we are called to travel. Our business, moving along the road to perfection, is progress. While we are expected to have the true goodwill to be perfect, it's O.K. not to be.

THE NEGOTIATION:

Can we be content with our progress?

THE PRAYER:

Dear Lord, our God, in whom all perfection lies, we pray that Your goodwill for us may become our goodwill without our putting ourselves in Your place. Help us that our lives may be consistent with the level of progress we have made by Your grace. Amen.

THE READING: Philippians 3:12-16

APRIL 22

THE ETERNAL THOU

THE INSPIRATION:

"Men have addressed their eternal Thou with many names. In singing of Him who was thus named they always had the Thou in mind: the first myths were hymns of praise. Then the names took refuge in the language of It; men were more and more strongly moved to think of and to address their eternal Thou as an It. But all God's names are hallowed, for in them He is not merely spoken about, but also spoken to." --Martin Buber

THE MEDITATION:

The revelation of God in the Scriptures is always in terms of a person. This revelation reaches its climax in Jesus Christ who called God his Father. A personal God is one who possesses personality. God is a person with whom we persons can communicate. We cannot communicate with an It. Communication is only possible with a Thou. Being created in God's image makes it possible for us to have an I-Thou relationship with Him. It is only through such a personal relationship that he gives us the strength to achieve sobriety and serenity.

If, however, "personal" means simply an enlarged replica of what we consider the best in human persons, then the adjective is inappropriate. "Personal" implies the capacity to communicate, awareness and self-awareness, action and reaction, and freedom and responsibility.

THE NEGOTIATION:

Is God personal or a vague indefinite blur?

THE PRAYER:

We thank You, O Lord, that You have personally revealed Yourself to us as One who cares for us and solicits our communication. Inspire us by Your Holy Spirit to know You more clearly and experience You more deeply. Amen.

THE READING: Jeremiah 31:31-34

APRIL 23

WHAT IS LOVE?

THE INSPIRATION:

"Lucy: Do you know what love is?

Schroeder: Love is a noun, which means, to be fond of, or attachment to, or devotion to, a
person or persons.

Lucy: On paper he's good."   --Charles Schultz

THE MEDITATION:

There are many definitions of love, none of which adequately describe what we mean by the
word. Even when we are "in love" we cannot articulate what we mean. Love is not so much a noun as it
is a verb. Love can only be perceived and experienced as action.

We use the world love in many ways: "I love apple pie, I love my spouse, God loves me." In the
Greek language in which the New Testament was written, there are three words for love: eros (sexual
desire and sensual longing), philia (affection for persons), and agape (God's kind of loving). Agape is a
giving love. "God loved the world so much he gave . . ." (John 3:16). It is this agape-love that Jesus
speaks about and demonstrates in his life. Agape-love is the essence of the Gospel.

Agape-love is totally undeserved. Perhaps we can begin to comprehend God's love when we
recall that he reached out to us in our helplessness, hopelessness, and powerlessness when we were
caught in the grips of alcohol. God's undeserved love comes to us most powerfully in our
unloveableness. Our attempts to define this love on paper may sound good but are inadequate. We
can only experience this love and demonstrate it in our relationship with others.

THE NEGOTIATION:

How will our experience of God's love affect our lives today?

THE PRAYER:

Continue to pour out upon us Your love, O Lord, that we may reflect the power of Your love in
all that we do and say and think. Amen.

THE READING: 1 John 4:7-16

APRIL 24

OPTIMISM

THE INSPIRATION:

> "He who, from zone to zone.
> Guides through the boundless sky thy certain flight,
> In the long way that I must treat alone,
> Will lead my steps aright."   --William Bryant

THE MEDITATION:

In Charles Dickens' novel "Great Expectations" Pip is a poor peasant boy who has little going for him except his expectations. Through many tragic events Pip grows to maturity and those expectations become reality. We know that the cruelties of life often interfere with our great expectations. Nevertheless, if our expectations are worthy, and if we hold on to them, we will have a far greater chance of their becoming reality. If we desire to become the persons God intends us to be, and if we trust in his strength to bring us to those expectations we will experience the reality of fulfillment. If we truly desire sobriety and serenity and expect to find them with God's help they will be ours.

We waste an awful lot of time in negative thinking. We play the game "What if": "What if I lose my job?; What if I lose my sobriety?; What if the roof caves in?" We waste time chasing phantoms that do not exist.

Everything is not going to work out exactly as we wish. Yet we have every reason to be optimistic because no matter what transpires God is behind us, ahead of us, and with us, leading our steps aright.

THE NEGOTIATION:

How optimistic are we about our future?

THE PRAYER:

O Lord, we thank You that You have brought us to this time and place in our search for sobriety and serenity. Fill out hearts with hope that we might walk optimistically into the future with You leading our steps. Amen.

THE READING: Psalm 23:1-6

APRIL 25

ST. MARK

THE INSPIRATION:

"Here begins the Gospel of Jesus Christ the Son of God."   --Mark 1:1

"Pick up Mark and bring him with you, for I find him a useful assistant."   --2 Timothy 4:11

THE MEDITATION:

John Mark was a companion of and assistant to both Peter and Paul. He is the author of the earliest of the four gospels. Both Matthew and Luke relied upon Mark's earlier work when they wrote their accounts of the Gospel.

The greatness of Mark was in his willingness to assist Peter and Paul who were always in the limelight. Mark was big enough to take a back seat. His way of serving the Lord was by assisting the great leaders of the Early Church. This doesn't mean that Mark was not a leader. Leadership in the Church means assuming responsibility. Those who are spokespersons for the Church and make important decisions need to be supported and assisted. The Church needs its' Marks. Marks survey the needs and respond where they can best be of service to the Lord. This is the leadership to which each of us is called.

Mark is the first to give us a written account of the Gospel. It is the power of that Gospel which is responsible for our sobriety and serenity. The life and message of Jesus speaks to our most fundamental question: is life absurd or does it have a purpose? The Gospel proclaims life has a purpose which is seen in the generous, forgiving, saving love announced and lived by Jesus Christ.

THE NEGOTIATION:

How can the inspiration of Mark's life be meaningful to us?

THE PRAYER:

"Almighty God, You have enriched Your Church with Mark's proclamation of the Gospel. Give us grace to believe firmly in the good news of salvation and to walk daily in accord with it. Amen."
--Collect for St. Mark's Day

THE READING: Mark 1:1-15

APRIL 26

REVENGE

THE INSPIRATION:

"Pass no judgment, and you will not be judged; do not condemn and you will not be condemned; acquit and you will be acquitted; give, and the gifts will be given to you. Good measure, pressed down, shaken together, and running over, will be poured into your lap; for whatever measures you deal out to others will be dealt to you in return." --Luke 6-37-8

THE MEDITATION:

Paul puts it most simply when he says, "Do not seek revenge" (Romans 12:19). One of the characteristics of persons who abuse alcohol is a persecution complex. In order to defend ourselves we deny that our troubles are our fault. We blame others and come to believe that they are out to get us. When others have harmed us, or we believe they have, we seek to "get even." A lot of violence and destructive words and deeds are condoned under the guise of revenge. We need to be reminded time and again that vengeance belongs to God; and cease trying to play his role.

To feel revenge in one's heart is the unhealthiest of human emotions. Those who harbor feelings of revenge greatly increase the risk of breakdown of their health. Revenge is a destructive emotion. Even when there is no attempt to act out the emotion by "getting even," revenge is destructive to those who harbor it. Revenge threatens our sobriety and makes serenity impossible.

THE NEGOTIATION:

Are we harboring any revenge in our hearts?

THE PRAYER:

O Lord, forgive us for our futile attempts to play Your role. Remove from us all feelings of hate and revenge that threaten to destroy us. Help us to deal with others as You deal with us in love and forgiveness. Amen.

THE READING: Luke 6:28-38

APRIL 27

SITUATION ETHIC

THE INSPIRATION:

"The law of love is the ultimate law because it is the negation of law; it is absolute because it concerns everything concrete. . . The absolutism of love is its power to go into the concrete situation, to discover what is demanded by the predicament of the concrete to which it turns. Therefore, love can never become financial in a fight for the absolute, or cynical under the impact of the relative."
--Paul Tillich

THE MEDITATION:

Love is the beginning and the end of the Christian Gospel. It begins with the truth that God is love and that this love is proclaimed and lived in the message and life of Jesus Christ. For the Christian everything is seen in the light of the overruling principle of love.

Too often we base our ethical decisions on the terms "right or wrong." We want to do the right thing. By the right thing we often mean the thing that the rest of the people are doing. Just because the majority, or everyone else for that matter, is doing something doesn't make it the good thing for us to do. We can readily understand the implications of drinking in this regard.

Rather than asking what is the right thing, let us ask what is the good thing, the most loving thing to do in a given situation. We face many ethical decisions which are difficult to make. There are often no clear-cut answers. "What would Jesus do in this situation?" is a good question to ask. Let us allow him to guide us doing the most loving thing in the moral dilemmas we face.

THE NEGOTIATION:

Can we think of times when the right thing has not been the good thing?

THE PRAYER:

Dear Lord of love, when we face very difficult decisions, we pray that You would fill us with the Spirit of Your love that we might be guided to think and act in the most loving manner. Amen.

THE READING: 1 Peter 4:7-11

APRIL 28

OPENNESS

THE INSPIRATION:

"You will find, on really looking honestly, that your mind is little better than a rough wilderness, neglected and stubborn, partly barren, partly overgrown with pestilent bushes and venomous wind-sown herbage of evil surmise; and the first thing to do is eagerly and scornfully to set fire to this, burn all the jungle into wholesome ask heaps, and then plough and sow." -- John Rushkin

THE MEDITATION:

There is a lot of garbage that accumulates in the minds of alcohol abusers. We, who would never allow garbage at our table, are too willing to allow it to be served into our minds. Openness is required for sobriety and serenity. If we are to have open minds and hearts the garbage must first be removed.

Closedness is sin. To close our minds to new ideas or close our hearts to God and to other people disallows us from growing to our potential. We need to let our minds be cleaned out and remade by God so that our whole nature may be transformed. Then we "will be able to discern the will of God, and to know what is good, acceptable, and perfect" (Romans 12:2).

My God's grace let us be open to the new, open to other people, open to God. A predominate mark of Jesus' life and message is inclusiveness. He never excluded anyone from God's love and grace; nor will we as we grow in openness.

THE NEGOTIATION:

What garbage in our minds keeps us from openness?

THE PRAYER:

Dear Lord, we thank You that You are always open to hear our prayers. We pray that we may be open to the continued and always fresh revelation of Your love and grace; and help us to respond with open minds and open hearts to the needs of others. Amen.

THE READING: Romans 12:1-2

APRIL 29

KNOWING GOD

THE INSPIRATION:

"O righteous Father, although the world does not know Thee, I know Thee, and these men know that Thou didst send me. I made Thy name known to them, and will make it known, so that the love Thou hadst for me may be in them, and I may be in them." --John 17:25-6

THE MEDITATION:

Thus Jesus concludes his "High Priestly Prayer." The reality of Jesus' experience of the Father is amazing. To Jesus God is not simply an object which is worshiped or thought about. God is "known" in the inner experience of Jesus. This God, who is an immediate and living reality, is made know to us by Jesus.

We too can directly perceive God. We can practice his present in our lives, not as an abstract concept, but as "our Father." We cannot adequately speak of God as we conceive him, but we can nonetheless experience him and know him.

It is this experiencing and knowing of God that is so essential to our sobriety and serenity. The more we practice this presence of God in our lives the deeper our awareness of him becomes. It is in this ever deepening compulsion for alcohol, to grow in serenity, and to increase of effectiveness and productivity in responding to the needs of others.

THE NEGOTIATION:

Are we learning to practice the presence of God more constantly?

THE PRAYER:

We thank You, Dear Lord, that through Your Son Jesus, You have made Yourself known to us. As we come to know You more deeply we pray that we may be so filled with Your love that our lives may be increasingly productive in Your service. Amen.

THE READING: John 17:20-26

APRIL 30

LOOKING FOR CHRIST

THE INSPIRATION:

"The importance of the Resurrection is that . . . something perfectly new in the history of the universe had happened. Christ had defeated death. The door which had always been locked had for the first time been forced open . . . The resurrection narratives are not a picture of survival after death; they record how a totally new mode of being has arisen in the university." --C.S. Lewis

THE MEDITATION:

As they were walking through a cemetery, a boy asked his father, "Is Jesus buried under one of those stones?" The women on Eastern morning looked for Jesus . . . he is not here . . . he will go before you . . ." (Mark 16:6-7). They were looking for Jesus in the wrong place.

We too sometimes look for Jesus in the wrong places. Jesus sometimes gets buried in history and tradition. As the little poem says:
>Jesus kept within a book
>Is not worth a passing look;
>Jesus prisoned in a creed
>Is a fruitless Lord indeed.
>But Jesus in the hearts of men
>Makes his presence known again.

Where then shall we look for Jesus? In the hearts of people wherever love and peace and reconciliation are proclaimed and lived—there is the Christ. "He will go before you." Whenever we follow him—there is the Christ.

THE NEGOTIATION:

Where will we find Christ today?

THE PRAYER:

Dear Lord, we thank You for this new mode of living and being which has arisen in our world through the Resurrection of Your Son. Help us to share in that Resurrection, that we might overcome the temptations that threaten us and service others in serenity. Amen.

THE READING: Mark 15:1-8

MAY 1

ST. PHILIP AND ST. JAMES

THE INSPIRATION:

"Seeing then that we have been entrusted with this commission, which we owe entirely to God's mercy, we never lose heart. We have renounced the deeds that men hide for very shame; we neither practice cunning nor distort the word of God; only by declaring the truth openly do we recommend ourselves, and then it is to the common conscience of our fellow-men and in the sight of God." --2 Corinthians 4:1-2

THE MEDITATION:

Philip, together with Peter and Andrew, was from Bethsaida and was one of the original disciples. He may have been the only Gentile among the twelve. James, the son of Alphaeus is called "the less" to distinguish him from the brother of John and the brother of Jesus. These two disciples are commemorated together because their remains were placed in the Church of the Apostles in Rome on May 1st 561.

The epistle for the day speaks of the apostle's commission. We, like they, have been entrusted with a commission. We, who have renounced the shameful deeds of alcohol abuse, have been given, by the grace of God, a commission to utilize our experience in the service of others. God's truth and grace are proclaimed through what we do and say. We are commissioned to be apostles—we are sent by God to display and declare his power in our lives.

THE NEGOTIATION:

Do we see ourselves as apostles—those sent by God?

THE PRAYER:

Almighty God, to know You is to have eternal life. Grant us to know Your Son as the way, the truth, and the life, and guide our footsteps along the way of Jesus Christ our Lord. Amen.
                    —Collect for St. Philip and St. James.

THE READING: 2 Corinthians 4:1-6

MAY 2

THE GREAT COMMANDMENT

THE INSPIRATION:

"'Master, which is the greatest commandment in the Law?' Jesus answered, 'Love the Lord your God with all your heart, with all your soul, with all your mind. That is the greatest commandment. It comes first. The second is like it: Love your neighbor as yourself. Everything in the Law and the prophets hangs on these two commandments.'" –Matthew 22:36-40

THE MEDITATION:

How fortunate we are to have some definite fixed points in our religious heritage to which we may turn again and again for guidance and direction. The Great Commandment, in which Jesus summarizes the Ten Commandments, is one of these fixed points upon which we anchor our Christian lives.

The Great Commandment is not true because it is in the Bible; it is in the Bible because it is true. The Ten Commandments have been tried and tested and found satisfactory for thousands of years. Generation after generation has learned that obedience to God's law brings serenity and disobedience brings trouble.

Those of us who are seeking sobriety and serenity cannot afford to ignore the guidance of these great landmarks of our religious heritage. Disobedience can only lead to disaster; obedience leads to a peace which the world cannot give.

THE NEGOTIATION:

What do the Commandments have to do with our sobriety and serenity?

THE PRAYER:

We thank You, O Lord, for the great principles for living abundantly that You have laid down before us. As we grow in our love for You, O Lord, enable us to display this love in our relationships with our neighbors. Amen.

THE READING: James 2:8-13

MAY 3

THE TEN COMMANDMENTS: INTRODUCTION

THE INSPIRATION:

"I am the Lord your God who brought you out of Egypt, out of the land of Slavery." --Exodus 20:2

THE MEDITATION:

In ancient times when a king had conquered a city, he would gather the defeated people before him and say, "I am your conqueror, therefore you shall . . ." In introduction to the Ten Commandments, God's right to give commandments is laid out. The framework for all his commands is "I am the Lord your God." A relationship between the giver and receivers of the commandments is established. The Ten Commandments are not orders from a conquering ruler, but rather a part of a covenant which the God of love is establishing with his people. Because he is our God and because he has delivered us, therefore his claim upon our lives requires a response which coincides with his will for us.

We can identify with being delivered out of the land of slavery. Our slavery was not in Egypt but rather to alcohol. It is by God's power that we are freed of our slavery. Because God has delivered us he has a claim upon our lives. That claim requires obedience on our part. Obedience means productive, useful, meaningful living. When God says "I am the Lord your God" he is not only speaking corporately but also individually. God has a plan for each one of us.

THE NEGOTIATION:

Are we ready to accept God's claim upon us?

THE PRAYER:

O Lord, our God, we thank You that you have delivered us from slavery. We pray that we might use our freedom in ways that please You. Help us to respond to Your love by faithfully and joyfully obeying Your commandments. Amen.

THE READING: Exodus 19:17-20:2

MAY 4

FIRST COMMANDMENT

THE INSPIRATION:

"You shall have no others gods." --Exodus 20:3

"My sin was this, that not in Him but in His creatures—myself and others—I sought for pleasures, honors, and truths, and so fell headlong into sorrows, confusions, errors." --Augustine

THE MEDITATION:

Because God has a claim upon our lives, he therefore asks that we respond with undivided loyalty to him. God himself admits the existence of "other gods." We may make a god out of anything or anyone in all creation. But we are commanded to worship the creator rather than the Creation.

We live in a polytheistic culture. There are many gods calling for our allegiance. These gods are not so much 'graven images" or pagan gods as they were in ancient cultures. Our gods are whatever we have ultimate concern for. Our experience has taught us that alcohol can and perhaps has been our god. Idolatry is to give ultimate concern to that which is not ultimate.

Life, therefore, consists of a continuous sorting out of priorities. A "graven image" is a concern if we allow it to take priority over God. The First Commandment calls us to re-evaluate our priorities and values and then, remembering who god is and what he has done for us, loving and trusting in him above anything else.

THE NEGOTIATION:

What or who are the gods that call for our allegiance?

THE PRAYER:

O Lord, You are our God. We know that in the past we have had other loyalties that were more important to us that You. Keep us from giving ultimate concern to anything or anyone but You. Give us the strength to worship You with all our heart, soul, and mind. Amen.

THE READING: Exodus 20:3-6

SECOND COMMANDMENT

THE INSPIRATION:

"You shall not make wrong use of the name of the Lord your God." --Exodus 20:7

"If you call upon me in time of trouble, I will come to your rescue, and you shall honour me."
--Psalm 50:15

THE MEDITATION:

We are not to take God's name lightly. Certainly the commandment deals with misusing God's names as expletives. But the commandment has to do with more that cursing. It also has to do with using God's name to bless our personal causes and concerns. When we use God's name to justify our prejudice, or condone our violence and injustice, or bless other behavior contrary to God's revelation in Jesus Christ, we are grossly misusing his name.

Each commandment is to be seen not only in its narrow negative form as something we should refrain from doing, but also in light of the Gospel in its broader positive sense as something to be done. Certainly God forbids cursing, swearing, lying, and deceiving by his name. But, on the positive side he also commands action. He commands us to call upon him for his rescuing power and worship him with prayer, praise and thanksgiving.

The name of God is a symbol for the God who gives us the power we need in our search for sobriety and serenity. Our worship of his holy name is our response.

THE NEGOTIATION:

What is God saying to us in the Second Commandment?

THE PRAYER:

O Lord, it is good to give Thee thanks,
to sing psalms to Thy name, O Most High,
to declare Thy love in the morning
and Thy constancy every night. Amen. --Psalm 92:1-2

THE READING: Psalm 50:1-23

MAY 6

THIRD COMMANDMENT

THE INSPIRATION:

"Remember to keep the Sabbath day to keep it holy. You have six days to labour and do all your work. But the seventh day is a Sabbath of the Lord Your God." --Exodus 20:8-10

"The Sabbath was made for the sake of man and not man for the Sabbath." --Mark 2:27

THE MEDITATION:

Because the Lord is our God who has called us into a covenant relationship with him through Jesus Christ, he commands a worship response. Worship is the subject of the Third Commandment. Too often people miss this subject and see the commandment as having to do with mowing one's lawn on Sunday.

In response to God's love and grace we worship him. Just as we need these daily periods of private devotion and meditation, so we need regular corporate worship with our fellow believers. We need public worship to praise and thank God, to be nurtured through his Word, to communion with him and our fellow worshipers, and to be motivated and organized for more effective service in the world. Our communion with God is incomplete without inspiration or regular pubic worship.

Many alcohol abusers draft away from public worship. Remembering the Sabbath is an important part of the recovery process. In public worship we experience the forgiveness and acceptance which we so desperately need. Worship stimulates the involvement of God's people in his world.

THE NEGOTIATION:

What place does public worship play in our lives?

THE PRAYER:

How dear is Thy dwelling-place
Thou Lord of Hosts!
Happy are those who dwell in Thy house;
They never cease from praising Thee. Amen.   --Psalm 84:1,4

THE READING: Psalm 84:1-12

FOURTH COMMANDMENT

THE INSPIRATION:

"Honour your father and your mother." --Exodus 20:12

"Obey your leaders and defer to them." --Hebrews 13:17

"We must obey God rather than men." --Acts 5:29

THE MEDITATION:

The first three commandments, called the First Table of the Law, like the first three petitions of the Lord's Prayer deal with our relationship to God. As Jesus points out in the Great Commandment (Matthew 22:35-40), love to God comes first and because of this love we are able to love our neighbor. With the Fourth Commandment we begin the Second Table of the law which deals with our relationship to other people.

We begin with our relationship to our parents which certainly includes other superiors who have authority over us. One of the characteristics of those of us who abuse alcohol is our inability to deal with authority. In our self-centeredness we resent anyone telling us what to do. Being unable to trust ourselves we have difficulty believing that anyone can be trustworthy.

While honor, respect, and esteem are due to persons in superior positions, our ultimate authority must always be God. There may be times when early authorities must be disobeyed in order to obey God. Our serenity is dependent upon his authority and presence in our lives.

THE NEGOTIATION:

Can we honor and respect the authority of our superiors when they are consistent with God's law?

THE PRAYER:

Dear Lord, You sent Your Son to proclaim Your love by teaching as one with authority. Give us the grace to honor and respect others with authority in keeping with Your Will; and give us the authority to carry out Your mission for us. Amen.

THE READING: Matthew 15:1-9

FIFTH COMMANDMENT

THE INSPIRATION:

"You shall not commit murder." – Exodus 20:13

"Everyone who hates his brother is a murderer." --1 John3:15

"You have learned that our forefathers were told, 'Do not commit murder.' . . . But what I tell you is this: Anyone who nurses anger against his brother must be brought to judgment." --Matthew 5:21-2

THE MEDITATION:

When we consider the Fifth Commandment in light of the Gospel we discover that more is involved than the taking of human life. God's will for us includes doing others no bodily harm not causing them any suffering. And even beyond that, Jesus includes the desire in anger to harm another. The alcohol induced anger and resentments are feelings with which we are familiar. These wishes of harm for others, even when not acted out, are destructive to us and pose a threat to sobriety.

As always there is a positive side to the commandment. It isn't merely refraining from doing or wishing harm to others, but helping and befriending them that is included in God's concern for us. The man on the Jericho road was beat, robbed, and left half dead. The culprits who committed this act of violence were obviously breaking God's Fifth Commandment. But so were the priest and Levite who passed by on the other side without lifting a hand to help.

THE NEGOTIATION:

How have we in our thoughts, words, and deeds broken the Fifth Commandment?

THE PRAYER:

O Lord, You have created us and all people in Your image and reserved for us a dignity and holiness in Your sight. Help us in our relationships with others to share the love and concern for them that You revealed in the life and message of Your Son. Amen.

THE READING: Luke 10:30-37

SIXTH COMMANDMENT

THE INSPIRATION:

"You shall not commit adultery." --Exodus 20:14

"The fornicator sins against his own body." --1 Corinthians 5:18

"Marriage is honourable; let us all keep it so." --Hebrews 13:4

THE MEDITATION:

God created us male and female and "it was very good" (Genesis 1:30) in his sight. Certainly among the good was the sex instinct. Besides the obvious reason of procreation, the purpose of this instinct is to demonstrate love. Yet this instinct can run wild and dominate us. It can cause us to regard other persons as less than human, minimizing them into sex objects.

Alcohol abuse and abuse of our instinct for sex often go hand in hand. The effects of alcohol abuse dehumanize ourselves and others, and sometimes results in the mistaken notion that all problems can be solved with our genitals. The relationship of alcohol and sexual abuse has long been recognized. The writer of Ecclesiastes warned:

"Never sit at table with another man's wife
Or join her in a drinking party,
For fear of succumbing to her charms
And slipping into fatal disaster." (9.9).

Furthermore, Shakespeare observed, "It (strong drink) provokes the desire, but it takes away the performance." In other words, lushes are lousy lovers.

For our own sakes, God calls us to honor marriage and live chaste and pure lives in word and deed. Without this sobriety is threatened and serenity is impossible.

THE NEGOTIATION:

How do we react to frustration in sexual matters?

THE PRAYER:

We thank You, O Lord, for the beautiful, intimate, creative, and love demonstrating sexual capacity You have given to us. Forgive us for our abuse of the sex instinct and create in us clean hearts and minds. Amen.

THE READING: Ecclesiastes 9:1-9

SEVENTH COMMANDMENT

THE INSPIRATION:

"You shall not steal." --Exodus 20:15

"You shall not pervert justice." --Leviticus 19:35

"The man who can be trusted in little things can be trusted also in great; and the man who is dishonest in little things is dishonest also in great things." --Luke 16:10

THE MEDITATION:

Our inclination is to think of the commandment concerning stealing in terms of great things. We congratulate ourselves by saying, "I have never held up a bank, or I have never robbed a liquor store." But God has something more in mind than grand larceny. God is concerned about our attitudes toward other people and their possessions. He is concerned about our injustice, our unfair dealings, our fraud. God, in short, is concerned about us.

The law, with its concern for the protection of society, says, "You shall not steal." This concern is primarily for the potential victim of theft. God's concern goes further. He is concerned not only with the potential victim, but also with the potential thief. He is concerned with us and our feelings about others and their possessions.

Even though we do not consider ourselves thieves, there is, again, the positive side of the commandment, which calls us to improve and protect the property and living of other people. Any lack of respect for others and their possessions is threatening to our sobriety and serenity.

THE NEGOTIATION:

How important is honesty to our sobriety and serenity?

THE PRAYER:

O Lord, You are the giver of all good and perfect gifts. We thank you for what is ours and what belongs to others. Help us to be honest and industrious and loving and helpful to others. Amen.

THE READING: Luke 16:1-5

MAY 11

EIGHTH COMMANDMENT

THE INSPIRATION:

"You shall not give false evidence against your neighbor." --Exodus 20:16

"A good name is more to be desired than great riches; esteem is better than silver and gold."
--Proverbs 22:1

"Speak the truth to each other, for all of us are the parts of one body." --Ephesians 4:25

THE MEDITATION:

"We who have, to a greater of less degree, had our good name ruined through alcohol abuse, know the importance of reputation. We are fully aware of the lie in the often quoted ditty:
"Sticks and stones will break my bones
But names will never hurt me."
Names will hurt us and often have. Having been victims of gossip, there are two things we can do: first, begin rebuilding our reputations by showing God's power through Christian living; and secondly show mercy and forgiveness to those who have gossiped against us, remembering that they too have been harmed and are in need of God's grace.

We are also aware of the belying, betraying, backbiting, gossiping, and slandering that takes place in bars and at drinking parties. Let us ask God for forgiveness and make amends, if possible, with those whom we have harmed. Let us apologize for others, speak well of them and put the most charitable construction on all they do.

THE NEGOTIATION:

Are gossipers harmed as much as those who they gossip about?

THE PRAYER:

Set a guard, O Lord, over my mouth;
Keep watch at the door of my lips. Amen. —Psalm 141:3

THE READING: James 3:1-2

NINTH COMMANDMENT

THE INSPIRATION:

"You shall not covet your neighbor's house." --Exodus 20:17

"The love of money is the root of all evil things." --1 Timothy 6:10

"Beware! Be on your guard against greed of every mind, for even when a man has more than enough, his wealth does not give him wealth." --Luke 12:15

THE MEDITATION:

Happy are those who are content with what they have! During our days of abusing alcohol we found very little contentment is anything except the temporary and artificial relief we received from alcohol. Being on the road toward sobriety sometimes presents us with new dangers. With sobriety often comes more money and accumulation of things. The danger is that we may want to make up for lost time and desire more than is good for us.

Coveting is a lust, a greed, an envy, an evil desire for that which we have not. Whether we acquire that which we covet or not, or whether we gain possession by legal or illegal means, the coveting itself is a threat to sobriety and serenity.

Jesus asks, "What will a man gain by winning the whole world, at the cost of his true self?" (Matthew 16:26). To be content with our portion doesn't rule out ambition but it does rule out lust, greed, envy, and begrudgement. At the same time, on the positive side, God wills us to assist and serve others in keeping and improving their worldly goods.

THE NEGOTIATION:

What are the things that we covet?

THE PRAYER:

Dear Lord, we thank You for all the blessings that You have so richly bestowed upon us. Help us to be content with what we have and seek those things which bring abundant and eternal life. Amen.

THE READING: 1 Timothy 6:3-10

MAY 13

TENTH COMMANDMENT

THE INSPIRATION:

"You shall not covet your neighbor's wife." --Exodus 20:17

"As he (David) walked about on the roof of the palace, he saw from there a woman bathing, and she was very beautiful." --2 Samuel 11:2

"If a man looks on a woman with a lustful eye, he has already committed adultery with her in his heart." --Matthew 5:28

THE MEDITATION:

While the Ninth Commandment deals with coveting our neighbour's material possessions, the Tenth Commandment deals with coveting our neighbour's spouse or other members of their household. Perhaps there is more than a little truth in the old adage about the grass looking greener on the other side of the fence. Be that as it may, there is unequivocal truth in the destructiveness of coveting whether the object be the wife, husband, or whatever.

David's first glimpse of Bathsheba was innocent enough in itself, but coveting soon took over. This coveting led to adultery and lying and cheating and scheming and finally to murder. By the time David was finished he had broken almost all of the Ten Commandments. And it all began with an "innocent" covetous glance. Breaking one of the commandments often sets off a chain reaction. As we, like David, get in deeper and deeper the more we are separated from God.

For our own sake as well as that of our neighbor, let us rejoice with him or her over the happiness of their home and earnestly seek to promote their welfare.

THE NEGOTIATION:

How has coveting led to a chain reaction in our lives?

THE PRAYER:

Dear Lord, forgive us for our coveting and the evil that has resulted from it. Create in us clean hearts that our lives may be an inspiration for purity in others. Amen.

THE READING: 2 Samuel 11:1-21

LET NATURE SING

THE INSPIRATION:

"In nature we find God; we do not only infer from nature what God must be like, but when we see nature truly, we see God self-manifested in and through it . . . From the play of minutest particles to the sweep of stars in their courses, the work of Mind is found—of a mind so mighty in range and scope, so sure in adjustment of infinitesimal detail, that before it all our science is clumsy and precarious." – William Temple

THE MEDITATION:

The modern emphasis on ecology and conservation of our natural resources is indeed commendable and essential. This emphasis has brought many persons "back to nature" with the result of "meditating on nature" and "feeling close to the Creator." Without being judgmental, we must ask if this "meditating" and "feeling" is what Jesus was talking about when he said "consider the lilies" (Matthew 6:28), or the Psalmist when he said "I lift up my eyes to the hills" (Psalm 121:1), or Maltbie Babcock when he wrote "This is my Father's world, And to my list'ning ears, All nature sings, and round me rings, The music of the spheres."

There is no question that God can be found in nature. We may have missed this truth in the blindness of our abuse of alcohol. And yet God is not found fully in nature. His revelation of himself will be incomplete if we look for him only there. God's revelation is found everywhere: in nature, in other people, in Scripture, in public worship. Those who say they can worship on Sunday morning on the golf course must understand that that is about as difficult as it would be to play golf during a worship service.

THE NEGOTIATION:

How does God reveal himself to us in nature?

THE PRAYER:

I lift my eyes to Thee
Whose throne is in heaven.
Deal kindly with us, O Lord, deal kindly. --Psalm 123:1,3

THE READING: Psalm 121:1-8

MAY 15

WISDOM

THE INSPIRATION:

"Happy is the man who keeps to my ways,
happy the man who listens to me,
watching daily at my threshold
with his eyes on the doorway;
for he who finds me finds life
and wins favour with the Lord." --Proverbs 8:33-35

THE MEDITATION:

In the Proverb wisdom is personified and identified with the Word of God, the Law of God, and the Spirit of God. We are exhorted to seek wisdom. After a brief period of sobriety we begin to see how far we were from wisdom and how essential it is for serenity. In personifying wisdom the Proverb paves the way for Christ whom Paul calls "the wisdom of God" (1 Corinthians 1:24). We are called to listen to him.

But let us make sure it is the wisdom of God to which we are listening. In the precarious period of early sobriety we receive a lot of advice from a lot of people. Let us test that advice to ascertain if it leads to Christ and his fellowship. We are so easily fooled. Our prejudices so often get in the way.

Listening to the wisdom of God is essential for us. We need quiet periods of devotion, meditation, and negotiation. But contemplation is not to be favored over action. Contemplative listening to the wisdom of God always leads to action. Wisdom is not merely a head and heart trip but results in loving action toward others. It is not a question of either/or but both/and. Listening to the wisdom of God and acting it out in our lives are two facets of the Gospel.

THE NEGOTIATION:

Can we discern the wisdom of God from the wisdom of the world?

THE PRAYER:

O Lord, God of infinite wisdom, we stand before You in awe and wonder with finite minds. Open our hearts to receive Your wisdom revealed through the Gospel of Your Son. Amen.

THE READING: Proverbs 8:1-36

MAY 16

SELF-PITY

THE INSPIRATION:

"Self-pity is one of the most unhappy and consuming defects that we know. It is a bar to all spiritual progress and can cut off all effective communication with our fellows because of its inordinate demands for attention and sympathy. It is a maudlin form of martyrdom, which we can ill afford." --Bill W.

THE MEDITATION:

There are perhaps many things in our lives for which we pity ourselves. The game of "Poor Me" is played hard and well by most alcohol abusers. Even when we cease abusing alcohol it is not easy for us to shut off the self-pity pattern we had developed over the years. In the early days of sobriety who has not moaned, "Poor me, I can't drink like other people?"

Often times we are unaware of our self-pity. Feeling sorry for ourselves is sometimes subtle or unconscious. We need to take a long, hard look at ourselves to discover the defect.

The remedy for self-pity is thanksgiving. When we are feeling sorry for ourselves it is time to count our blessings and get down on our knees and thank God for what he has given us through his grace. Being thankful leads us to use what God has given us for the benefit of others. When we want sympathy let us give thanks and do something for someone else.

THE NEGOTIATION:

In what ways do we feel sorry for ourselves?

THE PRAYER:

We give thanks to You, O Lord, for all that we have and all that we are. Fill us with Your grace that we may keep from self-pity and be filled with Your love so fully that it will overflow into the lives of others. Amen.

THE READING: Psalm 147:1-7

MAY 17

PEACE

THE INSPIRATION:

"To the quiet mind all things are possible. What is the quiet mind? A quiet mind is one which nothing weighs on, nothing worries, which, free from ties and from all self-seeking, is wholly merged into the will of God and dead to its own." --Meister Eckhart

THE MEDITATION:

Peace is not simply the absence of war on the national level or the absence of turmoil on the individual level. Peace is the experience that is known to one whose mind is merged into the will of God even in the midst of war and turmoil. Peace is impossible to an alcohol abuser because his or her will is captured by the drug alcohol.

Even when sobriety is realized peace does not come easily. We fight hard to maintain our self-will. Much of our difficulty in finding peace is due to the mistaken notion that peace is something we achieve. Conversely, peace is a gift. Jesus says, "Peace is my parting gift to you, my own peace, such as the world cannot give" (John 14:27). The Prince of Peace gives us his peace. The key to Jesus' peace is his relationship with his Father. This relationship can become ours if we accept the gift. The world cannot give this peace. It only comes by being absorbed in God's will. As Dante put it, "In his will is our peace."

THE NEGOTIATION:

Are we open to accept the peace of Christ in our lives?

THE PRAYER:

O Lord, only from You can come peace. Fill our hearts with the joy of doing Your will that we may experience Your peace and send us as peacemakers into the world of war and turmoil. Amen.

THE READING: John 14:22-31

MAY 18

TOLERANCE

THE INSPIRATION:

"Love in all sincerity, loathing evil and clinging to the good. Let love for our brotherhood breed warmth of mutual affection. Outdo one another in showing honor." --Romans 12:9-10

THE MEDITATION:

Tolerance is not putting up with someone who is intolerable. Tolerance is a positive and cordial effort to understand another's beliefs, practices, and habits without necessarily sharing or accepting them. Tolerance, for a Christian, is always seen in the light of God's love. Christ never condoned sin but always loved the sinner.

Christian tolerance rules out an indifference which says, "You can believe and do whatever you want and you'll have to take the consequences, it's none of my business." This kind of supercilious tolerance has allowed the destruction of many alcohol abusers.

Christian tolerance says, "I care, your suffering is my business." Our own recovery from alcohol abuse is due in part to the tolerant love of others. We who have experienced toleration are in a unique position to practice tolerance toward others.

Within the Christian Church tolerance is essential for mutual spiritual growth. Even though we profess different doctrines, we all seek the same goal—the Glory of God and peace and goodwill among people. It's a tremendous task. Let us work together with tolerance for one another.

THE NEGOTIATION:

Are there persons we will not tolerate?

THE PRAYER:

Dear Lord, give us the mind of Christ that we may look upon other people as he did in love and forgiveness. Help us to loathe evil and cling to good as we display tolerance to others. Amen.

THE READING: Romans 12:9-16

MAY 19

ASCENSION

THE INSPIRATION:

"Men of Galilee, why stand there looking up to the sky? This Jesus, who has been taken away from you up to heaven, will come in the same way as you have seen him go." --Acts 1:11

THE MEDITATION:

The doctrine of Christ's Ascension has suffered attack because of its apparent presupposition of the three-deck universe. Modern science is too sophisticated to conceive of the universe simply in terms of heaven, earth and hell. Acts is not arguing science but rather affirming that Jesus' earthly work is ended and that that work is now turned over to his Church.

Jesus told his disciples, "It is for your good that I am leaving you. If I do not go, your advocate will not come, whereas if I go, I will send him to you" (John 16:7-8). Jesus does not turn his work over to us to do by ourselves. The Advocate, the Holy Spirit, comes to call the Church and gives it power to carry on the work of Christ's Gospel.

We are not to stand around looking up into the sky for something to happen. The Advocate is present within us. Let us get in touch with that divine Presence and heed his call to love and service. That Advocate is always with us and leads us to sobriety and serenity. Let us keep in touch with that Advocate as we live this day to the glory of God.

THE NEGOTIATION:

What does Jesus' Ascension have to do with us today?

THE PRAYER:

Almighty God, Your only Son was taken up into heaven, hidden from his disciple's sight, and in power he intercedes with You for us. May we also come to Your presence and live forever in Your glory. Amen.
     --Collect for the Ascension

THE READING: Acts 1:1-11

MAY 20

INTERRUPTIONS

THE INSPIRATION:

"My whole life I have been complaining that my work was constantly interrupted until I discovered that my interruptions were my work." --Henri Nouwen

THE MEDITATION:

We dislike being interrupted. When we make plans to do something and someone comes along and interferes with those plans it displeases us. It all depends, of course, on how much we wanted to do the thing we planned. Some of us can remember how irritated we become when someone interrupted our drinking. Our priority at that time was centered on alcohol. Anything or anyone that interrupted that most important activity was looked upon with disdain.

Only when our drinking has been interrupted by sobriety are we in a position to grow in serenity. One of the components of serenity is our ability to cope with interruptions. When we practice the presence of God our main priority is to do his work. It may very well be that interruptions are the work to which God is calling us.

Jesus was once interrupted by his mother and brothers and used this occasion to declare, "Whoever does the will of God is my brother, my sister, my mother" (Mark 3:35). As brothers and sisters of Jesus our top priority is to do God's will—and this often interrupts our plans.

THE NEGOTIATION:

Are we ready for the interruptions which we will face today?

THE PRAYER:

O Lord, as we make plans for the day before us, help us, when interrupted, to use our time in ways that will bring honor to Your name by service to others. Amen.

THE READING: Mark 3:31-35

MAY 21

KEEPING THE LINE OPEN

THE INSPIRATION:

"Prayer, crystallized in words, assigns a permanent wave length on which the dialogue has to be continued, even when our mind is occupied with other matters." --Dag Hammarskjold

THE MEDITATION:

The words we use before God in prayer should be our words. Let us not pretend that we feel no emotions. Let us be natural before God, and tell him whatever is on our heart and mind I whatever words are natural to us. God doesn't care about our sounding "pious," or "holy," or "spiritual;" he wants us to be honest. After all, God knows what we think and feel. We need make no pretence in his presence. An honest, natural expression of ourselves enables us to continue in a creative, free, and mature relationship with God.

Having established a relationship with God through the words of our prayers, "a permanent wave length" is formed. Now we can live through the day, give ourselves to our tasks, be productive, serve others, have fun, and all the while the dialogue with God is continuing. It is as if the telephone, after our talk with God, is not hung up but laid on the table. We do get involved with many things but we are always aware that the line is open. This open line is practicing the presence of God. We need this open line to strengthen the quality of our sobriety and enable us to grow in serenity.

THE NEGOTIATION:

Are we growing in our ability to practice the presence of God?

THE PRAYER:

Forgive us, O Lord, for trying to make ourselves the dictator and You the listener. Help us to carry on a joyful conversation with You by keeping the line open throughout the day. Amen.

THE READING: 1 Samuel 3:1-21

MAY 22

SERENITY

THE INSPIRATION:

"The Lord is near; have no anxiety, but in everything make your requests known to God in prayer and petition with thanksgiving. Then the peace of God, which is beyond our utmost understanding, will keep guard over your hearts and your thoughts, in Jesus Christ." --Philippians 4:6-7

THE MEDITATION:

Sobriety is the gateway to serenity. Sobriety does not automatically bring serenity, but without it serenity is impossible. Serenity is being at peace with God, with ourselves, and with other people. It all begins with the realizations that the Lord is near. This nearness removes from us our anxieties, and opens up communion with God. We learn, slowly perhaps and gradually, to make this communion more constant. Practicing this nearness is difficult at first. It requires a dedicated conscious effort. It becomes easier as the practice continues through the days, weeks, months and years.

Serenity is the result of the nearness of God. It cannot be adequately described because it is "beyond our utmost understanding" and it is of far more worth than human reasoning. Our total life's experience, including our tragic abuse of alcohol, has brought us to this moment when we can experience a peace with God beyond our understanding and too wonderful for words.

THE NEGOTIATION:

Can we enjoy the nearness of God even though we cannot understand it?

THE PRAYER:

"Grant to us, O Lord, the royalty of inward happiness, and the serenity which comes from living close to Thee. Daily renew us in the sense of joy, and let the eternal Spirit . . . dwell in our souls and bodies, filling every corner of our hearts with light and grace; so that, bearing about with us the infection of good courage, we may be diffusers of life, and may meet all ills and cross accidents with gallant and light-hearted happiness, giving Thee thanks always for all thanks. Amen." –Robert Louis Stevenson

THE READING: Isaiah 26:1-9

MAY 23

NEW LIFE TODAY

THE INSPIRATION:

"It is right that you should begin again every day. There is no better way to finish the spiritual life than to be ever beginning it over again, and never to think that you have done enough." --Francis de Sales

THE MEDITATION:

Every day new life is offered to us. Each morning begins a new day of grace. A new, fresh start is available now. Resurrection is a present possibility.

Resurrection has invariably been described as belonging to another time, another place. But when resurrection is considered in terms of geography or past and future, it is robbed of its impact in terms of the here and now.

When Jesus told Nicodemus that he must be born over again, he answered, "But how is it possible for a man to be born when he is old? Can he enter his mother's womb a second time and be born?" (John 3:4). Nicodemus could only think of new life and new birth in physical terms of the past. Jesus assured Nicodemus that he could be born over again in the present.

Our main concern as individuals and as the Church is not with life after death, but rather life after birth. While we affirm our faith in life everlasting, that is not a reality for us now. It is life after birth that is our main concern because its reality is a present possibility. We have been resurrected from the abyss of alcohol abuse. New birth is ours. Let us grow in the new life as we are nurtured by God's love and grace each day.

THE NEGOTIATION:

Will we take advantage of the new life we have today?

THE PRAYER:

Dear Lord, we thank You that Your creative power is still at work in us and in the whole of your creation. Give us strength to take hold of the new birth, new life, and resurrection, which You offer us today that we may live in all the fullness of Your glory. Amen.

THE READING: John 3:1-12

MAY 24

A WORLD WITHOUT PAIN?

THE INSPIRATION:

"We live in a world in which innumerable creatures, subhuman as well as human, are constantly affecting one another. Not all the effects of this interaction are beneficial, since the agents are imperfect in or devoid of knowledge, wisdom, and goodness. But we cannot enjoy the values of such an order without also being exposed to its risks. Possibly the only way in which God could remove suffering would be to eliminate perilous freedom. However, this would impair rather than enrich the value of human life." --S. Paul Schilling

THE MEDITATION:

We know what pain is. We have experiences it in its physical and psychological forms. We also learned how to alleviate pain by consuming alcohol. Perhaps the pain was physical but more often it was psychological. Alcohol has been used historically as an anesthetic. It works, causing a loss of sensation. However, the effectiveness is temporary and artificial.

When we gain sobriety and seek serenity we soon discover that suffering and pain are still a part of life. Learning that there are no substitutes for alcohol, we look for alternative ways of dealing with the pain which is a part of the reality of living. While we seek to avoid pain and eliminate it if it comes we also use the experience to enrich the value of our lives. Each experience, whether it be joyful or sorrowful, is an opportunity to be drawn closer to God.

THE NEGOTIATION:

How does pain enrich the value of human life?

THE PRAYER:

Dear Lord, You have borne the pain of the world. Look with compassion upon us in our suffering and pain that we may be reassured of Your love and, by Your grace, be delivered from our distress. Amen.

THE READING: 1 Peter 2:19-25

PERMITTING THE TWILIGHT

THE INSPIRATION:

"Mysticism keeps men sane. . . The ordinary man has always been sane because he has always been a mystic. He was permitted the twilight. He has always cared more for truth than for consistency. The whole secret of mysticism is this: that man can understand everything by the help of what he does not understand. The morbid logician seeks to make everything lucid, and succeeds in making everything mysterious. The mystic allows one thing to be mysterious, and everything else becomes lucid." --G. K. Chesterton

THE MEDITATION:

We are called to love the Lord with all out heart, soul and strength (Mark 12:30). In other words, our response to and relationship with God is to be total. Neglect of any part of us would result in an unbalanced response. Alcohol abuse results in an imbalance of our various parts: emotional, spiritual, intellectual, and physical. Sobriety gives us the opportunity to function harmoniously.

We can go only so far with our mind and our senses. We need to learn to permit the twilight of spiritual experience which cannot be reasoned out to make intellectual sense. Then spiritual ecstasy begins to function. Love becomes spiritualized, the individual soul or spirit is united with the divine soul or spirit. In the center of Christian mysticism stands Christ. The mystic seeks to imitate him in his total, balanced response to his Father.

THE NEGOTIATION:

Are we willing to permit the twilight in our response to God?

THE PRAYER:

Dear Lord, whose thoughts and ways are not our thoughts and ways, help us to respond to You with our whole selves, and keep us from allowing our intellects to interfere with our experience of Your presence. Amen.

THE READING: Isaiah 55:1-12

MAY 26

LAUNCH OUT!

THE INSPIRATION:

> Take ship, my soul,
> Joyous launch out on trackless seas,
> Fearless for unknown shores to sail,
> Chanting a song pleasant of exploration.
> Away, brave souls!
> Farther, and farther sail!
> O, darling joy, but safe,
> Are they not all the seas of God?
> O farther, farther, farther sail." --Walt Whitman

THE MEDITATION:

Gold told Abraham to leave his home and go to an unknown land (Genesis 12:1). Jesus told his disciples to "launch out into the deep" and let their nets down for a catch of fish (Luke 5:4). Abraham was comfortable where he was. The disciples had been fishing all night and caught nothing—they thought it absolutely ridiculous to go fishing where they knew there were no fish. But Abraham and the disciples were willing to take the risk and launch out.

We too are called by God to launch out, to be willing to risk our comforts, our reasoning, our reputation. As sobriety comes only by taking risks of living without alcohol, so serenity comes only by taking risks. Only by "launching out into the deep," taking "the leap of faith," do we grow in serenity. The reason we are reluctant to launch out is because we forget that the unknown seas belong to God.

THE NEGOTIATION:

How does God want us to take the risk of launching out?

THE PRAYER:

O Lord, as we reluctantly and fearfully give heed to Your call to launch out into the darkness of the unknown, we pray that You would lead us by Your hand, and help us to know the serenity and excitement found only in serving You. Amen.

THE READING: Luke 5:1-11

MAY 27

CONSCIENCE

THE INSPIRATION:

"Conscience, instead of allowing us to stifle our perceptions and sleep on without interruption, acts as an inward witness and monitor, reminding us of what we owe to God and convicting us of departure from duty." --John Calvin

THE MEDITATION:

Without getting into the debate of whether conscience is due to environmental, hereditary, or other factors, let us concentrate on the reality of the moral sense that is in each of us. We are familiar with the anguish and pain of a wounded conscience. We also know that alcohol can, for a time, relieve that pain and anguish. However, when the effects of alcohol wear off, we discover the pain and anguish is not only still there, but it is intensified. Our experience has also taught us that the more we compromise our inner moral sense the more our conscience becomes conditioned and we are bothered less and less by the consequences of our immoral behavior; that is to say, we become less human.

With a growing hold on sobriety we perceive conscience as a positive rather than negative force. We need to be convinced of our departure from God's will for us. We need to be reminded of our duty to God. However, we define it, this inward witness and monitor is essential for our spiritual growth.

THE NEGOTIATION:

Do we regard conscience as one of God' great gifts to us?

THE PRAYER:

Dear Lord, open up our hearts that we might be convicted of our failures to serve You, and also that we might be reminded of Your duty to us. We pray for strength that we might do our best this day to have a clear conscience before You. Amen.

THE READING: Acts 24:1-16

MAY 28

MONEY

THE INSPIRATION:

"You cannot serve God and Money." --Matthew 6:24

"It is easier for a camel to pass through the eye of a needle than for a rich man to enter the Kingdom of God." --Matthew 19:24

THE MEDITATION:

Alcohol is a chemical in the solvent classification. Solvents have the capacity to dissolve other substances. Many of us have learned that alcohol also dissolves money and savings accounts. Money is important to alcohol abusers primarily because it is a means to buy alcohol. With sobriety money takes on new meaning, yet it is none the less important. Sobriety allows us to clarify our values as we grow in serenity.

Our ultimate priority must converge at a single point. To try to pay homage to more than one priority leads to a complicated and insecure existence rather than the simple life. Jesus stakes his teaching of the simple life upon only one principle, namely, that absolute personal loyalty to God must take precedence over anything and everything else.

Jesus does not suggest that the simple life is to be equated with poverty. His point is that money, and the things money can buy, can be good if used in support of our relationship with God rather than compete with it.

THE NEGOTIATION:

How can money be a curse and a blessing to us?

THE PRAYER:

Take my life, and let it be
Consecrated, Lord, to Thee;
Take my silver and my gold,
Not a mite would I withhold;
Take myself, and I will be
Ever, only, all for Thee. Amen. --Frances R. Havergal

THE READING: Matthew 19:16-26

MAY 29

PENTECOST

THE INSPIRATION:

"While the day of Pentecost was running its course they were all together in one place, when suddenly, there came from the sky a noise like that of a strong driving wind, which filled the whole house where they were sitting. And there appeared to them tongues like flames of fire, dispersed among them and resting on each one. And they were all filled with the Holy Spirit and began to talk in other tongues, as the Spirit gave them power of utterance." --Acts 2:1-4

THE MEDITATION:

The Church observes its birthday by looking back to that day almost 2,000 years ago when the Holy Spirit was poured out upon the disciples. The Spirit-filled disciples spoke so peculiarly that some of the people who heard them concluded they were drunk. But Peter assured them, "These men are not drunk, as you imagine; for it is only nine on the morning." Peter naively reveals his ignorance of alcohol abuse by supposing that people do not get drunk by 9:00 A.M. Some of us know differently! Peter's point is, of course, that these men are behaving as they are because they are filled with the Holt Spirit. In short, God's Spirit is intoxicating!

The Church does not, however, only look back on Pentecost. We look to the present time and place for that same Spirit to overpower and intoxicate us. Pentecost was not intended to be a once-and-for-all event in the life of the Church, but rather the beginning of a continuing process in which the Holy Spirit will intoxicate and possess us each day.

THE NEGOTIATION:

Are we ready and willing to become intoxicated by God's spirit?

THE PRAYER:

God, Father of Our Lord Jesus Christ, You sent upon the disciples the promised gift of the Holy Spirit. Look upon Your Church today and open our hearts to the full power of the Spirit. Kindle in us the fire of Your Love and strengthen our lives for service in Your Kingdom. Amen. –Collect for Pentecost

THE READING: Acts 2:1-39

MAY 30

MIRACLES

THE INSPIRATION:

"It is said . . . 'Miracles don't happen." Certainly they do not happen in ordinary circumstances. But the whole point of the Gospels is that the circumstances were far from ordinary. They were incidental to a quite spectacular situation . . . It was the inauguration of a new set of relations between God and man. A miracle in the sense of the New Testament is not so much a breach of the laws of nature, . . . but rather a remarkable or exceptional occurrence which brought an undeniable sense of the presence and power of God." --C. H. Dodd

THE MEDITATION:

The writers of the New Testament were not interested in miracle stories merely as records of marvels. For them the miracle stories were an integral part of the Gospel itself—the good news that God was active in Jesus Christ. If the Christian faith has meaning for us, the assumption that the laws of natural science must always have the last word is intolerably arbitrary. Our faith informs us that there are mysteries which science cannot fathom.

Those of us who are recovering from alcohol abuse will echo Augustine when he wrote, "I never have any difficulty in believing in miracles, since I experienced the miracle of change in my own life." A small girl, whose father was recovering from alcohol abuse, was asked my a friend if she believed Jesus changed water into wine. "I don't know about that," she answered, "but I do know that God changes whiskey into coffee at our house."

THE NEGOTIATION:

How can we help but believe in miracles when we are miracles?

THE PRAYER:

O Lord, how wonderful and glorious and mysterious are Your works! We thank You for the miracles that You have wrought in our lives. We pray that You would continue to bring about the miracle of change in us as we grow in serenity. Amen.

THE READING: John 2:1-11

MAY 31

SHAME

THE INSPIRATION:

"There smites nothing so sharp, nor smelleth so sour, as shame." --William Langland

"In thee, O Lord, I have taken refuge;
Never let me be put to shame." --Psalm 71:1

THE MEDITATION:

We understand guilt as that emotion we feel in ourselves and by ourselves when we have done something wrong or have failed to do something good. We understand shame to imply all the pain suffered by guilt plus the additional grief of others being aware of our failure or others being dishonored or disgraced by our behavior. Shame is both a noun which expresses our deep regret for our behavior which is known by others, and a verb which expressed the reproach or disgrace we bring to others. Whatever we call it, nothing smites so sharply as shame.

The painful shame we experienced in the clutches of alcohol abuse was almost unbearable at times. In the vicious cycle in which we found ourselves we often drank to relieve the shame which came from drinking. It is by the grace and power of God that we are delivered from that cycle. But even in sobriety we feel shame. As we turn our lives over to God and take refuge in him he removes our shame. If others are still ashamed by our behavior we can do nothing about that; it will have to be their problem. As for us, let us shamelessly take refuge in God.

THE NEGOTIATION:

Have we allowed God to remove our shame for past behavior?

THE PRAYER:

Restore me to honour, turn and comfort me, then I will praise thee . . .O God. Amen. —Psalm 71:21-22

THE READING: Psalm 71:1-24

JUNE 1

VICTORY

THE INSPIRATION:

"He said not: 'Thou shalt not be tempested, thou shalt not be travailed, thou shalt not be afflicted;' but He said: 'Thou shalt not be overcome.' God willeth that we take heed of these words, and that we be ever strong in such trust, in weal and woe. For he loveth and enjoyeth us, and so willeth He that we love and enjoy Him and mightily trust in Him, and all shall be well." --Julian of Norwich

THE MEDITATION:

Jesus says, "In the world you will have trouble" (John 16:33). And our immediate response is, "Come on now, Jesus, you don't have to tell us anything as obvious as that." We know trouble, tribulation, affliction, and sorrow both from our own making and from external events over which we have no control. Jesus, of course, doesn't stop with anything so trite. He continues, "But courage! The victory is mine; I have conquered the world." There is nothing obvious or trite about that!

Not only is the victory Christ's, but he allows us to share in his victory. His victory is our victory. As Paul puts it, "Overwhelming victory is ours through him who loved us" (Romans 8:37).

And yet, even though the victory has been won, the struggle goes on. We are winners by the grace of God in our struggle for serenity as we grow in Christlikeness toward the goal God has for us.

THE NEGOTIATION:

Can we rejoice in our victory even while our struggle goes on?

THE PRAYER:

Dear Lord, we rejoice in the victory which is ours. Give us courage to bear full witness with our lives to Your Son's victory over sin and death. Amen.

THE READING: John 16:25-33

JUNE 2

STRAIN AND STRESS

THE INSPIRATION:

"Drop thy still dews of quietness,
Till all our strivings cease;
Take from our souls the strain and stress,
And let our ordered lives confess
The beauty of thy peace." --John Greenleaf Whittier

THE MEDITATION:

An often repeated slogan in Alcoholics Anonymous is "Easy Does It." If there is anyone who needs to hear those words over and over again it is the alcohol abuser. We are people who do things to excess. We drink too much, we worry too much, we resent too much, we pity too much, we criticize too much, we are filled with too much "too-muches." In our anxiety, strain, and stress we need to be told over and over, "Easy Does It."

To learn how to relax, find quietness and calm, is not easy task. Perhaps we try too hard, which only leads to an increased tension, anxiety and frustration. Let us sit back, take a deep breath, and allow the Comforter to drop his "still dews of quietness" upon us.

There are two brief prayers which can be uttered in our hearts many times during the day in the midst of our busy activities: the first is "Lord, give me Your peace;" and the second is, "Lord, make me an instrument of Your peace." With God's help we can deal with the strain and stress we experience each day and, accepting his peace, we can bring it to others.

THE NEGOTIATION:

Can we trust God to bring us peace in our strain and stress?

THE PRAYER:

O Lord, we are anxious and troubled about many things. Breathe the coolness of Your balm upon us. Lord, give us Your peace. Lord, make us instruments of Your peace. Amen.

THE READING: Mark 4:35-41

JUNE 3

SATISFACTION

THE INSPIRATION:

"From the best bliss that earth imparts
We turn unfilled to Thee again." --Bernard of Clair Vaux

"The Lord is my Shepherd; I shall want nothing . . .
Thou has richly bathed my head with oil,
and my cup runs over." --Psalm 23:1, 5

THE MEDITATION:

We who have abused alcohol have a tendency to be hedonistic. Satisfaction for all of our wants and needs is sought after enthusiastically. Anything that brings pleasure and avoids discomfort is zealously pursued. We may have developed the philosophy that anything that brings satisfaction, by whatever means, is good. Alcohol, sex, money, possessions, prestige, anything that satisfies is good.

When our heads and hearts begin to clear from the confusion of alcohol abuse, we discover that serenity comes only when we reorder our values. This reordering does not mean that pleasure is outlawed. There is a phony piety which claims that if it feels good it must be wrong and if it hurts it must be good.

We continue to seek the satisfaction asked for by our needs. But now we know that all the bliss that earth imparts cannot bring fulfillment. Satisfaction comes only through our relationship with God. God not only fills out cup with satisfaction, our cup runs over. It is then that our unfulfilled desires become less important and we want nothing.

THE NEGOTIATION:

Is there any earthly thing that can bring full satisfaction?

THE PRAYER:

O Lord, You fill our hearts with Your love to the brink of overflowing. Help us to earnestly desire and zealously seek after a deeper satisfaction of Your love that we may want nothing. Amen.

THE READING: Philippians 4:15-20

JUNE 4

PUTTING PEOPLE IN CAGES

THE INSPIRATION:

"God has no favorites." --Acts 10:34

"A prejudice is a vagrant opinion without visible means of support." --Ambrose Bierce

"It is never too late to give up your prejudices." --Henry David Thoreau

THE MEDITATION:

Our prejudices begin with the labels we place on people: man, woman, white, black, liberal, conservative, doctor, lawyer, pastor, teacher, welder, senior citizen, adolescent, Lutheran, Jew, Roman Catholic, alcoholic, lush, etc. Labels get people arranged in their proper places on the jigsaw puzzle called prejudice. We don't like a piece out of place. We become anxious when a person doesn't act like his or her label dictates.

While there is a place for labels (we don't call a doctor to do a plumber's job), they can be very destructive. Putting labels on people is like putting people in cages. We put people in cages for the same reason we put animals in cages; to keep them under control, so we can watch them without their disturbing us.

Labels are destructive for two reasons: first they oppress people and sometimes people act as their labels suggest they should; secondly, by caging other people we cage ourselves. God calls us to freedom; there is living to be done. Let us not put people in cages or allow people to put us in cages. The only label we dare give or accept is "Child of God."

THE NEGOTIATION:

How do our labels affect our behavior?

THE PRAYER:

We thank You, O Lord, that You have no favorites. We pray that we might learn to see all people through Your eyes. Keep us from limiting the potential of ourselves and others. Amen.

THE READING: Acts 10:34-43

JUNE 5

"FRESH SKINS FOR NEW WINE"

THE INSPIRATION:

"No one tears a piece from a new cloak to patch an old one; if he does, he will have made a hole in the new cloak, and the patch from the new will not match the old. Nor does anyone put new wine into old wine-skins; if he does, the new wine will burst the skins, the wine will be wasted, and the skins ruined. Fresh skins for new wine!" –Luke 5:36-38

THE MEDITATION:

There has always been conflict between the old and the new. We who are recovering from alcohol abuse are keenly aware of this conflict. We generally prefer the old and familiar over the new and uncertain. Growth, however, means that we give up the old and take on the new.

Jesus had problems with his contemporaries because they wanted to hang on to the old when he thought it was time to let go. This is not to imply that the old is always bad or that the new is always good. Jesus came not to destroy the old but fulfill it. There are times when we cannot patch up the old—occasions which demand new garments and new wine skins.

The new wine is Jesus' metaphor for the new life in the Spirit. The Spirit ferments with God's love and cannot be contained by our old selves. The new life is an exciting journey. There are new situations, new possibilities, new challenges before us. We can expect to see strange and wonderful sights on the road ahead. Only persons with flexible spirits can survive such a journey.

THE NEGOTIATION:

How can the old, old story of Jesus and his love be always new?

THE PRAYER:

Dear Lord, we thank You for the new life in Christ. We pray that we might be inspired by Your Spirit to live out the excitement and challenges of that life, not fearing the new, but embracing it with flexibility and willingness to grow. Amen.

THE READING: Luke 5:29-39

JUNE 6

THE ULTIMATE QUESTION

THE INSPIRATION:

"That is what we are here for—to do God's will. That is the object of your life and mine—to do God's will. It is not to be happy or successful, or famous, or to do the best we can, and get on honestly in the world. It is something far higher that this—to do God's will." --Henry Drummond

THE MEDITATION:

To ask, "What are we here for?" is to ask the ultimate question. The question is born out of the "ontological shock" which we undergo. The ocean of purposelessness rages around purpose and threatens it. Meaninglessness chops away at meaning. Our attempts to relieve or ease the pain of the ultimate question with alcohol are futile.

What are we here for? Try as we may, the question cannot be avoided. We are here—to do God's will! But that is too simple, or too complicated, or too pious for some of us to swallow. God's will can only be perceived in his nature: God is love. We are here, therefore, to be agents of creative love. When we create love we are born to new life and also become agents to others of new life. Love always brings new life.

When we begin to recognize that we are here to be agents of creative love, we see for ourselves that all that separates and injures and destroys is overcome by that which unites and heals and creates. We shall no longer have to be plagued by the ultimate question for we shall know from first-hand experience that we are here to be agents of creative love.

THE NEGOTIATION:

Can we find serenity by ignoring the ultimate question?

THE PRAYER:

Dear Lord, You are the Ground of all being and all meaning. We pray that You would break into our temporal, early lives and let us see the signs of Your will and purpose for us and Your whole creation. Amen.

THE READING: 1 John 2:15-17

JUNE 7

PERSERVERANCE

THE INSPIRATION:

"Give yourselves wholly to prayer and entreaty; pray on every occasion in the power of the Spirit. To this end keep watch and preserve. . . " --Ephesians 6:18

THE MEDITATION:

"Hang in there," we are often told, and tell others and ourselves. The phrase implies that we muster up our strength or will power. The compulsion for alcohol cannot be dealt with by our strength or our will power. Our past failures ought to have taught us that. When Paul speaks of perseverance he excludes our strength and our will. It is giving ourselves wholly to prayer in the power of the Spirit that we can persevere. It is only by God's strength and God's will that we can face the compulsion of alcohol dependency and addiction.

What Mark Twain said about his smoking we can say about our drinking. It's easy to quit—we have done it many times. Easy to quit, but not so easy to stay quit. Sobriety and serenity are depending upon beginning and continuing. Perseverance means surrender of our lives and wills to the strength and mighty power of God. Through the misery and humiliation of our past we have been given the opportunity of learning perseverance. This is a beautiful lesson which enables us to live meaningfully, productively, and abundantly.

THE NEGOTIATION:

Do we acknowledge perseverance as a gift from God?

THE PRAYER:

O Lord, when Thou givest to Thy servants to endeavor any great matter, grant us also to know that it is not the beginning, but the continuing of the same until it be thoroughly finished, which yieldeth the true glory; through Him that for the finishing of Thy work laid down His life—Thy Son, Jesus Christ. Amen. –Francis Drake

THE READING: Ephesians 6:10-20

JUNE 8

"THE GREEN-EYED MONSTER"

THE INSPIRATION:

"O, beware, my lord, of jealousy;
It is the green-eyes monster which doth mock
The meat it feeds on." –Shakespeare

"Love is not jealous." --1 Corinthians 13:4 (RSV)

THE MEDITATION:

Jealousy is one of the most common and destructive of human emotions. This is especially true of alcohol abusers. The green-eyes monster has its base in insecurity. Lack of self-esteem brings us to demand exclusive affection and attention.

It is jealousy that led to the first murder (Genesis 3:4-5). It was jealousy which led to Joseph bring sold into slavery by his brothers (Genesis 37:28). Jealousy often results in violence toward others, but even when it does not the green-eyed monster is self-destructive.

Love, of course, is the answer to jealousy—love of God, love of self, and consequently love of others. To turn our lives and our wills over to God means to renounce our thoughts and feelings about others and accept God's instead. As we dwell upon God's thoughts and feelings for all his children, they become interwoven into our very fiber. In the spirit of Christ we can truly rejoice in the good fortune of others.

THE NEGOTIATION:

Are we harboring any jealousy in our heart?

THE PRAYER:

Forgive us, O Lord, for the jealousness in our hearts. Help us to see anew the overwhelming love, which You have for us, that we may look upon others through Your eyes, wishing and working for their happiness. We love, Dear Lord, because You first loved us. Amen.

THE READING: Genesis 37:1-11

JUNE 9

THE MINISTRY OF ACCEPTANCE

THE INSPIRATION:

"If we do something we are ashamed of it registers to our discredit, and if we do something honest or fine or good it registers to our credit. The net results ultimately are . . . either we respect and accept ourselves or we despise ourselves and feel contemptible, worthless, and unlovable." --Abraham Maslow

THE MEDITATION:

Alcohol serves as a solution to the abuser's guilt, remorse and feelings of worthlessness by depressing self-critique. The overwhelming conscience is relaxed by the drug, and it temporarily ceases to plague us.

Acceptance and absolution need to be heard, but they are never proclaimed in a vacuum. They are experienced in relationships. The ability to love comes as a result of having experienced love (1 John 4:19). Jesus saw his ministry as being anointed to "announce good news to the poor, to proclaim release for prisoners and recovery of sight for the blind; to let the broken victims go free" (Luke 4:18). He has passed this very ministry on to his Church. As a community of people we are forgiven and forgiving, so may they help others deal with feelings of guilt. This guilt must be accepted as it is, neither minimized nor magnified. The guilt having been accepted realistically, with a sense of need for mercy and understanding, makes it possible for grace and freedom to become the dominant feelings rather than guilt, remorse, and anxiety.

THE NEGOTIATION:

How can we help the Church to improve its ministry to alcohol abusers?

THE PRAYER:

Dear Lord, we thank You, that through Your grace You have accepted and forgiven us. We pray that this experience may motivate and equip us in our ministry to other broken victims that together we may grow in the freedom You intend for us. Amen.

THE READING: Luke 4:18-30

JUNE 10

THE FOUR DEGREES OF LOVE

THE INSPIRATION:

"First, then, man loves himself for his own sake. . . And when he sees that he cannot subsist by himself, he begins by faith to seek God as necessary (useful) to him . . . Then he loves God in the second degree . . . But when . . . he has begun to worship and approach Him, . . . little by little . . . God becomes known and consequently grows sweet, and thus . . . he passes into the third degree, so that he loves God, not now for being useful to him, but for Himself . . . I know now if the fourth is perfectly attained by any man in this life, . . . that is, a man loves himself only for the sake of God." --Bernard of Clair Vaux

THE MEDITATION:

As abusers of alcohol we have experienced a love-hate relationship with ourselves. The first step toward sobriety and certainly towards serenity is to love ourselves more than we hate ourselves. When we love ourselves for our own sakes, we begin an exciting journey. This journey will be short-lived, however unless we see God as necessary in our lives. As the journal continues, through worship, our love for God becomes for his sake rather than his usefulness for us. We see God less and less as an ecclesiastical bell-hop who exists to run errands for us, and more and more as the Being whose nature is love.

Loving God for his sake is what Paul is getting at when he says, ". . . that through faith Christ may dwell in your hearts in love. With deep roots and firm foundation . . ." (Ephesians 3:17). Love grows in depth.

THE NEGOTIATION:

Can we love ourselves only for the sake of God?

THE PRAYER:

O God of love, as You continue to pour out Your love upon us, we pray that we may experience greater expressions of that love in service toward others. Amen.

THE READING: Ephesians 3:14-19

JUNE 11

INFERIORITY

THE INSPIRATION:

"The feeling of inferiority rules the mental life and can be clearly recognized in the sense of incompleteness and unfulfillment and in the uninterrupted struggle both of individuals and of humanity."
--Alfred Adler

THE MEDITATION:

A woman kept complaining to her psychiatrist that she had an inferiority complex. Finally, the psychiatrist became fed up with her complaining and said, "Madam, you do not have an inferiority complex, you are inferior!" We are all inferior in one way or another. Our sense of incompleteness and unfulfillment often results in a false pride. The pain of inferiority, which results from the recognition that we can't be perfect, is certainly a factor in alcohol abusers.

Sobriety and serenity demands that the inferiority factor be dealt with realistically rather than with the false pride cover-up. It is through the acknowledgement of our inferiority and our incompleteness that we are able to take the first steps toward liberation. God doesn't ask us to be perfect, he asks that we make spiritual progress. He asks that we live humbly under his grace.

"What is it that the Lord asks of you? Only to act justly, to love loyally, to walk wisely before your God" (Micah 6:8). The uninterrupted struggle with inferiority is interrupted when we recognize who we are and who God is. It is by God's grace that we find fulfillment in our incompleteness.

THE NEGOTIATION:

How can our feelings of inferiority become a positive force in our lives?

THE PRAYER:

Dear Lord, we thank You that You accept us with all of our inadequacies. Give us strength to use all of the resources at our disposal to find fulfillment by utilizing Your gifts as we walk wisely in Your service.

THE READING: Micah 6:1-9

JUNE 12

JESUS

THE INSPIRATION:

"Don't just stand there! Go and walk toward him! . . . This Gospel can be preached with joy and confidence, because those who earnestly seek him and are ready to meet him are bound to meet him. . . But you, you must do it yourself. Don't look ahead or behind . . . Instead, fix your eye on him and go straight toward him. Don't wonder whether this path is safe or feasible, a way made smooth for the ordinary human being. Only make sure that it leads straight to Jesus." --Albert Schweitzer

THE MEDITATION:

The path to serenity is found by meditating on the life and messages of Jesus. But let us make sure it is the path of Jesus. There is a detour from the path that leads to a "meek and mild" Jesus, a passive household pet who never offends. The Gospels, however, in no way suggest a Mr. Milquetoast; they see him as an active revolutionary. Of course, he was kind and tender toward the suffering and oppressed. But he insulted the religious and political establishment. He associated with questionable people and they said of him: "Look at him! A glutton and a drinker, a friend of tax-gatherers and sinners!" (Matthew 11:19). He assaulted indignant business people and showed no proper deference for wealth and social position. He displayed a paradoxical humor that offended serious minded people and wept for the sorrowful and those who lacked the insight to weep for themselves. He came to call sinners to God's love and finally was executed as a dangerous threat to the status quo.

THE NEGOTIATION:

Are we maturing in our understanding and experience of Jesus?

THE PRAYER:

O Lord, we thank You for sending Your Son into the world that through his life and message we might find life and serenity. As we meditate upon his life we pray that we may be able to imitate him more fully. Amen.

THE READING: Matthew 11:12-19

JUNE 13

SELF-WORTH

THE INSPIRATION:

"No wonder we do not lose heart! Though our outward humanity is in decay yet day by day we are inwardly renewed. Our troubles are slight and short-lived; and their outcome an eternal glory which outweighs them by far. Meanwhile our eyes are fixed, not on things that are seen, but on the things that are unseen: for what is seen passes away; what is unseen is eternal." --2 Corinthians 4:16-18

THE MEDITATION:

A lack of self-worth and alcohol abuse go hand in hand. The more we drink the less we think of ourselves and consequently drink some more to relieve the pain of low self esteem.

The remedy is to see ourselves as God sees us. Each one of us is special to God; each one is his unique child. To see ourselves through God's eyes means that we see the inward as well as the outward, the eternal as well as the temporal, the unseen as well as the seen. We do indeed have troubles, aches and pains and groan with the deterioration of the physical. God is concerned with our temporal problems and speaks to us with words of comfort and love. Moreover God sees through our temporal problems into our eternal worth. God has temporal and eternal plans for us.

God loves us so much that he gave us his Son that we might have abundant life now and eternal life in glory. That's how much we're worth to God. No wonder we do not lose heart.

THE NEGOTIATION:

Do we see ourselves as having eternal worth in God's eyes?

THE PRAYER:

O Lord, Your love for us overwhelms us. Help us to grow in appreciation of Your love that we might never question our worth or the worth of all others. Amen.

THE READING: 2 Corinthians 4:16-5:10

JUNE 14

HYPOCRISY

THE INSPIRATION:

> "The devil can cite Scripture for his purpose.
> An evil soul, producing holy witness,
> Is like a villain with a smiling cheek,
> A goodly apple rotten at the heart;
> O, what a goodly outside falsehood hath!"

THE MEDITATION:

We often hear people say they stray from the Church because of all the hypocrites in it. They're right! The Church is full of hypocrites. Hypocrisy is an occupational hazard for those who call themselves Christians. None of us ever lives up to the faith that we profess. But it is in the Church that we hear the Gospel of forgiveness and reconciliation which speaks to our hypocrisy. There is always room for more hypocrites in the Church. We know we are hypocrites and we always seek God's help in dealing with our hypocrisy.

In the Church we also hear the Gospel which confronts and convicts us of our hypocrisy and calls us from this destructive defect. Jesus warns that when we do acts of charity we do not announce it with a flourish of trumpets, and when we fast we do not look gloomy so that our piety might be seen by other people. We cannot glorify ourselves and God at the same time. We do not perform Christian acts so that people will know how religious we are. We glorify God by bringing to all things and everyone we touch a new lift, openness, acceptance, optimism, and love.

THE NEGOTIATION:

How can we witness to others without parading our piety before them?

THE PRAYER:

Forgive us, O Lord, for our failure to live up to the faith we profess. Help us to glorify Your name in our lives and witness to others without parading our piety before them. Amen.

THE READING: Matthew 6:1-4, 16-18

JUNE 15

HELL

THE INSPIRATION:

"It has been said, that there is of nothing so much in hell as of self-will. For hell is nothing but self-will, and if there were no self-will there would be no devil and no hell. When it is said that Lucifer fell from Heaven, and turned away from God, . . .it means nothing else than that he would have his own will, and would not be of one will with the Eternal Will. And when we say self-will, we mean: To will otherwise as the One and Eternal Will of God's will." --Theologia Germanica

THE MEDITATION:

As alcohol abusers we know about hell; we know about self-will. To be raised from hell and experience resurrection means to surrender our own will. This is like giving up life itself. It is dying to self. It means a fundamental decision once taken and then renewed day by day to live by the Eternal Will.

The will is the expression of the big "I" around which the universe revolves. If the Eternal Will is to rule it means a complete reorientation, for then the universe revolves around God. We need this experience every day. As Paul said, "Every day I die" (I Corinthians 15:31). It's what Jesus meant by taking up our cross daily (Like 9:23). The big "I" is crucified and the Eternal Will takes over at the point where our will crosses God's will and we submit to it. This is an essential daily experience or else we submerge into the hell of self-will where we are separated from God.

THE NEGOTIATION:

Are we ready to surrender the big "I" for today?

THE PRAYER:

O Lord, we confess that there is a part of us that wants to follow our self will. Give us strength, O Lord, to give heed to the other part of us that wants to surrender our life and will to Your eternal Will, that we may live this day in union with You. Amen.

THE READING: 2 Peter 2:4-9

JUNE 16

THE NATURE OF HUMANITY

THE INSPIRATION:

"Man is but a reed, the most feeble thing in nature. But he is a thinking reed . . . If the universe were to crush him, man would still be more noble than that which killed him, because he knows that he dies and the advantage which the universe has over him; the universe knows nothing of this. All our dignity consists then in thought. By it we must elevate ourselves.

THE MEDITATION:

The creation stories in Genesis 1 and 2 tell us God created us in his own image (Genesis 1:27) and God formed us from the dust of the ground (Genesis 2:7). Humans, therefore, take on certain attributes of God and of the earth. From God, whose nature is love, we are given the capacity for love. Again, from God, we inherit his attribute of omnipotence. We are not satisfied with being human—we want to play God. The argument of the serpent that convinced Eve to eat the forbidden fruit was the tempting promise, "You will be like God" (Genesis 3:5). Alcohol has the power to bring feelings of omnipotence to human beings who are dissatisfied with being human.

From the ground we inherit various drives which are necessary for our survival and good when tempered by love and destructive when ruled by our desire for omnipotence. We also inherit from the ground a capacity for violence. Truly human persons are those who isolate their desire for omnipotence and capacity for violence and follow their drives tempered by love. To be human is to be humane and that is our highest calling.

THE NEGOTIATION:

Can we accept the fact that we are created to be neither God nor animals?

THE PRAYER:

O Lord, You have created us to be human. You sent Your Son to teach us what it means to be truly human. Help us to live up to the dignity of our human calling by elevating ourselves above an animal existence; and keep us from putting ourselves in Your place. Amen.

THE READING: Genesis: 2:5-3:7

JUNE 17

THE SOCIAL LUBRICANT

THE INSPIRATION:

> "See Social Life and Glee sit down
>> All joyous and unthinking,
> Till quite transmutify'd they've grown
>> Debauchery and Drinking." --Robert Burns

THE MEDITATION:

There is no question that alcohol in lesser amounts is a social lubricant. Alcohol loosens the tongue by helping people overcome social inhibitions. Some of us depended upon alcohol to help us be sociable. Some drink to socialize, others socialize to drink; neither of which are social drinking. Some of us, while attending a drinking party without imbibing, have discovered how shallow and ridiculous the conversation is.

There is a myth which says extraversion is good and introversion is bad. This myth causes some of us to try to be something we are not. Some people are more "outgoing" than others. We cannot put moral judgments on basic psychological types.

Our responsibility is to be true to ourselves by living up to our potential in interpersonal relationships. Jesus always had time for people and related to them on the level of their needs. His encounter with the Samaritan woman at Jacob's well exemplifies an intimacy which reaches out in love to meet her deepest needs. Jesus' life serves as a model for us as we seek to take time, reach out, give of ourselves, and respond to the needs of those with whom we have social encounters.

THE NEGOTIATION:

Does alcohol help or hinder our social relationships?

THE PRAYER:

O Divine Master, grant that we may not so much seek to be consoled as to console; to be loved as to love; to be understood as to understand. For it is in giving that we receive; . . . and it is in dying that we are born to eternal life. Amen. –Francis of Assisi

THE READING: John 4:1-30

JUNE 18

LONELINESS

THE INSPIRATION:

> *"Thou knowest what reproaches I bear,*
> All my anguish is seen by Thee
> Reproach has broken my heart,
> My shame and my dishonor are past hope;
> I looked for consolation and received none,
> For comfort and did not find any." --Psalm 69:19-20

THE MEDITATION:

Is there any human feeling that is more painful than loneliness? We can understand why alcohol abuse has been called "the lonely sickness." We have experienced the heartbreak of forsakenness. During those times we have felt that "no one cares" and "no one understands." But we were wrong. There are many who care, many who understand, who have experienced the same despair of isolation. We need fellowship with them: with those who have had a common experience with alcohol abuse and with the Church who has the *consoling Gospel of a Lord who knew the loneliness of complete rejection.*

There is an epidemic of loneliness today. It seems that the more urbanized we become, and the closer we live to other people, the lonelier we become. A Gallup poll reported that fifty-one percent of Americans fund life "dull and mundane." Christopher Morley commenting on The Lost Weekend said, "It becomes almost the history of a whole era of frustration."

Knowing that there are others who care and understand is extremely important. But beneath this knowledge is the trust expressed by Jesus: "The hour . . . has . . . come, when you are all to be scattered . . . leaving me alone. Yet I am not alone, because the Father is with me" (John 16:32).

THE NEGOTIATION:

Can our loneliness be alleviated by responding to the loneliness of others?

THE PRAYER:

In our loneliness, O Lord, help us to remember Your great love and the caring and understanding of others, and use us, O Lord, to respond to the loneliness of others. Amen.

THE READING: Psalm 69:1-36

JUNE 19

DRY BONES

THE INSPIRATION:

"The Lord . . . carried me out by his spirit and put me down in a plain full of bones . . . and they were very dry. He said to me, 'Man, can these bones live again?' I answered, 'Only thou knowest that, Lord God.' He said to me, 'Prophesy over these bones and say to them, O dry bones, hear the word of the Lord . . . I will put breath into you, and you shall live. '" --Ezekiel 37:1-5

THE MEDITATION:

The ministry of Ezekiel was about 593-597 B.C. in Babylon. He was in exile, the temple had been destroyed, and there was no hope; he lived in a valley of dry bones. It was then that the wind (the Spirit of God) blew over the valley and the bones rattled back together, took on flesh, and became living people.

As alcohol abusers we know the hopelessness and helplessness of the valley of dry bones. The most terrifying aspect of the vision is the reality that people exist without the breath of life. The tragedy is not that we die, but rather than we do not live. Ezekiel faces the situation at its worst for the sake of God. He speaks the Word of the Lord even when there is none to hear. He does not abandon the situation even when there is no hope for success.

The Wind, though invisible, is ever present. We must never estimate the situation merely by what can be seen. We live by a deeper reality than that which can be measured and calculated. Ezekiel keeps at it. In hopelessness he is willing to be God's agent. That's the way God works! Let us be faithful to his Word. At any moment God may break in and bring about the impossible.

THE NEGOTIATION:

Is there such a thing as hopeless hope?

THE PRAYER:

O Lord, give us a vision of hope in our hopelessness. Enable us to face the impossible by clinging to and speaking Your Word of life that we might be agents of Resurrection. Amen.

THE READING: Ezekiel 37:1-14

JUNE 20

MISPLACED HUMILITY

THE INSPIRATION:

"What we suffer from today is humility in the wrong place. Modesty has moved from the organ of ambition. Modesty has settled upon the organ of conviction, where it was never meant to be. A man was meant to be doubtful about himself, but undoubting about the truth; this has been exactly reversed . . . The part of a man that a man does assert is exactly the part he ought not to assert— himself. The part he doubts is exactly the part he ought not to doubt—the Divine Reason." --G. K. Chesterton

THE MEDITATION:

Naaman was a mighty man of valor, but he was also a leper. It wasn't until he put away his pride and humbled himself by washing seven times in the Jordon River that he was healed. There is a relationship between humility and healing. In our broken relationships and our alcohol abuse it is our pride that is an inevitable barrier to healing.

Humility is not claiming we can't play the piano when we can. False humility is subtle pride which seeks to shield us from exposure. It is a selfishness which refuses to share. Christian humility is defined by Paul: "Whatever you are doing, do all to the honour of God" (1 Corinthians 10:31). And then Paul goes on to say, "Follow my example" (1 Corinthians 11:1), and we respond by saying, "Such arrogance, pride audaciousness." Still, Paul doesn't stop, he continues, "as I follow Christ's (example)." Such humility is not humiliation, but a deeper freedom.

THE NEGOTIATION:

Do we dare to say to others, "Follow my example, as I follow Christ's?"

THE PRAYER:

Help us, O Lord, in all that we do, to do to Your glory. In our relationships with others keep us from asserting ourselves and enable us to asset Your honor and Divine Reason, that we may be imitated as we imitate Christ. Amen.

THE READING: 2 Kings 5:1-4

JUNE 21

SUMMER

THE INSPIRATION:

>"In the good old summer time,
>In the good old summer time,
>Strolling through the shady lanes,
>With your baby mine; . . ."   – Ren Shields

THE MEDITATION:

There is something nostalgic about the good old summertime. We remember the vacations, being out of doors, the warm days, the cool beer. It's true, we had some pleasant times while drinking; we also had some miserable times—and they increased as the years went by. We need always beware lest nostalgia seduce our memories by clinging to the good and forgetting the bad. It is through remembering the miseries of the past and counting the blessings of the present that we maintain sobriety.

Jesus advises us to "Look at the fig tree, or any other tree. As soon as it buds, you can see for yourselves that summer is near. In the same way when you see all this happening, you may be sure that the Kingdom of God is near" (Luke 21:29-31). As the spring is the time of new life and budding, so summer is the time for growth. The Church Year recognizes this as Pentecost Season and emphasizes our needs for growth through the teaching of Jesus. Summer has come! It is a time for growth, a time for maturing in the Christian life and faith. The Kingdom of God is near. Let us mature in our citizenship in that Kingdom.

THE NEGOTIATION:

What are the signs that the Kingdom of God is near to us?

THE PRAYER:

We praise You, O Lord, for the warmth and beauty of this season. Draw us ever closer to You that we might grow into a maturity that is pleasing to You. Help us grasp in our hearts and lives the nearness of Your Kingdom. Amen.

THE READING: Genesis 8:14-22

JUNE 22

JOY

THE INSPIRATION:

"Hasten unto God! Why? Not because we ought to. Fellowship with God isn't a bitter duty. Fellowship with God is the deepest joy of human existence. It is the Pearl of Great Price, for which we should sell all we have, and in joy, purchase the pearl . . . We are not our truest, deepest selves until we are selves in joyful fellowship with God. Religion isn't an accidental, beautiful spark, struck off as the hammers of history forge culture after culture upon the anvil of suffering and toil and hope. Religion is the life blood of the full self, the deepest necessity, the most imperious hunger . . ." --Thomas Kelly

THE MEDITATION:

This business of recovering from alcohol abuse is not to be considered a morbid, self-pitying martyrdom, but rather a joyful experience. When we look at what God has done and is doing and will do for us we can only respond with the excitement of joy and thanksgiving.

Fellowship with God is the deepest joy of human existence. "Christians" who walk around with long faces and give the impression that piety is a pain have not entered into the joy of their Master. The Christian life is not bitter duty but joyful response to the grace and love of God.

This doesn't mean that we do not know sorrow and tribulation, but rather, in spite of all, we are overpowered by God's love and respond with joyful thanksgiving for what we have rather than mourning what we have not. Joy is to be shared. If we run into people who don't have smiles today, let's give them one of ours. Smiling is fun and feels good and looks nice and doesn't cost a thing.

THE NEGOTIATION:

How can we share our joy of fellowship with God?

THE PRAYER:

Dear Lord, help us to go about our business today, with laughter and smiling face that our lives may truly reflect thanksgiving for all Your blessings. Enable us to share the joy we know in fellowship with You. Amen.

THE READING: Matthew 25:14-23

JUNE 23

HONESTY

THE INSPIRATION:

"Rarely have we seen a person fail who has thoroughly followed our path. Those who do not recover are people who cannot or will not completely give themselves to this simple program, usually men and women who are constitutionally incapable of being honest with themselves. There are such unfortunates . . . They are naturally incapable of grasping and developing a manner of living which demands vigorous honesty."
--Alcoholics Anonymous

THE MEDITATION:

The way to serenity through sobriety is a way which demands rigorous honesty. Active alcohol abusers are incapable of being honest with themselves, with others, with God. Only with a taste of sobriety do we have a chance to develop the rigorous honesty necessary for growth in serenity.

Most of us claim to be fairly honest people. But because honesty is relative, we ourselves control it. Therefore we assert that we never go beyond the limits of our honesty because we can always push those limits a little farther.

When honesty is not accepted as absolute, we are left with an honesty which is subordinate to our personal interests. Acceptance of an absolute honesty means we are willing to admit that we have a tendency to fit honesty into our self interests.

We cannot be interested in anything less than absolute honesty. Who wants to draw most of his or her salary? Who wants to eat hamburger that is moderately fresh? Who wants a roof that doesn't leak most of the time? The only kind of honesty that leads to serenity is absolute honesty.

THE NEGOTIATION:

Are we rigorously pursuing absolute honesty?

THE PRAYER:

Dear Lord, You know our secret thoughts and desires; there is nothing about us unknown to You. Help us to see through ourselves that we might become aware of and give up the games we play with ourselves, with You, and with others. Amen.

THE READING: Luke 8:11-15

JUNE 24

THE NATIVITY OF JOHN THE BAPTIST

THE INSPIRATION:

"You yourselves can testify that I said, 'I am not the Messiah; I have been sent as his forerunner!' It is the bridegroom to whom the bride belongs. The bridegroom's friend, who stands by and listens to him, is overjoyed at hearing the bridegroom's voice. This joy, this perfect joy, is now mine. As he grows greater, I must grow less." --John 3:28-30

THE MEDITATION:

John the Baptist provides a good model for us in our search for serenity. John's mission and purpose in life was to point to Jesus. He allowed himself to be subordinate to Jesus. His measure of greatness was his capacity to lose himself for Jesus' sake. As John put it, "As he (Jesus) grows greater, I must grow less."

John pointed to Jesus and his disciples followed Jesus – they exposed themselves to Jesus by accepting his invitation to "come and see." Through this exposure John's disciples became disciples for Christ. John's perfect joy is in pointing others away from himself to Jesus. He is willing to decrease as Christ increases.

We are called to live lives that point to Jesus. Others have pointed us to Jesus. We expose ourselves to his Gospel, and then we become pointers. The cycle continues.

John teaches us a basic fact of life: We cannot serve and glorify Christ while serving and glorifying ourselves. The more our lives point to Christ the more serenity we enjoy.

THE NEGOTIATION:

What opportunities will we have to point to Christ today?

THE PRAYER:

Almighty God, You once called John the Baptizer to give witness to the coming of Your Son and to prepare his way. Grant to Your people today the wisdom to see Your purpose and the openness to hear Your will, that we may witness to Christ's coming and so prepare his way. Amen. –Collect for the Nativity of John the Baptist

THE READING: Luke 1:57-67

JUNE 25

EPHPHATHA

THE INSPIRATION:

"They brought to him a man who was deaf and had an impediment in his speech . . . He (Jesus) took the man aside, away from the crowd . . . Then, looking up into the heaven, he signed and said to him, 'Ephphatha,' which means 'Be opened.'" --Mark 7:32-34

THE MEDITATION:

Jesus opens people up to the possibilities of maximum living. Alcohol abuse has a way of making us live minimally. Being possessed by alcohol we often ask, "How little can I get by with?"

Jesus lived life to the maximum. It was said of him: "All that he does, he does well" and again, "Having loved his own, he loved them to the end." He always had time for those whom society labeled "outcasts." He went around telling people "Ephphatha"—"Be Opened." He calls us from minimum to maximum giving of ourselves. Maximum living means we give not out of obligation but in response to God's love as demonstrated by Jesus.

Many people seem to measure out their minds and hearts with a medicine dropper. They appear to be saving themselves for something. They are meager spirits. When we respond to Jesus' call to "Be opened," we leave the minimum and get out of the realm of obligation, and enter into the joy of maximum living. Maximum living never asks, "How little can I get by with? But rather, "What can I give of myself?" Having heard and responded to the "Ephphatha" call, our lives will stimulate "Ephphatha" to others.

THE NEGOTIATION:

Are we opened to the call of maximum living today?

THE PRAYER:

Dear Lord, through Your Son You have opened up for us the possibilities of living life in all its fullness. We pray that we may respond by giving of ourselves that we may know the joy of our Master. Amen.

THE READING: Mark 7:31-37

JUNE 26

THE SPIRIT

THE INSPIRATION:

"'The Spirit' designates something we actually know . . . (It) does not refer . . . to an idea or doctrine, but to an experienced reality . . . The Spirit is compared with wind or fire. It can be 'poured out'; one can be 'filled' with it. It can be 'sent,' can 'come,' and can be 'given' and 'received.' These phrases we may take less literally than some did in the primitive communities, but we cannot talk about the Spirit without using such concrete terms. For 'the Spirit' has no meaning except with experience. To be known it must be felt."
--John Knox

THE MEDITATION:

The use of wine as a symbol of the Spirit is common in the Bible. At Cana (John 2:1-11) Jesus changed water into wine. The six stone jars, for the rites of purification, represent a watered-down, Spiritless religion. Jesus anticipated the giving of the Spirit by changing the water into wine. That the wine is intoxicating is attested to by the steward who says, "Everyone serves the good wine first (when people can tell the difference), then the poor wine; but you have kept the good wine until now." This sign, changing spiritless religion into the intoxicating wine (religion) of the Spirit anticipates the Pentecost Event, when the Spirit-filled disciples are accused of being intoxicated. This is a condition which is experienced, felt and known.

THE NEGOTIATION:

Have we allowed ourselves to experience the Spirit in our lives?

THE PRAYER:

Come, gracious Spirit, heavenly Dove,
With light and comfort from above:
Be Thou our guardian, Thou our guide,
O'er every thought and step preside. Amen. —Simon Browne

THE READING: Acts 8:14-24

JUNE 27

SEX

THE INSPIRATION:

> "Amoebas at the start
> Were not complex
> They tore themselves apart
> And started sex."   -Arthur Guiterman

THE MEDITATION:

No one would dispute the complexity or the power of that energy we call sex. Ours has been called a "sensate culture." This suggests that our culture accepts as real only those things which are perceived sensually. It is the physical, rather than the spiritual which dominates the behavior of our generation. We are such a sex-oriented culture that many people believe that sexual satisfaction is the only way to relieve our tensions. This orientation diminishes the sex act to a mechanical, inhuman function rather than its God given purpose as an expression of love. Dag Hammarskjold writes, "Your cravings as a human animal do not become a prayer just because it is God to whom you ask to attend to them."

Sex is a beautiful God-given gift. But it is very difficult for the alcohol abusers to recognize it as such. There are three things we can do with our sex energy. We can allow our instincts to overtake us and dehumanize ourselves *and other people by using them as sex-objects*. We can try to contain that tumultuous energy roaring with us. But in addition to indulgence and regression there is a third way. We can re-direct this God-given capacity and energy into a creative, caring expression of love.

THE NEGOTIATION:

Have we bought into the sensate culture which claims that sex can resolve all our problems?

THE PRAYER:

O Lord, we thank You for the mystery and wonder of Your gift of sex. We pray that we may use this gift in ways that are pleasing to You and in accordance with Your purpose. Amen.

THE READING: 1 Corinthians 13:1-13

JUNE 28

GRATITUDE

THE INSPIRATION:

"Even among men, gratitude creates an intimate communion. Gratitude is ultimately such a strong bond that nothing can break it. How much more so with God. Because we fail to give thanks, we do not have communion with him. This is why he seems so far away . . . To pray means first to give thanks, and many never achieve true communion with him in their prayers because they do not begin with thanksgiving."
> --Albert Schweitzer

THE MEDITATION:

While resentment is one of the most unhealthy and destructive human feelings, gratitude is one of the healthiest and constructive. Happy and serene people are thankful people. When we are feeling resentment toward another person the best thing we can do it to thank that person for something he or she has done for us. The best thing for us to do when we are feeling downcast is to give thanks. There is always something for which to be grateful. As the old song advises, "When you're tired and you can't sleep, count your blessings instead of sheep." And always, high on our list of blessings, will be our sobriety.

THE NEGOTIATION:

What blessings have we for which we have neglected to thank God?

THE PRAYER:

Almighty God, Father of all mercies, we Thine unworthy servants do give Thee most humble and hearty thanks for all Thy goodness and loving kindness to us and to all people. We bless Thee for our creation, preservation, and all the blessings of this life; but above all, for Thine inestimable love in the redemption of the world by our Lord Jesus Christ; for the means of grace, and for the hope of glory. And, we beseech Thee, give us that due sense of all Thy mercies, that our hearts may be unfeignedly thankful, and that we show forth thy praise, not only with our lips, but in our lives; by giving up ourselves to Thy service, and walking before Thee in holiness and righteousness all our days. Amen. — The General Thanksgiving

THE READING: Psalm 95:1-5

JUNE 29

ST. PETER AND ST. PAUL

THE INSPIRATION:

"Surely you know that you are God's temple, where the Spirit of God dwells. Anyone who destroys God's temple will himself be destroyed by God, because the temple of God is holy, and that temple you are."
-- 1 Corinthians 3:16-17

THE MEDITATION:

The two great apostles commemorated on this day exemplify what it means to be God's temple wherein the Spirit dwells. Their ministry embraced all the known Jewish and Gentile world, and they have been associated in Christian devotion since earliest times. The day of Peter and Paul have been observed since 258 A.D.

To see ourselves as God's temple wherein the Spirit dwells says something profoundly relevant about alcohol abuse. Our bodies, as temples of God's Spirit, are intended to be holy. We adulterate our bodies by adding that which is impure to God's temple. Alcohol is an impure element which destroys and adulterates the bodies of alcohol abusers. As we develop and mature in the practice of the presence of God we perceive our bodies to be more and more sacred and less and less secular. The more we meditate on the life and message of Jesus Christ, the more the physical and the spiritual become fused; and the less distinction we make between earthly and holy functioning. God's Spirit dwells in his temple; and that temple we are.

THE NEGOTIATION:

Can we distinguish between the sacred and the secular?

THE PRAYER:

Almighty Father, You gave the apostles Peter and Paul the strength to lay down their lives for the sake of Your Son. Give us the same strength to be ready to at anytime to lay down our lives for the one who gave his life for us. Amen. —Collect for Peter and Paul

THE READING: 1 Corinthians 3:16-23

JUNE 30

IDLENESS

THE INSPIRATION:

"Why are you standing about like this all day with nothing to do?" --Matthew 20:6

"Woe to those . . . who sing idle songs, and . . . drink wine in bowls." --Amos 6:4-6 (RSV)

"Go to the ant, you sluggard, watch her ways and get wisdom." --Proverbs 6:6

THE MEDITATION:

One of the discoveries of sobriety is the realization of how time-consuming alcohol abuse was and how much extra time we suddenly have on our hands. This new found time can very easily lead us to be an idleness which is threatening to our sobriety and contributes nothing to serenity Idleness often slips into boredom, frustration, and self-pity which we can ill afford.

We need to learn to fill the new-found time, which comes with sobriety, with constructive activity. This activity must take two directions: inner and outer. Constructive inner activity includes all that which results in self-improvement especially in the area of spiritual growth through our meditation, devotion, and worship. Constructive outer activity includes all that which benefits other people.

At the same time, there is always the danger of our becoming overly involved so that we end up "harried." By negotiating with ourselves and God we will not allow this to happen.

THE NEGOTIATION:

How do we use of "leisure" time?

THE PRAYER:

Dear Lord, we thank You for the days, hours, and moments which are ours. Help us to use this time in ways that are beneficial to ourselves and others. Amen.

THE READING: Matthew 20:1-6

JULY 1

EVENNESS

THE INSPIRATION:

"One ought to keep hold of God in everything and accustom his mind to retain God always among his feelings, thoughts and loves. Take him with you among the crowds and turmoils of the alien world. Maintain the same mind, the same trust, and the same earnestness toward God in all your doings. Believe me, if you keep this kind of evenness, nothing can separate you from God-consciousness." --Meister Eckhart.

THE MEDITATION:

Our practice of God's presence begins perhaps with our desperation to find sobriety. This is perfectly legitimate. All seeking after God begins with a desperation of one kind or another. But as we learn more and more to retain God's presence, the original cause for desperation becomes less and less. The Presence becomes less a means to an end and more an end in itself.

God consciousness is not a pre-occupation, which disallows our thinking or involvement in other things or activities. It is rather an occupation, which we bring into other thoughts, feelings and activities.

This evenness in all of our doings is our goal. To retain God as the center of all we do and say and think and feel is the objective we seek. The goal and objective of evenness does not come easily; yet, that is the direction toward which we daily proceed.

THE NEGOTIATION:

Is God-consciousness a means to an end or an end in itself?

THE PRAYER:

Dear Lord, we Thank you for this moment of consciousness of Your Presence. Enable us to take Your presence with us this day as we face the turmoils of an alien world. Amen.

THE READING: Psalm 16:1-11

JULY 2

THE VISITATION

THE INSPIRATION:

> "Tell out, my soul, the greatness of the Lord,
> Rejoice, rejoice, my spirit, in God my savior; . . .
> His name is Holy;
> His mercy sure from generation to generation, . . .
> The arrogant of heart and mind he has put to rout, . . .
> But the humble have been lifted high." – Luke 1:46-52

THE MEDITATION:

The visit of Mary to Elizabeth, first observed in the thirteenth century, is a comparatively recent festival. Some church calendars have moved the festival from this traditional date to May 31st. Whenever observed, it is an occasion to ponder the magnificent.

The Son of Mary praises God for doing such great things through a humble person. God does not work through those of arrogant hearts and minds. It is only when we surrender our arrogance that God begins to work in us and sobriety and serenity become possible. Humility is the only attitude through which God's mercy is displayed. The greatness of God can only be perceived by the humble in heart and mind.

When we look back in honest appraisal of our lives we come to realize it is when we gave up, or had the arrogance beat out of us, and accepted humiliation, it was then that God began to do great things for us and through us.

THE NEGOTIATION:

Do we sometimes forget to praise God for what he has done for us?

THE PRAYER:

Lord God, You give us signs of Your presence in the events of our lives. Grant that we may readily recognize Your gracious visitation and always proclaim Your greatness and the great things You have done for Your people. Amen. – Collect for The Visitation

THE READING: Luke 1:39-56

JULY 3

TEMPTATION

THE INSPIRATION:

"If you feel sure that you are standing firm, beware! You may fall. So far you have faced no trial beyond what man can bear. Good keeps faith, and he will not allow you to be tested above your powers, but when the test comes he will at the same time provide a way out, by enabling you to sustain it."
-- 1 Corinthians 10:12-13

THE MEDITATION:

Paul doesn't say "if" but rather "when" the test comes. Temptation is inevitable. We know this so well in relation to alcohol abuse. The compulsion, the addiction, the dependency, the test, the temptation, no matter what we are less aware of is the threat to us when we feel we are "standing firm;" when we think we "have it made." We need to remind ourselves that temptation, whether it be blatant or subtle, is always a threat to us.

Martin Luther once remarked, "I cannot keep birds from flying over my head, but I can keep them from building under my hat." While temptation is inevitable we can and must do some things to avoid it. Let us not become overly confident and let us do those things that we have learned from our experience and the experience of others that avoid tempting situations. We always need fellowship with others who share our experience with alcohol abuse. And let us practice God's presence confidently knowing that with every temptation he will provide a way out.

THE NEGOTIATION:

Are we willing to let God provide us with a way out of temptation?

THE PRAYER:

O Lord, grant us grace never to parley with temptation, never to tamper with conscience; never to spare the right eye, or hand, or foot that is a snare to us; never to lose our soles, though in exchange we should gain the whole world. Amen.

THE READING: Matthew 18:8-9

JULY 4

DECLARATION OF DEPENDENCE

THE INSPIRATION:

"The God who gave us life, gave us liberty at the same time." --Thomas Jefferson

"Where the spirit of the Lord is, there is liberty." --2 Corinthians 3:17

THE MEDITATION:

As we celebrate our national independence, it may be well for us to reaffirm our declaration of dependence upon God. We made that declaration for the first time when we admitted our powerlessness over alcohol and turned our lives and wills over to God. It is a declaration that we need to reaffirm over and over again.

Jesus said, "If you dwell within the revelation I have brought, . . . you shall know the truth, and the truth will set you free" (John 8:31-32). Those who heard Jesus speak these words didn't understand. The only freedom they could comprehend is of a political nature. Jesus points out to them that anyone who sins is a slave to sin and that he offers and even more authentic freedom than political forces can muster.

The freedom Jesus offers is from something and for something: freedom from sin, death, and fear, to be sure; but also freedom demands responsibility. We are responsible for ourselves and responsible to God and all others in our human family. As we dwell on our dependence upon God we know and live the truth, which makes us authentically free.

THE NEGOTIATION:

Are independence and freedom the same thing?

THE PRAYER:

We thank You, O Lord, for the freedom and independence, which is ours. Help us to responsible use these gifts that we might grow in our willingness and effectiveness in service You. Amen.

THE READING: John 8:31-36

JULY 5

PAYING OUR RESPECTS

THE INSPIRATION:

"We come to prayer, purely and simply to pay our respects to God and to prove our loyalty. If it pleases him to speak to us by granting us his inspirations and interior consolations, that would be a great honour and delight, but if he does not show us such favour and leaves us there unnoticed without so much as speaking to us, we must not leave on that account, but on the contrary remain quietly and devoutly in His presence . . . It is honour enough for us, just to be near him." --Francis de Sales

THE MEDITATION:

The idea of prayer as paying our respects to God is foreign to most of us. Our usual motivation for prayer is found in some need we wish to be satisfied. We would speculate that most prayer consists of petitions: "Give me this; give me that." Not that "give me" has no place in prayer, but that place need not dominate our prayer life. Oscar Wilde once quipped, "When the gods wish to punish us they answer our prayers."

People generally make their plans and carry them out the best they can. Or, having made their plans, they ask God to help them carry them through. Another way is open to us: to ask God what his plans are and then offer ourselves to carry out his purposes.

In our search for serenity we need to learn to pay our respects to God, who knows what our needs are before we ask him (Matthew 6:8). Paying our respects to God is being in his presence for his sake. This is an honor he reserves for us which never fails to give us serenity.

THE NEGOTIATION:

Can we pay our respects to God without asking something of him?

THE PRAYER:

We come into Your presence to pay our respects to You, O Lord. We love You and praise You. It feels good to be with You, Dear Lord. We are honored to be in Your presence. Thank You for the privilege. Amen.

THE READING: Psalm 14:1-10

JULY 6

SIMPLICITY

THE INSPIRATION:

"The true explanation for the complexity of our (lives) is an inner one . . . The outer distractions .
. . reflect an inner lack of integration . . . Life is meant to be lived from a Center . . . where the Eternal
dwells at the base of our being . . . Many of the things we are doing seem so important to us . . . But if
we 'center down' . . . and take out life program into the Silent places of the heart, with complete
openness, ready to do, ready to renounce according to His leading, then many of the things we are
doing lose their vitality to us; . . . There is a re-evaluation of much that we do or try to do, which is done
for us, and we know what to do and what to let alone." --Thomas Kelly

THE MEDITATION:

We are complicated people who live in a complicated world. Moreover, we have all the
complexities of alcohol abuse. We don't know which "experts" to listen to. We can hardly keep up with
the fast changing world. Max Coots has said, "Nothing stays the way it was or will remain the way it will
become." Hope and faith struggle to keep ahead of fear and anxiety.

One attempt to deal with complexity is with oversimplification. We can tell each other to "keep
it simple," and seek simple and pat answers to our problems. But if we are to be intellectually honest
we discover that there is no easy attic in which to store our confusions.

And yet we need some simplicity to balance our complexity. As we learn to "center down" to
where the Eternal dwells we discover a rearrangement of our values and priorities and experience a
serenity in simplicity.

THE NEGOTIATION:

Have we allowed ourselves the simplicity of centering down?

THE PRAYER:

Lord, temper with tranquility
Our manifold activity
That we may do our work for Thee
With very great simplicity. Amen. –Sixteenth Century Prayer

THE READING: John 14:1-6

MONOTONY

THE INSPIRATION:

"I will greatly rejoice in the Lord,
    my soul shall exult in my God;
For he has clothes me with the
    Garments of salvation
He has covered me with the robe
    of righteousness." --Isaiah 61:10

THE MEDITATION:

It is not uncommon, after the excitement of the early days of sobriety wears off, for alcohol abusers to experience a sense of monotony. After all one of the factors in our turning to alcohol was to escape monotony. We must admit that alcohol did provide excitement in spite of the misery we caused ourselves and others. With that kind of excitement behind us and the realization that sobriety must be our new way of life, we sometimes revert to the old feelings of monotony. Back to the old routine, the mundane, boring, monotonous, existence.

It is then that we need a word of excitement. And that word is the Word of God. The Word of God says "no" to monotony and "yes" to life. The Word becomes flesh. God touches us with Word and Sacrament. He reaches into our routine, dull, mundane, boring, monotonous existence with his love. We begin to experience with enthusiasm the excitement of his presence. It is then that we can say, "I will greatly rejoice in the Lord."

There is nothing monotonous about the new life in Christ. It is life, which is always new, refreshing, and challenging. And this excitement and zest for living becomes intensified the more we meditate on the life and message of Jesus.

THE NEGOTIATION:

How can we best deal with feelings of monotony?

THE PRAYER:

Teach me, my God and King,
In all things Thee to see,
And what I do in anything,
To do it as for Thee. Amen. –George Herbert

THE READING: Isaiah 61:10-62:3

JULY 8

INTERCESSORY PRAYER

THE INSPIRATION:

"Our prayers for others flow more easily than those we offer on our own behalf . . . I detect two
. . . reasons for the ease of my own intercessory prayers. One is that I am often . . . praying for others
when I should be doing things for them. It's so much easier to pray for a bore than to go and see him.
And the other is like unto it. Suppose I pray that you may be given grace to withstand your besetting sin
. . . Well, all the work has to done by God and you. If I pray against my own besetting sin, there will be
work for me." --C.S. Lewis

THE MEDITATION:

Our own suffering, besetting sin, and powerlessness over alcohol are properly subjects of our
prayers. But what about other people? While we are unique individuals who experience life in our own
peculiar way, others have similar experiences. The need our prayers, we need to pray for them, we
need their prayers, and they need to pray for us. There is no experience in the human family with which
we cannot identify, for we have had similar experiences.

Our prayer life would be enriched if we would give at least as much time and effort in
intercession as we give to our own needs. And let us beware lest our intercessory prayer become a
pious cop-out, which satisfies a "religious" need in us and placates our conscience so that we feel we
don't have to do something for others. True prayer, in Jesus' name, always results in some kind of
action. We do not truly pray for the man lying in the gutter unless we try to help him. We do not truly
pray for our own needs unless we make the effort, with God's help to change.

THE NEGOTIATION:

Is it easier for us to pray for ourselves or others?

THE PRAYER:

Dear Lord, we pray for Your children who are suffering, who are facing besetting sin, who are
abusing alcohol. Help us to respond to their needs by being Christs to them. Amen.

THE READING: John 17:11-19

JULY 9

THE POOR IN SPIRIT

THE INSPIRATION:

"When he (Jesus) saw the crowds he went up the hill. There he took his seat, and when the disciples had gathered round him he began to address them. And this is the teaching he gave: 'How blest are those who know that they are poor; the Kingdom of Heaven is theirs.'" --Matthew 5:1-3

THE MEDITATION:

Jesus begins his Sermon on the Mount with a series of short and precise teaching statements, which we have come to know as the Beatitudes. The Beatitudes are promises of the Kingdom of God and descriptions of those who receive the promises.

The poor in spirit are those who are aware of their spiritual needs. One of the blessings that can come out of alcohol abuse is that we have such a sense of powerlessness that we become profoundly aware of our spiritual poverty. This awareness can be the beginning of a Spirit-filled life.

Jesus is not blessing poverty as such, but rather those who are aware of and respond to their need for spiritual growth. He's talking about those who are open to learn and grow; those who come eagerly like children to the great book of life; those who are content with simplicity in a world dominated by the complications of science and technology.

The first Beatitude is a condemnation of pride, which is so threatening to alcohol abusers. Pride is the root of all sin. Poverty of spirit is the root of all virtue.

THE NEGOTIATION:

Are we aware of our need for spiritual growth?

THE PRAYER:

We come to You, O Lord, in powerlessness and hopelessness. We are deeply aware of our poverty and need for spiritual growth. Help us to be receptive to Your Presence that we might even now know the blessings of Your Kingdom. Amen.

THE READING: Psalm 40:1-7

JULY 10

THOSE WHO MOURN

THE INSPIRATION:

"How blest are the sorrowful; they shall find consolation." – Matthew 5:4

"You have no more right to consume happiness without producing it than to consume wealth without producing it." --George Bernard Shaw

THE MEDITATION:

The word "blessed" or "how blest" denotes the highest kind of happiness and well-being, and literally means "how happy." The Beatitudes describe those who are happy in God's sight.

That the sorrowful or those who mourn are happy is a paradox. The world says, "Enjoy!" Jesus says, "Grieve!" He calls for a sharp denial of the world's values and priorities. Those who mourn their own sins and shortcomings, as well as the wickedness of the world, shall be comforted by God.

Consolation comes to those who accept their own sorrow with resolve to be strengthened and with God's help to make the sorrow an oblation. Our tendency is to rebel against the pain of mourning, or to pretend it doesn't exist, or to repress it through busy activity or in the pursuit of pleasure. True happiness comes to those who work through their sorrow.

Paul counsels us to "Help one another to carry these heavy loads, and in this way you will fulfill the law of Christ" (Galatians 6:2). We are to share our neighbors sorrow, expose ourselves to the world's misery, and show compassion where there is injustice, oppression, and suffering. Let us never fall into the trap, which says, "It's none of my business; my own recovery from alcohol abuse is all the problems I need." Happiness is found by producing it in others.

THE NEGOTIATION:

Can we be happy and sorrowful at the same time?

THE PRAYER:

O Lord, fill us with sorrow for our own failures and the wickedness of the world. Bring to us Your consolation; and inspire us to show compassion toward others by bearing their burdens. Amen.

THE READING: Isaiah 61:1-9

JULY 11

THE MEEK

THE INSPIRATION:

"How blest are those of a gentle spirit; they shall have the earth for their possession." -- Matthew 5:5

"'The meek,' said Christ, 'inherit the earth.' They do not buy it; they do not conquer it, they inherit it."   --Henry Drummond

THE MEDITATION:

We often think of the words "meek" and "meager" as synonyms. But true meekness knows nothing of meagerness. Meekness is not weakness. The meek are those who are so overcome by God's greatness that they see the purpose of their lives only in giving of themselves for love's sake. The Greek word for meek means goodwill toward all people in reverent obedience to God.

The self-centered life that goes along with alcohol can only be eliminated by learning meekness. The more we learn meekness the greater God becomes to us. Water rests only when it gets to the lowest place. So do we. Meekness is a necessary ingredient of serenity.

Meekness has an astonishing reward: inheritance of the earth! An inheritance is a gift, it cannot be bought or seized by force. The opposite of meekness is aggression. Aggressors are at odds with themselves. The meek in reverent lowliness center down on God's will for themselves and the world. The earth if the Lord's; he puts down the mighty from their seats and exalts them of low degree (Luke 1:52).

THE NEGOTIATION:

What can we do to learn meekness?

THE PRAYER:

Dear Lord, we come before Your greatness in humble thanksgiving and praise. We thank You that by Your grace You overwhelm us with the power of Your love. Help us, in all meekness to live this day for Your sake. Amen.

THE READING: Psalm 37:10-40

JULY 12

HUNGER AND THIRST FOR RIGHTEOUSNESS

THE INSPIRATION:

"How blest are those who hunger and thirst to see right prevail; they shall be satisfied." -- Matthew 5:5

"Preserve in right conduct and loyalty and you shall find life and honour." --Proverbs 21:21

THE MEDITATION:

The word "hunger" implies an intense desire. The word "thirst" has perhaps even a stronger implication for us. Not that we so much physically thirsted for alcohol, but the intense desire for a drink has an implication with which we can readily identify. It is this intense desire that Jesus is talking about in regard to righteousness.

But who among us, even with sobriety, can claim righteousness? Notice that the requirement in this beatitude is not righteousness, but rather a hunger and thirst for righteousness, i.e. an intense desire to see right prevail. We seek not perfection but spiritual progress. As Robert Louis Stevenson remarked, "To travel hopefully is a better thing than to arrive." Here Jesus takes the intense desire for the deed.

The hunger and thirst about which Jesus speaks is righteousness within ourselves and seeing right prevail in our world. Longing for and working for that which is right in God's sight comes through meditating on the life and message of Jesus. The satisfaction comes in practicing the presence of God. It is not the physical satisfaction of eating nor the psychological satisfaction of drinking but the spiritual satisfaction of living in God's presence.

THE NEGOTIATION:

Is our desire to do God's will as intense as was our desire for alcohol?

THE PRAYER:

O Lord, create in us a hunger and thirst to want and do that which You require of us; and when we fail give us the satisfaction of turning our failures into our strengthening. Amen.

THE READING: John 6:41-58

JULY 13

THE MERCIFUL

THE INSPIRATION:

"How blest are those who show mercy; mercy shall be shown to them." --Matthew 5:7

"The quality of mercy is not strain'd,
It droppeth as the gentle rain from heaven
Upon the place beneath; it is twice blest;
It blesseth him that gives and him that takes." --Shakespeare

THE MEDITATION:

Mercy lays claim on us whenever and wherever there is suffering. We, who have found some semblance of sobriety through the mercy of God and others, know that true mercy seeks to restore physical and spiritual health. Mercy is needed by the physically suffering, but also for the morally crippled, those poor in honor and diseased by greed. Mercy is called for whether or not the suffering, crippling, poverty, imprisonment, or disease was brought on by an individual. Mercy never says, "It's your fault; therefore I withdraw," or "You got yourself into this, therefore it's your problem." Mercy responds to suffering whatever the cause.

Mercy is not "feeling sorry for" someone or "having pity on" someone. Mercy embraces action; if untranslated into deeds it becomes septic. If deeds are impossible, words may help. If words are impossible, tears may help.

The merciful are too aware of their own failures and needs for mercy to pass judgment on others. They know that their receptiveness to God's mercy is directly related to the mercy they practice toward others. "Twice blest!"

THE NEGOTIATION:

What situations will we encounter this day that will call for our mercy?

THE PRAYER:

Teach me to feel another's woe
To hide the fault I see;
That mercy I to others how
That mercy show to me. –Alexander Pope

THE READING: Psalm 51:1-9

JULY 14

THE PURE IN HEART

THE INSPIRATION:

"How blest are those whose hearts are pure; they shall see God." --Matthew 5:8

"To the pure all things are pure; but nothing is pure to the tainted winds of disbelievers, tainted alike in reason and conscience. They profess to acknowledge God, but they deny him by their actions. Their detestable obstinacy disqualifies them for any good work." --Titus 1:15-16

THE MEDITATION:

When contemplating the Sixth Beatitude our immediate response is to wonder which is more inaccessible—the condition or the promise, purity of heart, or seeing God. Even in our state of recovering from alcohol abuse we question the possibility of either. Purity of heart need not be thought of as moral perfection, but rather progress in that direction. The extent of our serenity is directly related to our degree of purity of heart.

The word "heart" in Biblical usage refers to our whole personality. It involves our mind and will as well as our emotions. The pure in heart see God's activity in themselves and in the world around them. They are aware of God's presence in their lives even in the midst of temptation and suffering. They are open to experience God's spirit working in and through them.

James Reid says that to the impure person life is like a stained-glass window seen from the outside, but that the pure person sees it from the inside. We are not mocked by the beatitude: God does purify our minds and wills and emotions when we turn to him in repentance and confession. In practicing his presence he keeps us pure and we can indeed see him.

THE NEGOTIATION:

Is there a difference between purity and "puritanism?"

THE PRAYER:

Lord, make me pure.
Only the pure shall see Thee as Thou art
And shall endure. Amen. –Christina Rossetti

THE READING: James 4:1-10

JULY 15

THE PEACEMAKERS

THE INSPIRATION:

"How blest are the peacemakers; God shall call them his sons." --Matthew 5:9

"Like the bee, we distill poison from honey for our self-defense—what happens to the bee if it uses its sting is well known." --Dag Hammarskjold

THE MEDITATION:

The central theme of the Gospel is found in the angels' song when they hailed Jesus' birth: "Peace on earth" (Luke 2:14). That theme is repeated and lived out in Jesus' life. In the Seventh Beatitude Jesus says the children of God are peacemakers, and later in the Sermon on the Mount he admonishes those who would hear to "love your enemies" (Matthew 5:44). And finally, Jesus last bequest is, "Peace is my parting gift to you" (John 14:27).

While abusing alcohol we know little peace; much less are we in a position to be peacemakers. Peace has its basis in reconciliation with God. With this established we are in a position to be reconciled with others. Peacemakers are makers of peace. They are not passive but actively involved in the things that make for peace.

Peacemakers abhor violence of any kind whether it be physical or mental. They believe that the power of God's love is the strongest force in the world. They are philosophically non-violent and actively anti-violence. They search for alternatives to violence and never condone cruelty in any form. God calls them his sons and daughters. They know true serenity.

THE NEGOTIATION:

Who is hurt by hurting another person?

THE PRAYER:

Lord, make us an instrument of Your peace; where there is hatred, let us sow love; where there is injury, pardon; where there is doubt, faith; where there is despair, hope; where there is darkness, light; where there is sadness, joy. For it is in giving that we receive; it is in pardoning that we are pardoned; and it is in dying that we are born to eternal life. Amen. –Francis of Assisi

THE READING: Matthew 5:43-48

JULY 16

THE PERSECUTED

THE INSPIRATION:

"How blest are those who have suffered persecution for the cause of right; the kingdom of Heaven is theirs.

"How blest are you, when you suffer insults and persecution and every kind of calumny for my sake. Accept it with gladness and exultation, for you have a rich reward in heaven; in the same way they persecuted the prophets before you." –Matthew 5:10-12

THE MEDITATION:

Jesus asks his followers to remain true even at the risk of losing their lives. Christians are condemned when they are so tepid that they are not insulted or persecuted, but simply ignored. When the Gospel of peace and love is proclaimed and lived out it is threatening to the world. There are good reasons for keeping our alcohol conditions anonymous. But there is no such thing as "Christians Anonymous." Christians are compelled to witness to the Gospel in word and deed. This witness often involves risk. The Eighth Beatitude is not outdated, but very relevant to our generation.

It's hard for us to conceive of gladness and exultation in the face of insults and persecution. But Jesus asks us to trust him and tells us we are in the good company of the prophets. Not all persecution is blest: Jesus is talking about "for the cause of right" and "for my sake."

As alcohol abusers most of us suffered from a persecution complex. But Jesus is not talking about that kind of morbid self-pity. Persecution for his sake brings gladness and exultation.

THE NEGOTIATION:

Are we members of "Christians Anonymous?"

THE PRAYER:

Dear Lord, we thank You that through the Gospel of Your Son You have granted to us salvation and life that has meaning, purpose and direction. Give us the courage, O Lord, to speak and live this precious Gospel, that, being willing to take risks, we may know the gladness and exultation which You promise. Amen.

THE READING: John 15:18-27

JULY 17

A RISING TIDE

THE INSPIRATION:

"When observed through sufficient depth of time life can be seen to move. Not only does it move but it advances in a definite direction . . . Research shows that from the lowest to the highest level of the organic world there is a persistent and clearly defined thrust of animal forms toward species with more sensitive and elaborate nervous systems . . . What else can this mean except that . . . there is a continual heightening, a rising tide of consciousness which visibly manifests itself on our planet in the course of ages?" --Pierre Teilhard de Chardin

THE MEDITATION:

Meditation on the Beatitudes can leave us with a guilt-ridden depression. But if we see life as "a rising tide of consciousness" and ourselves as being "in process" we need not be left with such lowness of spirit. Augustine once wrote, "Man was created in order that a beginning might be made." In our arrogance we look upon ourselves as some kind of finished product. Montaigne was contemptuous about a species that could not create a worm bur could make gods by the hundreds.

If we think of ourselves as a beginning rather than as an end of God's creative design, perhaps we can forgive ourselves for not being perfect. Among all of God's species humans are the only ones who kill their own kind wholesale. Obviously this is not fitting for a finished product. If we see ourselves in the beginning of a process in rising consciousness, perhaps we can forgive ourselves and accept God's forgiveness of us.

There is a preordained spiritual evolution. In spite of our failures God reacts and moves us toward his end. He is the "Source, Guide, and Goal of all that is" (Romans 11:36).

THE NEGOTIATION:

Do we see ourselves as "in process" rather than finished products?

THE PRAYER:

O Thou who maketh all things new, and having made man, canst yet more wonderfully remake him; O Thou who art ever waiting to change lives of selfishness into lives of service, we praise Thee, O Lord. Amen.
            —John Hunter

THE READING: Ezekiel 11:14-21

JULY 18

TENTATIVENESS

THE INSPIRATION:

"One God, one law, one element.
And one far-off divine event,
To which the whole creation moves." --Alfred Tennyson

THE MEDITATION:

We are tentative rather than completed creatures. We are pioneers rather than settlers. We live in a forest of doubt rather than in a sea of certainty. And yet, in this doubt and tentativeness we live by faith in God toward whom the whole creation moves. We decidedly have not grieved, but we are on the way. As Christians we are "people of The Way."

We sometimes wonder how we got to where we are today. As we recall the horrors of alcohol abuse, some of us marvel that we have survived at all. And yet here we are today, at this moment, meditating and negotiating with God and ourselves. Somehow, by the grace of God, we have arrived at this moment. But the moment is tentative and we are tentative.

God is indeed the "Source, Guide, and Goal" of our lives and "of all that is" (Romans 11:36). He is behind us, we came from him. He is before us, we move toward him. He is with us, we are led by him. This does not mean we are puppets or robots. God does not control us but respects the freedom of our wills with which he created us. We are free to ignore God and his will for us. We often do. And yet he reacts to our failures and moves us along toward his goal for us, which is himself. But this movement is dependent upon our willingness to be moved.

THE NEGOTIATION:

Do we acknowledge God as our Source, Guide, and Goal?

THE PRAYER:

God of our fathers, and our God, give us the faith to believe in the ultimate triumph of righteousness. We pray for the bi-focals of faith that see the despair and the need of the hour, but also see further on, the patience of our God working out his plan in the world He has made. Amen. –Peter Marshall

THE READING: Proverbs 16:1-9

JULY 19

BEAUTY

THE INSPIRATION:

"There is in the universe a higher kind of beauty. It is the beauty of sacrifice, of giving up for others, of suffering for others . . . A man has not found his highest beauty until his brow is tinged with care for some cause he loves more than himself. The beauty of sacrifice is the final word in beauty." -- Frank C. Laubach

THE MEDITATION:

That which we call beautiful is usually that which is perceived to be so visibly or audibly or with one more of our sense. However, when we talk about "a beautiful person" we normally refer to characteristics other than those, which are sensually perceived. The beauty of Jesus was not in his physical appearance, whatever that may have been like, but rather in his self-giving, self-emptying manner of living. Our Beautiful Savior calls us to be beautiful. "As thou has sent me into the world," he prayed to his Father, "I have sent them into the world" (John 17:18).

As authentic beauty is seen in Jesus' self-emptying life, so it is seen in our self-giving. In this beauty we find meaning. The purpose of our lives is found in giving of ourselves to others. When in the grips of alcohol abuse we are not able to give much of ourselves, we need all of ourselves for ourselves. The degree of serenity we reach is directly related to our willingness to sacrifice ourselves for the sake of others. As we grow in loving the cause of Christ more than ourselves and taking that cause upon ourselves, the more beautiful we become.

THE NEGOTIATION:

Is authentic beauty a gift?

THE PRAYER:

Beautiful Savior, King of Creation,
Son of God and Son of Man!
Truly I'd love Thee, truly I'd serve Thee,
Light of my soul, my joy, my crown. –Munster Gesangbuch

THE READING: Isaiah 52:7-12

JULY 20

THE MOON LANDING

THE INSPIRATION:

"There are heavenly bodies and earthly bodies; and the splendor of the heavenly bodies is one thing, the splendor of the earthly bodies, another. The sun has a splendor of its own, the moon another splendor."
--1 Corinthians 15:40-41

THE MEDITATION:

It was on a Sunday, July 20, 1969, that the astronauts landed on the moon. This landing has been hailed as the greatest of all human scientific accomplishments. We are the heirs of centuries of scientific materialism, which made the moon landing possible. We are also heirs of an intense spiritual anguish, created by a pre-occupation with the truth of science and a corresponding neglect of spiritual truth. Only matter has been recognized as real. There are no absolute truths, no ultimate values, and no awareness of the spiritual. The result is a meaninglessness, which drives many to despair and escape into alcohol and other drug abuse.

There seems to be appearing, however, new developments. The insights of modern physicists have challenged the world view of classical physics. There is once again room, and necessity, for faith and mystery. We seem to be living in a generation, which is in-between cultures with drastically different world views. These are exciting times to be alive.

If we fund truth in walking on the moon we are still left with the question, "what does it mean?" Absolute truth and ultimate values can only be found in the reality of the spiritual.

THE NEGOTIATION:

Do mystery, grace, and faith enter our strivings to comprehend reality?

THE PRAYER:

Dear Lord, we are the confused children of an age of confusion. Come to us in the midst of the meaninglessness of our culture with insight into Your ultimate and absolute truth, that we might know and live out Your purpose for us. Amen.

THE READING: Luke 21:25-28

JULY 21

LUKEWARMNESS

THE INSPIRATION:

"I know all your ways; you are neither hot nor cold. How I wish you were either hot or cold! But because you are lukewarm, neither hot nor cold, I will spit you out of my mouth." --Revelation 3:15-16

THE MEDITATION:

Where the Church is sub-Christian, let us oppose it and seek to improve it. Where the church is true to the Gospel, let us give everything we've got to support it. We cannot be neutral about the Church, nor can we be lukewarm about the Lord of the Church. Christ has called us into fellowship with him through his body—the Church.

Jesus was very blunt when he said, "He who is not with me is against me, and he who does not father with me scatters" (Matthew 12:30). There is an either-or in Christ's call. The middle ground is non-existent.

One of the characteristics of alcohol abuse is resentment. These resentments go out in all directions. Naturally the Church will be among the targets of these resentments. While harboring resentments sobriety becomes very difficult and serenity impossible. As we begin to deal with our resentments there is a tendency to ease off once neutrality has been reached. In our search for serenity we sometimes become content with lukewarmness. We have a continuing need for reconciliation, a perpetual need to gather with Christ.

The Church is indeed sub-Christian in some areas. That's because the Body of Christ is made up of imperfect people like us. We can't be neutral about Christ's Church. We must always seek to make his Body more Christ-like.

THE NEGOTIATION:

Have we dealt with our resentments only to the point of neutrality.

THE PRAYER:

Dear Lord, You have called us into the fellowship of Your Son, through his Body, the Church. Keep us from lukewarmness toward this fellowship, and inspire us to deeper commitment in making Your Church more Christ-like. Amen.

THE READING: Revelation 3:14-22

JULY 22

MARY MAGALENE

THE INSPIRATION:

"Early on the Sunday morning, while it was still dark, Mary of Magdala came to the tomb. She saw that the stone had been moved away from the entrance . . . Mary stood at the tomb outside, weeping . . . Jesus said ,'Mary!' She turned to him and said, 'My Master!' . . . Mary of Magdala went to the disciples with her news: 'I have seen the Lord!'" –John 2:1,10,16,18

THE MEDITATION:

Mary Magdalene traveled with Jesus and his disciples and provided for them with her own resources. She was present at the crucifixion and burial of Jesus. She was a principal witness to the Resurrection. In the gospels of Mark and John she is the first one to see the risen Christ. There is one other fact we know about Mary of Magdala: Jesus cured her of possession of seven demons (Luke 8:2).

What were the seven demons with which Mary was possessed? We don't know, but they could be emotional disturbance, prostitution, alcohol abuse, or any number of other demons. As alcohol abusers we know what it means to be possessed by demons. We can identify with Mary as being in need of the same healing power that Christ brought to her. God's healing power solicits a response. Mary followed Jesus to the end and was the first to witness his Resurrection.

As we allow God's healing power to work in us our demon is expelled. We experience the new life in Christ, and, like Mary become witness to his Resurrection.

THE NEGOTIATION:

What is our response to the expulsion of our demons?

THE PRAYER:

Almighty God, Your Son Jesus Christ restored Mary Magdalene to health of body and mind, and called her to be a witness of his Resurrection. Heal us now in body and mind, and call us to serve You in the power of the Resurrection of Your Son. Amen. –Collect for Mary Magdalene

THE READING: John 20:1-2, 11-16

JULY 23

KNOWLEDGE

THE INSPIRATION:

"Knowledge is not a couch whereon to rest a searching and restless spirit; nor a terrace for a wandering mind to walk upon with a fair prospect; nor a tower of state for a proud mind to raise itself upon; nor a sort of commanding ground for strife and contention; nor a shop for profit and sale; but a rich storehouse for the glory of the Creator, and the relief of men's estate." -Francis Bacon

THE MEDITATION:

Alcohol abuse often results in an insecurity which believes that the best defense is a strong offense. This offensive sometimes comes in the form of a pretention that we know it all. Fuzzy minds try to impress others and ourselves with our vas storehouse of knowledge.

With sobriety and growing serenity we become less interested in impressing others. We begin to agree with Montaigne that "all other knowledge is hurtful to him who has not honesty and good nature." We can admit with Paul that our knowledge is imperfect (1 Corinthians 13:9).

This is not to imply that we should become agnostic. Our search for knowledge takes on new meaning. We seek to know the love of Christ "though it is beyond knowledge" (Ephesians 3:19). We seek to love the Lord with all out mind (Mark 12:30). Knowledge then becomes a rich storehouse for the glory of the Lord and is used to life up other people in mind and spirit.

THE NEGOTIATION:

Is there any knowledge which cannot be used for the benefit of others?

THE PRAYER:

We are aware, O Lord, that we think our knowledge is greater than it is. Forgive us for our arrogance and full us with a thirst for the knowledge of Your love that we may be able to feed others to Your glory. Amen.

THE READING: Psalm 119:65-72

JULY 24

HOPE

THE INSPIRATION:

"The potentialities of development in human souls are unfathomable. So many who seem irretrievable hardened have in point of fact been softened, converted, regenerated, in ways that amazed the subjects even more than they surprised the spectators, that we never can be sure in advance of any man that his salvation by the way of love is hopeless. We have no right to speak of human crocodiles . . . as of fixedly incurable being." --William James

THE MEDITATION:

As alcohol abusers many of us have experienced the agonizing pain of hopelessness. Our plight was expressed by Robert Frost: "Nothing to look backward to with pride, and nothing to look forward to with hope." Hopelessness expresses a depressing state where, not only do others give up on us, we give up on ourselves.

And yet somehow in our despair of hopelessness we, by the grace of God, heard and responded to a word of hope. Somehow we fixed our hope on the gift of grace through Jesus Christ (1 Peter 1:13). By the way of love hope came to us and we followed. We continue to follow. Hope urges us on toward greater depths of serenity.

It is healthy for us to recall our past hopelessness. Such recalling brings praise to God and helps us in dealing with others who experience hopelessness. Through our experience we have a special calling to minister to the hopeless. Even when others give up a person as a hopeless case, we cannot for we know it only takes a spark of love to begin a changing and growing process.

THE NEGOTIATION:

Is there anyone whom we have given up as hopeless?

THE PRAYER:

Lord of hope, we thank You that by Your grace we heard a word of hope in our hopelessness. Use us, O Lord, to bring hope to others in their despair. Amen.

THE READING: Hebrews 6:11-20

JULY 25

ST. JAMES

THE INSPIRATION:

"When he (Jesus) had gone a little further he saw James son of Zebedee and his brother John, who were in the boat overhauling their nets. He called to them; and, leaving their father Zebedee in the boat with the hired men, they went off and followed him." --Mark 1:19-20

THE MEDITATION:

James responded to Jesus' call. Little did he realize that day what was in store for him as he took the leap of faith and followed Jesus. James' discipleship had its up and downs. James, together with his brother, wanted to call down fire from heaven to consume a village that would not accept them (Luke 9:54). On another occasion James and his brother had the audacity to ask Jesus if they might sit at his right and left in his glory (Mark 10:37). Even after accepting Jesus' invitation to follow, James did not quickly lose desire for his revenge and his pride. But James followed and in his association with Jesus learned love and humility. He learned Christlikeness to the extent that he was willing to make the ultimate sacrifice. James is the only apostle whose martyrdom is recorded in Scripture (Acts 12:2).

When we make a commitment to follow Jesus we do not immediately become Christlike. It is through association with him that we learn and grow. It is by meditating on the life and message of Jesus that we grow in love and humility. We, Like James, have our ups and downs as we journey through life in Jesus' steps, but we make progress on that journey each day.

THE NEGOTIATION:

Can we see the results of our associating with Jesus?

THE PRAYER:

We thank you, O Lord, for the lives of people like James who give us inspiration. As we seek to associate with Your Son, we pray that we may grow in grace, love and humility. Amen.

THE READING: Acts 11:27-12:3

JULY 26

INTIMACY

THE INSPIRATION:

"I am the good shepherd; I know my own sheep and my sheep know me—as the Father knows me and I know the Father—and I lay down my life for the sheep." --John 10:14-15

THE MEDITATION:

One of the basic needs of all human beings is intimacy. Our experience has taught us that alcohol abuse plays havoc with social and interpersonal relationships. Intimacy with other people is difficult enough to achieve without the added interference of alcohol abuse. What we need is to be able to be ourselves and give ourselves in relationships with others. We have a deep need to remove our masks and share ourselves with other human beings. And yet, the thing we so desperately need, we often fight against. We don't want to remove our masks; we feel safer behind them.

Intimacy involves the risk of rejection. We would rather others see only our dimples—our beauty spots. We don't want them to see our warts. We all have warts which we would rather conceal. We need to remove our masks and stand exposed in the presence of certain select persons. When we do, our ugly warts may bring rejection. That's the risk we take. But it's the only way to find satisfaction for our intimacy needs. While we do not have the time or energy to achieve intimacy with everyone we meet, let us not neglect our needs with those select few.

THE NEGOTIATION:

With what persons are we willing to risk intimacy?

THE PRAYER:

Dear Lord, we know that You know all there is to know about us. Keep us from wearing masks in Your presence, and give us the courage to risk being known, with all of our virtues and vices, by others. Amen.

THE READING: John 10:1-18

JULY 27

ETERNITY WITHIN

THE INSPIRATION:

"Deep within us all there's an amazing inner sanctuary of the soul, a holy place, a Divine centre, a speaking voice, to which we may continuously return. Eternity if at our heart, pressing upon our time-worn lives, warning us with intimation of an astounding destiny, calling us home into itself. Yielding to these persuasions is the beginning of true life." --Thomas Kelly

THE MEDITATION:

Probably the last place we would look for Eternity is "at our hearts." Eternity is usually regarded as something external, something over and above us. The Gospel proclaims otherwise. "This is eternal life: to know thee who alone art truly God, and Jesus Christ whom thou has sent" (John 17:3). Eternity is knowing God. Eternity is, therefore, not only a futuristic concept but also a present reality.

Our search for serenity must therefore be directed toward the amazing inner sanctuary of the soul. George Herbert puts it like this: "By all means use sometime to be alone. Value thyself; see what thy soul doth wear." God says, "Be still, and know that I am God" (Psalm 46:10).

This holy place is where we can know God and ourselves. This Divine center is where we can negotiate with God and ourselves. This place and center is within us and always at our disposal. As we grow in our ability to practice God's presence and yield to his eternal voice we experience serenity and are able to live more abundantly the true life of service.

THE NEGOTIATION:

Are we more continuously returning to God's presence?

THE PRAYER:

Breathe on me, Breath of God,
Unit my soul with Thine,
Until this earthly part of me
Glows with Thy fire divine. Amen. –Edwin Hatch

THE READING: John 17:1-8

JULY 28

CONDUCT AND CHARACTER

THE INSPIRATION:

"It is quite idle, by force of will, to seek to empty the angry passions out of life. Who has not made a thousand resolutions in this direction, only with unutterable mortification to behold them dashed to pieces with the first temptation? The soul is to be made sweet not by taking the acidulous fluids out, but by putting something in—a great love, God's great love." --Henry Drummond

THE MEDITATION:

As alcohol abusers we know from first hand experience how futile our will power can be. We have failed in thousands of resolutions in this direction. The force of our wills is not powerful enough to bring us sobriety and serenity. There is, however, another force available to us: it is the force of God's love—which is the greatest power in all existence. This force and power can and does renovate and regenerate us.

We are not merely talking about a change of conduct which comes from trying harder, because that is not the basic problem. Even with a change of conduct, there will still be conflict until there is a basic change of character. This will profoundly affect our conduct as a by-product. We may be frightened at times because it seems God's love is not working in our lives. We may be terrified at other times because it is.

Paul says, "we are transfigured into his likeness, from splendor to splendor; such is the influence of the Lord" (2 Corinthians 3:18). This transfiguration includes conduct and character.

THE NEGOTIATION:

Can we achieve sobriety and serenity by our own will power?

THE PRAYER:

Dear Lord, we thank You for the all-powerful gift of Your love. Enable us to utilize this gift to our growth in grace and righteous living. Amen.

THE READING: Ephesians 5:1-14

JULY 29

CHEAP AND COSTLY GRACE

THE INSPIRATION:

"Cheap grace is the grace we bestow on ourselves. Cheap grace is the preaching of forgiveness without requiring repentance, baptism without church discipline, Communion without confession, absolution without personal confession. Cheap grace is grace without discipleship, grace without the cross, grace without Jesus Christ, living and incarnate...

"Costly grace is the gospel which must be sought again and again, the gift which must be asked for, the door at which a man must knock. Such grace us costly because it costs a man his life, and it is grace because it gives a man the only true life."

THE MEDITATION:

While the grace of God is given freely, it is not cheap. Even though God's grace is unmerited and undeserved and has no strings attached, our responses determine its values. We put the price tag on God's grace. We decide whether it is cheap or costly. Our response to God's free gifts displays the worth we place on them.

Except for the grace of God many of us would be dead or lying in some gutter. If we fully appreciate that fact we will not accept it cheaply. It will cost us something as we in response turn our lives and wills over to God. God's love revealed in Jesus Christ will be costly to us if it means something to us. Life and love is from God. Let us not deflate their value but live in a response which is worthy of the gifts and the giver.

THE NEGOTIATION:

Do our lives reflect the value of God's grace?

THE PRAYER:

O God of grace, giver of all we have and all that we are, help us to respond to Your gifts with lives that are given wholly to Your glory in self-giving service to others. Amen.

THE READING: Ephesians 2:1-10

JULY 30

DEFINING GOD

THE INSPIRATION:

"One philosopher says, 'Whatever we can say of God, God is', and another declares, 'God is nothing that we can express'; and both of them are right. . . In the scriptures God is given many names . . . because his majesty cannot be expressed in any words at all: he is above and beyond nature. He transcends all categories. They call him this or that because he is not really any of these things . . . God is far above aught that we can say; were God not so lenient and had the saints not given and God accepted it from them I would never dare to give him praise in words." --Meister Eckhart

THE MEDITATION:

People have been trying to define God since their first consciousness of him. This is not a totally unworthy occupation so long as God is never limited or put into a box. In the final analysis the Infinite is undefinable by the finite. And yet the Scripture uses many names and metaphors for what we call God: Shepherd, Father, Potter, Jehovah, Yahweh, Lord, King, Love, Source, Guide, Goal, etc. Theologians have extended the list. Each of the names, metaphors, and concepts of God tell us something of his nature, but none of them, nor the total of them define his essence.

Our own personal definition of God must always be kept open. It must always be a growing and expanding concept which knows no limits. As much as we would like to create God in our image and keep him safely in our containers, he will not be confined. Our growth in serenity is related to our willingness to expand our concept of God.

THE NEGOTIATION:

Do our favorite names for God restrict our concept of him?

THE PRAYER:

Immortal, invisible, God only wise,
In light inaccessible hid from our eyes,
Most blessed, most glorious, the Ancient of Days,
Almighty, victorious, Thy great Name we praise. Amen. –Walter Chalmers Smith

THE READING: Colossians 2:1-7

JULY 31

SALT

THE INSPIRATION:

"Salt is a good thing . . . Have salt in yourselves, and be at peace with one another." --Mark 9:50

"You are salt to the world." --Matthew 5:13

THE MEDITATION:

According to the encyclopedia sodium chloride (salt) has over 14,000 uses. It is used in everything from manufacturing chemicals to refrigeration. In Jesus' day salt, although it had fewer uses, was even more important than it is today. So precious was salt in Biblical times that it was used for money. We get the word salary from the Latin "salarium." Those who do not earn their wages are said to be "not worth their salt."

The usefulness of salt to which Jesus refers is seasoning and healing. His followers are to be a seasoning and healing force in the world. King Herod died from worms because he usurped the honor due God (Acts 12:23). It is by salt that the worm dies.

"Have salt in yourselves," says Jesus. But when we apply salt to a wound, it hurts. It hurts to be healed, to give up our self-righteousness, our pride, our resentments. It hurts when God's salt is applied to our alcohol abuse. It hurts to face the truth about ourselves. There is pain in our healing.

When the pain subsides and we are in the process of being healed, we are called to be "wounded healers." As the worms of addiction and dependence die from God's good, but painful, salt, we are sent to be salt to the world.

THE NEGOTIATION:

To whom will we bring God's healing and seasoning today?

THE PRAYER:

We thank You, O Lord, for Your healing power. Help us through our experience to be Your agents and bring Your healing and peace to others. Amen.

THE READING: Matthew 10:1-8

AUGUST 1

DIFFERENT GOSPELS

THE INSPIRATION:

"I am astonished to find you turning so quickly away from him who called you by grace, and following a different gospel. Not that it is in fact another gospel; only there are persons who unsettle your minds by trying to distort the gospel of Christ." --Galatians 1:6-7

THE MEDITATION:

Instead of the usual thanksgiving with which Paul begins his epistles, to the Galatians he writes, "I am astonished . . ." The precise identity of the opponents of the Gospel is unclear. What is clear is that they are proclaiming a "different gospel." In the midst of this confusion in the Galatian churches, Paul hammers out the major themes of the Gospel.

The "different gospel" preached in Galatia has its modern equivalents. How shall we know the true Gospel in the midst of our modern confusion? In the first place the Gospel is the good news that God so loved the world that he gave (John 3:16). Solutions comes through the self-giving and self-emptying of Jesus Christ. "All are justified by God's free grace alone" (Romans 3:24). Any "different gospel" which teaches otherwise is not the Gospel of Jesus Christ.

Secondly the Gospel is inclusive not exclusive; universal not particular. Jesus spent much time and energy ministering to the "outcasts." Any racism, sexism, age-ism, physicalism, or any other "ism" which excluded anyone is not the Gospel.

The third mark of the Gospel is seen in the theme of Jesus' life and message: Peace on earth and good will towards all people. When these three marks are missing, we are hearing a different gospel."

THE NEGOTIATION:

Can we discern between the "different gospels" we hear?

THE PRAYER:

Dear Lord, we thank You for Your all-inclusive grace and peace revealed to us in the life and message of Your Son. Help us to live by the power of this Gospel. Amen.

THE READING: Galatians 1:1-12

AUGUST 2

GREED

THE INSPIRATION:

"It is that spirit of greed which Jesus said God hated more than any other. It is so diametrically opposed to the spirit of God. For God forever lavishes His gifts upon the good and bad alike, and finds all his joy in endless giving. —Frank Laubach

THE MEDITATION:

Greed is that which goes beyond what we normally term "wishing for" or "ambition." Greed is an avaricious and inordinate desire for something or someone. Greed and alcohol abuse go hand in hand. While abusing alcohol, it is ourselves, our own deeds and wants that take precedence over everything and everyone else. Drinking makes giving very difficult for us; receiving becomes our top priority.

With sobriety and serenity we begin to sense the truth in Jesus' words, "Happiness lives more in giving than in receiving" (Acts 20:35). It is in giving, not getting, that we begin to find meaning and purpose in our lives. As God gave and gives, as Jesus spent his life in self-giving, so our purpose is found in giving. Not only in giving money and things but also in giving of our very selves is found true happiness. There was a time when we were incapable of giving. That time has passed.

In addition to giving we also need to learn the grace of receiving. We need to learn to be able to graciously accept gifts from God and others. Life is a two-way street. We must guard against over-dependence and over-indulgence. Serene human beings are always interdependent.

THE NEGOTIATION:

How does greed threaten our sobriety and destroy our serenity?

THE PRAYER:

Dear Lord, fill us with Your spirit which ever lavishes gifts upon Your beloved; and keep us, O Lord, from greed which You despise. Teach us the grace of giving and receiving. Amen.

THE READING: Acts 20:25-35

AUGUST 3

WHATEVER BECAME OF SIN?

THE INSPIRATION:

"In all of the laments and reproaches made by our seers and prophets, one misses any mention of sin; a word which used to be a veritable watch-word of prophets . . . Does that mean that no sin is involved in all our troubles . . . Is no one any longer guilty of anything? Guilty perhaps of a sin that could be repented and repaired or stoned for? Is it only that someone may be stupid or sick or criminal—or asleep? . . . Anxiety and depression we all acknowledge, and even vague guilt feelings; but has no one committed any sins? Where, indeed did sin go? What became of it?" --Karl Menninger

THE MEDITATION:

An over-emphasis of the medical and psychological aspects of alcohol abuse has robbed many persons of assuming responsibility for their behavior. In a culture that talks about no-fault insurance we seem to be developed a no-fault theology. No-fault theology echoes Eve's cop-out: "The devil made me do it" (Genesis 3:13). Secondly no-fault theology says, "Society forced me, everyone is doing it, I was just following the crowd." Thirdly, "I'm a victim of heredity, my parents messed me up, my uncle drinks too much." Fourthly, "I'm only human, what can you expect from me."

Sin in the New Testament means missing the mark—God's mark for us. God created us to be free and humane creatures. We are responsible for our thoughts, words and deeds. When we fall short of God's mark and turn to him in repentance, he forgives us. Our broken relationship with him is reconciled by love. Sin is still around. It's real! We are responsible for it and for turning to God in repentance.

THE NEGOTIATION:

Are we responsible for our sinful thoughts, words, and deeds?

THE PRAYER:

Be merciful to us, O Lord, for we have sinned. Both in our actions and in our failure to act we have fallen short of Your mark for us. Forgive us and strengthen us that we might walk in Your way this day. Amen.

THE READING: Romans 5:12-17

AUGUST 4

DOUBTS AND MESSENGERS

THE INSPIRATION:

"To deny the existence of God may . . . involve less unbelief than the smallest yielding to doubt of his goodness. I say yielding; for a man may be haunted with doubts, and only grow there by in faith. Doubts are the messengers of the Living One to the honest. They are the first knock at our door of things that are not yet, but have to be, understood. . . Doubt must precede every deeper assurance." -- George Macdonald

THE MEDITATION:

Over confidence, complacency, and taking for granted have resulted in the demise of many a tear, many a marriage, and many a friendship. Unhealthy contentment with sobriety often results in the destruction of alcohol abusers. Self-satisfaction in spiritual matters brings a stunted faith where growth is halted.

Doubts are messengers of God to the honest. To doubt our relationships, our sobriety, our faith is to honestly appraise them. This appraisal not only wards off destruction, but stimulates growth. We need to work at our relationships, work at our sobriety, work at our faith. Doubt, honest doubt, puts us to work.

Tennyson has written: "There lives more faith in honest doubt, believe me, than in half the creeds." This does not eliminate the assurance and conviction which is a part of a living faith, but rather motivates growth. Let us remember too, that all doubt is not honest.

THE NEGOTIATION:

Do we acknowledge doubts as messengers of God?

THE PRAYER:

Ever insurgent let me be,
Make me more daring that devout;
From sleek contentment keep me free,
And fill me with a buoyant doubt. Amen.

THE READING: Hebrews 12:14-29

FRIENDS

THE INSPIRATION:

"Blessed is the man who bears with his neighbor according to the frailty of his nature as much as he would wish to be borne with if he should be in a like case . . . Blessed is that brother who would love his brother as much when he is ill and not able to assist him as he loves him when he is well and able to assist him.   Blessed is the brother who would love . . . his brother as much when he is far from him as he would when with him, and who would not say anything about him behind his back that he could not with charity say in his presence." --Francis of Assisi

THE MEDITATION:

Alcohol abusers usually have a long list of broken friendships. The active alcohol abusers try very hard to establish friendships but find these relationships difficult, if not impossible. After a period of sobriety we often discover how shallow our relationships with our drinking "friends" really were.

We have a deep need for authentic friendships. We use the word "friends" very lightly; we number them by the hundreds. What we generally mean by "friends" is acquaintances or associates. Friends are those with whom we have a mutual loyalty, honesty and trust. Friendship does not come easily. It involves work and time and risk. We discover that friendship is worth our endeavors.

John writes, "Let us love one another, because love is from God" (1 John 4:7). Within the context of the Christian faith we acknowledge that God's love is the source of all our relationships: friends, associates, acquaintances, and all humanity.

THE NEGOTIATION:

Who among our relationships are potential friends?

THE PRAYER:

Dear Lord, You have created us to be interdependent creatures. We thank You for our friends. Give us the courage and strength to enlarge that circle, and enable us, by Your love, to love all people. Amen.

THE READING: 1 John 3:13-24

AUGUST 6

TRANSFIGURATION

THE INSPIRATION:

"Jesus took Peter and James and John . . . and led them up a high mountain where they were alone; and in their presence he was transfigured . . . And they saw Moses and Elijah appear . . . Then Peter spoke: 'Lord,' he said, 'how good it is that we are here! If you wish it, I will make three shelters . . .'"
– Matthew 17:1-4

THE MEDITATION:

The Transfiguration, traditionally commemorated on August 6, is now observed on the Last Sunday after Epiphany. Whenever remembered the Transfiguration says something about our fundamental human need for transcendence. There are many synonyms and ways of expressing this need: a need to be lifted up above ourselves, a need to get out of touch of our horizontal earth-boundness and get in touch with the vertical dimensions of life, the need for a peak experience, a happening, an Event, a Presence, a mountain top experience, getting high.

Certainly, Peter, James and John experienced transcendence on the Mount of Transfiguration. Peter was elated by the experience: "How good it is that we are here!" He apparently wanted the "high" to last: "I will make three shelters." We alcohol abusers know of our needs to get high. We also know that alcohol and other drug produced highs are temporary and artificial. There are alternative highs which are real. But even authentic transcendence is momentary. We must come down. Their lives were more abundance having been to the holy mountain.

THE NEGOTIATION:

How do we deal with our needs for transcendence?

THE PRAYER:

Almighty God, on the mountain You showed Your glory in the transfiguration of Your Son. Give us the vision to see beyond the turmoil of our world and glimpse the King in all his beauty. Amen. – Collect for the Transfiguration

THE READING: Luke 9:28-36

AUGUST 7

BELIEVING "IN"

THE INSPIRATION:

"How many have been driven into outer darkness by empty talk about faith as something to be rationally comprehended, something "true" . . . There is a pride of faith, more unforgivable and dangerous than the pride of the intellect. It reveals a split personality in which faith is 'observed' and appraised, this negating that unity born of a dying-unto-self, which is the definition of faith." --Dag Hammarskjold

THE MEDITATION:

Our creeds begins with "I believe in . . ." not 'I believe that . . ." To believe "in" something or someone is to trust them, to depend upon them, to die-unto-self for. There is a tremendous difference between believing "that" something is "true" and believing in something. The former has to do with the mind, the latter with the soul. St John of the Cross has said that "Faith is the marriage of God and the Soul;" faith is not the marriage of God and the mind.

We can believe "that" George Washington has wooden false teeth, but that belief doesn't have anything to do with our lives. However when we believe "in" something or someone our hearts, wills, and souls are involved.

Our sobriety and serenity become real when we turn our lives and wills over to the power of God. This means we believe "in" God. It is a marriage of God with our souls. It involves a dying-unto self. It has profound relevance for us in our daily lives. As Paul says, "He shall gain life who is justified through faith" (Romans 1:17).

THE NEGOTIATION:

What is our own definition of faith?

THE PRAYER:

Forgive us, O Lord, for our pride of faith. Enable us in all humility to accept Your gift of faith that we may die-unto-self and live according to Your hold will. Amen.

THE READING: Galatians 3:7-12

AUG 8

IDENTIFICATION

THE INSPIRATION:

"'Lord, when was it that we saw you hungry and fed you, or thirsty and gave you drink, a stranger and took you home, or naked and clothed you? When did we see you ill or in prison, and came to visit you?' And the King will answer, 'I tell you this: anything you did for one of my brothers here, however humble, you did for me.'" –Matthew 25:37-40

THE MEDITATION:

We could add to the question: "When did we see you in the despair of alcohol abuse, and bring healing and hope to you?" The metaphor of the King breaks down here. A King is served, he doesn't serve; a King wears a crown of gold, not thorns; a King sits on a throne, he doesn't die on a cross. All nations are not gathered before him at the cross. There are no angels gathered before him at the cross. At the cross he is simply there, there in the agony of the suffering, the oppressed, the outcasts. All that seems to remain at the cross is a prayer: "Father, forgive them" (Luke 23:24). The King identifies with his brothers and sisters who are hungry, thirsty, strangers, naked, sick, imprisoned, drunk.

And yet the title over the cross is ironically true. He is the King! Faith claims him to be King. Faith acknowledges his Kingdom. A Kingdom not of this world. Then where is his Kingdom? Wherever and whenever we take time to be with people in need. As we minister to, and bring the hope and healing of God's love to the suffering, the oppressed, the outcasts—there is the Kingdom of God. When we identify with less fortunate brothers and sisters, the Kingdom of God is among us.

THE NEGOTIATION:

Are we willing to identify with those with whom Jesus identified?

THE PRAYER:

Dear Lord, we thank You that through Your Son, You have identified with us in our deepest need. Grant us the grace to identify with others who are suffering and thus make the presence of Your Kingdom known to them. Amen.

THE READING: Isaiah 58:1-12

AUGUST 9

FOLLOW ME

THE INSPIRATION:

"Discipleship means allegiance to the suffering Christ, and it is therefore not at all surprising that Christians should be called upon to suffer. In fact it is a joy and a token of his grace. The acts of the early Christian martyrs are full of evidence which shows how Christ transfigures for his own . . . the unspeakable assurance of his presence . . . They are made partakers in the perfect joy and bliss of fellowship with him. To bear the cross proves to be the only way of triumphing over suffering. This is true for all who follow Christ, because it was true for him." --Dietrich Bonhoeffer

THE MEDITATION:

Two words which are often found on the lips of Jesus are "follow me." The words always include the cost of following: self-denial and cross-bearing. "Follow me" is no respecter of denominational lines or ecclesiastical ties. "Follow me" is the invitation of one who is going someplace. But the words threaten to dislocate us. We always feel safer to stay where we are. "Follow me" is an invitation to grow, learn, develop, mature, serve, suffer, move on. There is a bumper stick which says, "Don't follow me, I'm lost." Jesus knows where he's going; he has a plan, a purpose, in history and beyond. He wants to cut us in. "Follow" comes from the Greek word for "road." To follow Jesus is to share his road. Our prayer is not for a longer stay with God, but for a closer walk with God.

The one who says "Follow me" is more interested in the present and future than in the past. With Jesus it is not where we've been that matters but where we are and where we're going; it is not that we have fallen, but that we get up; not who we hurt, but who we will help.

THE NEGOTIATION:

Can we harmonize the suffering and joy of following Jesus?

THE PRAYER:

At the invitation of Your Son, O Lord, we rise up to follow You. Grant us the endurance and strength to deny ourselves and the joy of Your presence. Amen.

THE READING: Matthew 8:18-22

AUGUST 10

SPIRITUAL FITNESS

THE INSPIRATION:

"Man is curious to wash, dress and perfume his body, but careless of his soul. The one shall have many hours, the other not so many minutes. This shall have three or four new suits a year, but must wear its old clothes still." --William Penn

THE MEDITATION:

We are more than what we eat or drink or wear. There is more to us than our bodies, therefore we do not live by bread alone (Matthew 4:4). All parts of us must be nourished. If our bodies are not properly fed, we suffer from malnutrition. If our minds are not fed by intellectual stimulus, they become limited and closed. If our imaginations are not fed, life loses its zest, wonder and joy. If our emotions are not fed, something within us deteriorates from lack of love. If our souls are not fed, our purpose, direction, and meaning for living dries up for want of the grace of God.

There is a lot of talk these days about physical fitness, and surely, this is not without value. But what about spiritual fitness? Paul advises Timothy to "keep yourself in training for the practice of religion" (1 Timothy 4:7). This is done by exercising: our daily devotions and Scripture reading and prayer, our weekly worship, and our on-going practice of the presence of God.

Perhaps there was a time when we thought we could live by drink alone. But that time has passed—alcohol, our friend, turned enemy and betrayed us.

THE NEGOTIATION:

Do we expend as much time and energy in spiritual exercises as we once did in pursuit of alcohol?

THE PRAYER:
Dear Lord, help us to recognize and nurture our many needs. And above all, I Lord, let us not neglect training for the practice of religion, and enable us to be aware of Your presence this day. Amen.

THE READING: 1 Timothy 4:1-10

AUGUST 11

THE STING OF ALCOHOL

THE INSPIRATION:

"Whose is the misery? Whose the remorse?
Whose are the quarrels and the anxiety?
Who gets bruises without knowing why?
Whose eyes are bloodshot?
Those who linger late over their wine,
Those who are always trying some new spiced liquor.
Do not gulp down the wine, the strong red wine,
When the droplets form on the side of the cup;
In the end it will bite like a snake
And sting like a cobra." --Proverbs 23:29-32

THE MEDITATION:

The writer of the proverb was either one of us, or else possessed an uncanny insight into alcohol abuse. As long as alcohol has been known to humans there have been those who abused it. One would think that with such wisdom around for so many years people would know better by now. Our lives attest to the fallacy of this naïve thought.

Alcohol abuse is not identified by how much, or what, or when, or how often, or where an individual drinks. Alcohol abuse can only be defined by what the drug does to a person. This takes two forms: (1) loss of control over alcohol, where we cannot decide when to drink or when to stop drinking; and (2) interference with normal functioning, i.e. marriage, family, interpersonal relationships, employment, finances, health. Whether alcohol abuse be identified as a physical addiction or a psychological dependence, we know that it does sting like a cobra.

When delivered from such a sting by the Grace of God, we can only respond with humble thanksgiving and dedicate ourselves to his glory through service to others.

THE NEGOTIATION:

What can be done to overcome the sting of alcohol?

THE PRAYER:

Dear Lord, we pray that the misery of alcohol abuse is behind us. We thank You for Your healing power. Enable us to show our thanksgiving by lives given wholly to Your service. Amen.

THE READING: Proverbs 23:29-24:10

AUGUST 12

ENVY

THE INSPIRATION:

"Envy is called a passion; and means suffering. Envy is a mysterious and terrible disease. The nerves of sensation within the man are attached by some unseen hand to his neighborhood all around him, so that every step of advancement which they make tears the fibers that lie next to his heart. The wretch enjoys a moment's relief when the mystic chord is temporarily slackened by a neighbor's fall; but his agony immediately begins again, for he anticipates another twitch as soon as the fallen is restored to prosperity." --W. Arnot

THE MEDITATION:

Who are they whom we envy? Are they those who have more money or possessions than we? Are they those who have higher positions than we? Are they those who have greater talents than we? Are they those who can drink and "handle their liquor?" Who are they? In order to measure the envy that may be in us we must be specific. Envy in the abstract is a poor inventory.

It is important for us to search our souls for the subtle passion we call envy. Important because this mysterious and terrible disease can destroy us. Envy threatens our sobriety and makes serenity impossible.

Once, through self-diagnosis, envy is discovered, let us deal with it. Let us take it to the Lord in prayer. Sincere and humble thanksgiving is the remedy for our envy. With our hearts so full of thanksgiving for all that we have and are, we are no longer bothered by what others have or are. What bothers us now are others who have less than we—and we seek to do something about it.

THE NEGOTIATION:

Are we alert to envy in us and willing to deal with it?

THE PRAYER:

Give us grateful hearts, O Lord, for all that we have and all that we are. Keep us from the self-destructive passion of envy, and help us to respond to the human needs that lie in our paths. Amen.

THE READING: Galatians 5:19-26

AUGUST 13

GOD'S INSTRUMENTS

THE INSPIRATION:

> "A wonderful thought
> In the dawn was given . . .
> And the thought
> Was this;
> That a sacred plan
> Is hid in my hand; . . .
> That God.
> Who dwells in my hand,
> Knows this sacred plan
> Of the things he will do
> For the world,
> Using my hand." --Toyohiko Kagawa

THE MEDITATION:

God's way of creating is to make a creative creation. All nature attests to this way of God. God works always with instruments. And this was Jesus' way when he undertook the finishing of humanity. It was a great and noble task which required a multitude of instruments. Jesus' instruments were people. His first item of business was to make a collection of people—he called that collection his Church. Being collected by Jesus, we are God's instruments.

What a wonderful revelation: to discover that we are God's instruments; that God uses us to carry out his sacred plan. How thrilling it is to know that the Creator wills to use us, in spite of our past failures, to carry out his plan for the world. He who has the whole world in his hands asks us to give him a hand.

THE NEGOTIATION:

Do we agree with Augustine: "Without God, we cannot; without us, God will not?"

THE PRAYER:

We thank You, O Lord, for the thrilling and terrible call to be Your instruments. We are filled with awe that You want us to share in Your creative process. Help us to know and carry out Your sacred plan. Amen.

THE READING: Jeremiah 1:4-19

AUGUST 14

OUR DAILY DEVOTIONS

THE INSPIRATION:

"Out from . . . a holy Center came the commissions of life. Our fellowships with God issues in world concern. We cannot keep the love of God to ourselves. It spills over. It quickens us. It makes us see the world's needs anew. We love people and we grieve to see them blind when they might be seeing, asleep with all the world's comforts when they ought to be awake and living. Sacrificially, accepting the world's goods as their right when they really hold them only in temporary trust." -- Thomas Kelly

THE MEDITATION:

Out of these daily devotions, if they authentically reach "a holy Center," will come a compassion, which encompasses the world of life. What takes place during these devotional periods has to do with the way life is lived out in commitment to God. The Latin word from which we get the term "devotion" means to vow or consecrate something to the deity. What we do during these devotional periods describes only a small patch in the whole plot of land. These quiet moments are important insofar as they contribute something to the enhancement and fulfillment of the larger consecration.

In "Christian" daily devotions we are referring to the relationship of that activity to the living of life in view of one's commitment and consecration to God, who has manifested himself and his purpose uniquely in the person of Jesus. This activity inspires us to see and respond to the world's needs as Jesus did. This is truly the road to serenity.

THE NEGOTIATION:

How important are these devotional periods for us?

THE PRAYER:

We thank You, O Lord, for these precious moments of prayer, devotion, meditation, and negotiation with You and ourselves. Help us to carry the inspiration we receive from You with us this day that we might be more compassionate toward Your world and more deeply consecrated to You. Amen.

THE READING: Psalm 1:1-5

AUGUST 15

ST. MARY

THE INSPIRATION:

"Mary treasured up all these things and pondered over them." --Luke 2:19

THE MEDITATION:

Mary, the mother of Jesus, has been commemorated on this date since early times. Mary was present at the most important events in Jesus' life: at his birth (obviously), at the first of his signs in Cana, at the cross, at the tomb, and with the apostles after his ascension waiting for the promised gift of the Spirit. The Church Year, from the First Sunday in Advent through the Last Sunday after Pentecost, enables us to be present at these events—and more. The Church Year is an important map which makes it possible for us to travel with Jesus and meditate on his life and message. This age old system of contemplating the Gospel can be a tremendous help to us in our search for serenity.

Probably the most outstanding characteristic of Mary, the handmaid of the Lord, is her humility. Possessing a mighty faith, Mary was willing to be a servant of the Lord. Her son said, "The greatest among you must be your servant" (Matthew 23:11). How inside-out this is compared to the standards of our culture which says, "Whoever is served is the greatest." We live in a society in which humility is regarded as a weakness. Not so, says the Gospel. From our own experience we know that it was when we begin to humble ourselves that we found the strength for sobriety. Our degree of serenity goes hand in hand with our growth in humility.

THE NEGOTIATION:

Are we growing in humility as we contemplate the life and message of Jesus?

THE PRAYER:

O God our Father, we rejoice with Mary whom You chose to be the mother of Your Son, and we join her song of praise. Let the mighty be overthrown, and honor the lowly who serve You in humility and joy. Amen. —Collect for St. Mary

THE READING: Psalm 45:10-15

DEPRESSION

THE INSPIRATION:

"My depression deepened unbearably, and finally it seemed to me as though I were at the very bottom of the pit . . . All at once I found myself crying out, 'If there is a God, let him show himself! I am ready to do anything, anything!'

"During acute depression, avoid trying to set your whole life in order all at once. If you (do) . . . you will continue to make sure of your failure, and when it comes you will have another alibi for still more retreat into depression." –Bill W.

THE MEDITATION:

While actively abusing alcohol, depression is an almost constant condition. Once we sober up, we would expect that we would rid ourselves of depression. This is seldom the case. Most of us continue to experience periods of depression even after years of sobriety. These periods are sometimes referred to as "dry-drunks or "dry-benders." We sometimes experience the same unbearable depression that we experienced while drinking. As sobriety continues and serenity increases these periods of depression become shorter in duration, further apart, less severe, and finally disappear.

Understanding our depression can help alleviate it. Depression has been defined as anger turned inward. When we find ourselves at the "bottom of the pit," let us seek to determine the outward source of our anger and discover how it has turned inward. Then let us turn to God, who understands us, and loves us, and forgives us. It is then time for action—not setting our whole lives in order, but taking a step in spiritual progress.

THE NEGOTIATION:

Are we growing in our ability to deal with depression?

THE PRAYER:

Dear Lord, we thank You that we can turn to You when we experience the unbearable pain of depression. Help us to practice Your Presence in our lives that, by Your grace, we may ward off the pain by giving thanksgiving and service to You. Amen.

THE READING: Psalm 77:1-20

AUGUST 17

EXCUSES

THE INSPIRATION:

"When we fail, how often we try to hide from ourselves the truth. We call our collapse by some less serious name, as though that changes its nature. We highlight some mitigating circumstances, hoping that a mumbled alibi will ease the pain . . . Jesus allows no escape. He calls on us to face our failures . . . He wants no inner festering which can retard recovery. He wants a clean wound for healing. . . Then, having laid bare the need he applies the salve of . . . the deep full forgiveness of God."

THE MEDITATION:

It is obvious, as Pascal observed, that "the heart has reasons of which reason has no knowledge." We alcohol abusers are masters of the alibi. We need only recall the unreasonable reasons we gave ourselves and others for our drinking to perceive our proficiency in making excuses. To retain this proficiency results in an "inner festering which can retard recovery."

We have been slaves to two giant masters: heredity and environment. Our excuses take two forms: "I was born that way" or "circumstances have made me that way." From either of these masters there seems no hope of escape from our slavery. But the experience of thousands who have recovered from alcohol abuse shows us there is an escape route. The route demands "rigorous honesty" and leads to God. To put God first and cease to do those things which we know are contrary to his will, and to begin to do those things which we know he desires, is the escape route. Once this decision is made, heredity and environment lose their power, and we become God's free, responsible children.

THE NEGOTIATION:

Are we losing our proficiency in making excuses?

THE PRAYER:

Dear Lord, help us to break the chains of heredity and environment which keep us from the freedom You desire for us; and enable us to grow in responsibility for ourselves and to You. Amen.

THE READING: Romans 2:1-15

AUGUST 18

DEDICATION

THE INSPIRATION:

"Do not stand still, even for a moment, for to stand still in the way of holiness and perfection is, not to take breath or courage, but to fall back and become weaker than before." –Lorenzo Scupoli

THE MEDITATION:

Jesus tells about "A merchant looking out for fine pearls (who) found one of very special value; so he went and sold everything he had and bought it. (Matthew 13:45-46). Jesus is saying that God's Kingdom is of such superior value to everything else in this world, that once discovered, a person will not allow anything to interfere with securing its possessions. The way of holiness requires total dedication.

In a sense, we alcohol abusers have an advantage over other people. For us, our dedication on the way of holiness is essential for our sanity, and may very well be a matter of life and death. Most people do not have this urgency for survival. In order to gain sobriety and serenity we must be dedicated to the way of holiness.

Whether we are aware of it or not, every human being is engaged in a search for something that enables us to make sense out of the mystery we call life. That something is God's Kingdom, which Jesus likens to a pearl of very special value. God places the pearl where it can be found. We may go through life expecting little, and then suddenly, there it is! A glimpse of that pearl results in a life dedicated to possess all that God has in mind for us.

THE NEGOTIATION:

How dedicated are we to the way of holiness?

THE PRAYER:

Teach us, good Lord, to serve Thee as Thou deserves;
To give, and not to count the cost--. . .
To toil, and not to ask for any reward
Save that of knowing that we do Thy will. Amen.   --Ignatius Loyola

THE READING: Matthew 13:44-52

AUGUST 19

FREE WILL

THE INSPIRATION:

"God cannot seize our wills or force us to use our trials advantageously, but neither can the devil. We are absolute dictators, in deciding whether we wish to offer our will to God. And if we turn it over to him without reservation, he will do great things in us. The phrase which sanctifies any moment is 'Thy will be done.' Those who make every Now and occasion for thanking God live in an area of love greater than their desire to 'have their own way.'"

THE MEDITATION:

God respects his creation. He highly regards the freedom of will with which he created human beings. But where there is freedom of will there is also the possibility of the tragic misuse of freedom. Our freedom to respond to God's call is also freedom to reject him. We are absolutely free to say "Yes" or "No" to God, to accept or reject life, to make choices, to drink or not to drink. Freedom is our opportunity and our tragedy.

The possibilities of values achieved, however, always outweigh the risks of tragedy. If God would completely control us, and take away our freedom and spontaneity, he would have a world of robots incapable of love; for where there is no freedom there can be no love.

Isaiah says "we are the clay, thou the potter" (Isaiah 64:8). And Paul says, "Surely the potter can do what he likes with the clay" (Romans 9:21). Of course God can! God can do any and all things. But God, as Love, cherishes a loving response. As clay, we are molded by the Potter only when we allow it.

THE NEGOTIATION:

Do we finally appreciate the great things God can and will do in us?

THE PRAYER:

Have Thine own way, Lord! Have Thine own way!
Thou art the Potter; I am the clay.
Mould me and make me after Thy will,
While I am waiting, yielded and still. Amen. —George Stebbins

THE READING: Romans 9:19-33

AUGUST 20

THE VALUE OF TIME

THE INSPIRATION:

> "Lost, yesterday, somewhere between Sunrise and Sunset,
> Two golden hours, and set for sixty diamond minutes.
> No reward is offered for they are gone forever." --Horace Mann

THE MEDITATION:

To mourn the loss of two measly hours seems ridiculous to us who have had our lost week-ends, weeks, months, and years. And yet with sobriety and serenity comes a new appreciation of time—hours are golden and minutes are diamonds! This new appreciation, rather than depressing us with time lost, impresses us with the preciousness of time as an invaluable gift of God. We have also learned with Longfellow:

> Nor deem the irrevocable Past
> As wholly wasted, wholly vain,
> If, rising on its wrecks, at last
> To something nobler we attain.

Perhaps lost time can be redeemed if we learn from it. Santayana has written, "Those who cannot remember the past are condemned to repeat it." There is much time that we cannot remember: "those memory lapses", those alcoholic blackouts. Even these can be of value, if we learn from them. We dare not forget the past in order to ward off its repetition.

While the past has meaning and instruction for us, we cannot live there. We can only live here and now. Jesus says to us as he said to Zacchaeus, "Salvation has come to this house today!" (Luke 19:9). When we perceive salvation as a present reality, life is authentic and abundant and time is of the utmost value.

THE NEGOTIATION:

Are we growing in our appreciation of the value of now?

THE PRAYER:

Dear Lord, we thank You for this precious moment of time. As salvation comes to our home this day, enable us to abide in Your presence and make the most of Your gift of time. Amen.

THE READING: Luke 19:1-10

AUGUST 21

THE FAMILY

THE INSPIRATION:

"If it does not please you to worship the Lord, choose here and now whom you will worship: the dogs whom your forefathers worshipped besides the Euphrates, or the gods of the Amorites in whose land you are living. But I and my family, we will worship the Lord." --Joshua 24:15

THE MEDITATION:

There was a time when the family was recognized as the basic unit of society. But even with the recognition gone, the truth remains: we need the support and strength that the family can provide. Even those who have no biological family need persons whom they regard as their "family."

Our experience has taught us that alcohol abuse plays havoc with family relationships. There are many whose drinking has caused them to permanently lose their families. Family relationships are not restored and healed immediately, as we would wish, after a few weeks of sobriety. Sometimes the damage done is irrevocable. And yet we ought to go as far as possible in making amends and reconciling relationships.

Our needs do not change; we need those who provide the life-nurturing qualities of the family. Joshua and his family chose to worship the Lord. While the ideal is not always possible, it is our goal. When we, and those whom we call our family, share a mutual desire to worship the Lord, we experience the family as God intended it to be. Here is a unit which provides life-giving and creative capacities.

THE NEGOTIATION:

"Is your home a place of rest and refreshment where God himself becomes more real to those who enter it?" --Friend's Book of Discipline

THE PRAYER:

Dear Lord, we thank You for those whom we call our family. Give us the strength to make You more real to our families that we might mutually worship and service You. Amen.

THE READING: Joshua 24:14-28

AUGUST 22

TEAMWORK

THE INSPIRATION:

"They learnt the difference between the little things they could do alone and the magnificent things they might do together. With some pain and much joy they discovered the fascination and power of a team." --Alan Thornhill

"The task is too heavy for you: you cannot do it by yourself." --Exodus 18:18

THE MEDITATION:

The key to teamwork is the recognition of dependence. In this business of finding sobriety and serenity it is extremely difficult, if not impossible, to make it alone. We are dependent creatures. We need the understanding and the strength of others who share our experience with alcohol. Two men, a stock broker from New York and a doctor from Akron, Ohio, were losing the battle with alcohol. They got together one day in 1935 and discovered a magnificent thing: together they could stay sober. And so Alcoholics Anonymous was born. We are no different. We are dependent people who need the power of a team.

In addition to our need for horizontal dependence and interdependence with others, we have a need for vertical dependence with God. Moses walked with God and depended upon him. But Moses had to be taught dependence on other people by Jethro. Moses thought he could do it all by himself. At Jethro's suggestion Moses humbled himself and found the power of a team. Dependence does not imply weakness but rather strength. We need others. We need God. Others need us. God needs us.

THE NEGOTIATION:

Does our ego sometimes interfere with out dependency needs?

THE PRAYER:

Forgive us, O Lord, for our pride which causes us to think that we make it in this world on our own. Give us the humility to recognize our dependence on You and other people. Amen.

THE READING: Exodus 18:13-27

AUGUST 23

DISCIPLINE

THE INSPIRATION:

If one were asked to single out the one weakness which, more than any other, has robbed both individual and corporate Christian life of power, one would say it is that unwillingness to endure rigorous self-denial which is so characteristic of our age." --E. Herman

THE MEDITATION:

Self-denial or self-discipline does not mean giving up something. To give up something implies a loss. Self-discipline leads to gaining something rather than losing something. Jesus did not ask us to give up things, but rather to exchange them for things of greater value. The self-discipline involved in our giving up alcohol results in the gaining of sobriety and serenity. We exchange alcohol for those things which make living abundant.

Paul likens the Christian life to the training an athlete undergoes in order to win a contest (1 Corinthians 9:25). The training is never considered loss, but rather gain. We too train to gain, to win. For the Christian, self-discipline is actually self-expression—expression of all that is best and highest in self.

Arnold Toynbee tells us that, out of twenty-one civilizations which have vanished, sixteen collapsed because of inner decay. Civilizations are not often murdered; they more often commit suicide. Individuals unwilling to discipline themselves do not gain the new life Jesus talks about. He tells us we enter this life by the narrow gate: "The gate that leads to life is small and the road is narrow" (Matthew 7:14).

THE NEGOTIATION:

Do we understand self-discipline as gaining rather than losing?

THE PRAYER:

God harden me against myself,
This coward with pathetic voice
Who craves for ease, and rest, and joys. Amen.
            --Christina Rossetti

THE READING: 1 Corinthians 9:19-27

AUGUST 24

ST. BARTHOLOMEW

THE INSPIRATION:

"Philip went to find Nathanael, and told him, 'We have met the man spoken of by Moses in the Law, and by the prophets: it is Jesus son of Joseph, from Nazareth.' 'Nazareth!' Nathanael exclaimed; 'can anything good come from Nazareth?' Philip said, 'Come and see.' When Jesus saw Nathanael coming, he said, 'Here is an Israelite worthy of the name; there is nothing false in him.'" --John 1:45-47

THE MEDITATION:

Bartholomew is included in the lists of Jesus' disciples in Matthew, Mark, and Luke. In John's gospel the name Nathanael replaces Bartholomew. Beyond the episode describing his call to discipleship in the first Chapter of John, nothing is known of Nathanael, alias, Bartholomew.

The passage does, however, cause us to speculate concerning two things about Nathanael's character. First, he was a snob. He was prejudice against the insignificant town of Nazareth. We sometimes allow our snobbishness and prejudice to interfere with our inquiry and growth. Sobriety and serenity cannot be gained with closed minds. Nathanael was, however, open enough to respond to Philip's invitation to come and see Jesus for himself.

The second thing about Nathanael is his conceit. When Jesus remarked that there was nothing false in him, Nathanael's vanity caused him to agree. We know the danger, to our sobriety and serenity, which an exaggerated self-esteem can bring. Nathanael swallowed his pride and became a faithful and loyal disciple of Jesus. Pride stands in the way of discipleship.

THE NEGOTIATION:

Do we allow snobbishness and pride to keep us from being open to the Gospel?

THE PRAYER:

O Lord, give us an openness of our hearts and minds to be lead by Your calling. Grant us courage to investigate and ponder that we might grow in our relationship with You. Amen.

THE READING: John 1:43-51

AUGUST 25

LOSING AND WINNING

THE INSPIRATION:

"YANK: Sure! Lock me up! Put me in a cage. Dat's de on'y answer ya know. G'wan lock me up!

POLICEMAN: What you been doin?

YANK: Enough to gimme life for! I was born, see? Sure dat's de charge. Write it in de blotter. I was born, get me?" --Eugene O'Neill

THE MEDITATION:

Sometimes people, like Yank, believe they were born to lose. Especially is this true of alcohol abusers. Alcohol makes us believe we are losers. Our crime is being born, and for that crime we must lose in the game of life. One man actually had a tattoo on his arm which read "Born to Lose!" After achieving sobriety he went to great expense and endured much pain to have his life's slogan removed. No human being is born to lose; we are born to win. God does not create losers, but winners.

The New Testament assures us that "Every child of God is victor . . . The victory that defeats the word is our faith" (1 John 5:3-4). Faith can remove mountains of alcohol abuse and set us on a winning way in life. Victorious living is betting out lives that God is who Jesus declares him to be. We win at the game of life when we trust and love God above anything else. Winning at life means recognizing life as God's gift and living it according to his will. Winners are authentic and autonomous human beings who are awed and excited and challenged by the mystery of life. Winners see life as God meant it to be.

THE NEGOTIATION:

Who is responsible for writing the script we follow in life?

THE PRAYER:

We thank You, O Lord, that through Your son we are victorious. Keep us from following a losing script and enable us to live as the winners You want us to be. Amen.

THE READING: 1 John 5:1-12

AUGUST 26

CRITICISM

THE INSPIRATION:

"The human mind is so construed that it resists vigour and yields to gentleness." --Francis de Sales

"The one of you who is faultless shall throw the first stone." --John 8:7

THE MEDITATION:

In a eulogy a man said of another, "I can say one good thing about him, he wasn't always as much trouble as he was sometimes." There are times when we must strain ourselves to be generous in our judgments of others. It is difficult for we alcohol abusers not to be critical, but chronic critics never get down to positive action. They are miserable and useless persons.

There is something attractive to us about the game of "Blemish." We are like the woman who criticized how dirty everyone's car was until she had her own windshield cleaned. Much of our criticism is projection: we condemn in others what we fail to recognize in ourselves. Our criticism is also based on our insecurity: we have the mistaken notion that we can build ourselves up by tearing others down.

Longfellow suggests that "if we knew the secret history of our enemies we would find enough sorrow and suffering to disarm all our hostility." Criticism diminishes when we, as Native Americans say, "Walk in another's moccasins."

There is, however, a place for constructive criticism. If we are genuinely concerned about helping and improving others, we will with gentleness criticize them. But, this involves risk. It also builds solid relationships.

THE NEGOTIATION:

Have we honestly considered the reasons behind out criticism of others?

THE PRAYER:

It's me, it's me, it's me, O Lord,
Standin' in the need of prayer—
Not my brother, nor my sister,
But it's me, O Lord,
Standin' in the need of prayer. Amen. –Negro Spiritual

THE READING: John 7:53-8:11

AUGUST 27

OUR SUPREME DUTY

THE INSPIRATION:

"There are only two duties which our Lord requires of us, namely, the love of God, and the love of our neighbor . . . In my opinion, the surest sign for discovery whether we observe these two duties, is the love of our neighbor; since we cannot know whether we love God, though we may have strong proof of it; but this can be more easily discovered respecting the love of our neighbor. And be assured, that the further you advance in that love, the more you will advance in the love of God likewise." --Teresa of Avila

THE MEDITATION:

John of the Cross has said, "When the evening of this life comes, we shall be judged by love." We are judged by Love for our love. Therefore our supreme duty is to learn love. Every day everyone has many opportunities for learning love. The world is not a playground; it is a classroom. Life is not a vacation, but an education. Our one duty and lesson is to learn how to love God and others.

Learning takes place by practicing the content of the lesson. The pianist learns to play the piano by practice. We learn love by practice. There is no way we can practice the love of God outside of loving deeds directed toward others. The only way to show our love for God is by loving our neighbors. The only way to thank God for our sobriety is by loving and helping those who still suffer from alcohol abuse. Our experience makes us fit for this task.

Jesus says, "If there is love among you, then all will know that you are my disciples" (John 13:35). Love among us is nothing less than our love for God.

THE NEGOTIATION:

Do we try to separate our love for God from our love for others?

THE PRAYER:

O God of Love, who will not let go of us, we pray that we may learn Your love. Help us to practice love toward others that we might grow in our love towards You. Amen.

THE READING: 2 Corinthians 5:11-17

AUGUST 28

THE STRUGGLE

THE INSPIRATION:

"I said mentally, 'Lo, let it be done now.' And as I spoke, I all but came to a resolve. I all but did it, yet I did not. Yet I did not fall to my old condition, but took up my position hard by, and drew breath. And I tried again, and wanted but very little of reaching it, and somewhat less, and then all but touched and grasped it; and yet came not at all, nor touched, not grasped it, hesitating to die to death, and live to life; and the worse, to which I had been accustomed, prevailed more with me than better, which I had not tried. And the nearer the moment in which I was to become another man approached me, the greater horror did it strike into me." --Augustine

THE MEDITATION:

Augustine's description of his struggle is one with which we can easily identify. Perhaps we have uttered similar sentiments in our struggle with alcohol. That struggle continues until in self-surrender we intellectually and emotionally stop struggling and turn our lives and wills over to God's power. Receiving the power to deal with our drinking problem does not, however, mean that our struggles are over. It means that we are now in a position to begin the struggle of saying, "Thy will be done." This is not a once-and-for-all commitment, but the beginning of a life-long struggle. We continually struggle toward the goal which is a perpetual prayer in our hearts saying, "Thy will be done."

Paul expressed the struggle like this: "The good which I want to do, I fail to do; but what I do is the wrong which is against my will" (Romans 7:19). Paul found consolation in his struggle through the "indwelling Spirit," which is another way of saying, practicing the presence of God. To reach perfection in that practice is our goal, to make progress is our struggle.

THE NEGOTIATION:

Are we growing in our conscious and unconscious contact with God?

THE PRAYER:

Dear Lord, we thank You that, by Your grace, we are engaged in the struggle for practicing Your presence more continuously. May "Thy will be done" be the theme song in our hearts this day. Amen.

THE READING: Romans 7:19-8:13

AUGUST 29

DEATH

THE INSPIRATION:

"For everything its season, and for every activity under heaven its time: a time to be born and a time to die." --Ecclesiastes 3:1-2

"It is man only who is able to face his own death consciously; that belongs to his greatness and dignity. . . Man's knowledge that he has to die is also man's knowledge that he is above death." --Paul Tillich

THE MEDITATION:

One of the Kings of France once ordered that he did not want to see or hear anything that would remind him of death. He willed to avoid it completely. Every morning his servants would bring fresh flowers to his room and remove them each evening. One night the servants slipped up on their duty; by morning the flowers had withered and died. It is impossible to avoid the fact if death. Some of us, in the throes of intoxication, have been very near death many times. Death is obvious, real and near. We don't need the Scripture to remind us "All mankind is grass . . . The grass withers" (Isaiah 40:6-7). We are children of the earth. "Dust you are, to dust you shall return" (Genesis 3:19).

Jesus says, "If a man has faith in me, even though he die, he shall come to life; and no one who is alive and has faith shall ever die" (John 11:25-26). Even Jesus could not talk realistically about life without also talking about death. Death seems to have the last word. "But surely," some in us says, "we were meant for something better than the grave." The days are not meant for dying and weeping. Thorns were not meant for crowns, trees were not meant for crosses. But still death is a reality. Death is a burglar who knows his way into everyone's house of living and snatches from us what is precious. Until a power greater than death appears we will go on weeping. But the Gospel proclaims a power greater than death has appeared: he is the Resurrection and the Life.

THE NEGOTIATION:

Do we believe that we will never come to terms with our life until we come to grips with our death?

THE PRAYER:

Dear Lord, even though we fight to avoid it, we know that one day we will die. Help us to accept the truth that death is a part of life, and live this day as though it were our last. Amen.

THE READING: 1 Corinthians 15:23-28

AUGUST 30

CREATIVITY

THE INSPIRATION:

"Stop lying to one another, now that you have discarded the old nature with its deeds and have put on the new nature, which is constantly renewed in the image of its creator and brought to know God."
--Colossians 3:9-10

THE MEDITATION:

God is love, and love, among other things, is that which creates. Being created in the image of our creator, we too have the capacity to love—to be creative. If there is anything that is stifled by alcohol abuse, it is our ability to be creative. Having put on the "new nature," we are renewed in the image of our Creator. It is Love that holds everything together. God invites us to love and thereby share in his plan for creation. We love, therefore we are creative.

There are four marks of creativity. First, there is a passion for process. What we are now becoming is seen as more important that the finished product. As Alcoholics Anonymous says, "We claim spiritual progress rather than spiritual perfection." We are people of "The Way." Second, creativity means holistic thinking. We can see more from a mountain top than we can when we are in the valley. Creative thought is not compartmentalized or exclusive. There is an at-one-ment which goes far beyond our petty concerns. Thirdly, creativity demands tolerance for ambiguity. Open people do not always have to be right—they wonder! God is too big to be put into a box. Creativity relies more on faith and less on knowledge of the facts. In the fourth place, creativity means originality of form. Creative persons look for new answers to old questions and new questions that have never been asked. We are called to worship God with our whole heart, mind, soul, and strength.

THE NEGOTIATION:

How can we increase the creative activity God wills for us?

THE PRAYER:

Dear Lord, we thank You for allowing us to share in Your creative activity. Help us to sense the excitement of living as creative persons in Your Kingdom as we are daily renewed by Your love for us. Amen.

THE READING: Colossians 3:1-17

AUGUST 31

VANITY

THE INSPIRATION:

"And the name of that town is Vanity; and at the town there is a fair, called Vanity Fair." --John Bunyan

"Vanity of vanities! All is vanity." --Ecclesiastes 1:2 (RSV)

THE MEDITATION:

We know about the place called Vanity Fair, for we have spent much time there. Indeed, "all is vanity" in the shallow pride of alcohol abusers. Our desperate desire for admiration resulted in a phony conceit. As conceited persons we tried to convince others of our value in hopes they would tell us something about ourselves which we really didn't believe. Vanity must vanish if we are to find sobriety and serenity.

Bunyan furthermore tells us: "He that is down needs fear no fall, he that is low, no pride." If we are to be sober, serene, and productive persons we will get down off of our high horses and realistically view ourselves as we are. We are the offspring of God in whom we live and move and exist (Acts 17:28). As offspring of God, we are not God—we sometimes forget that. We are not the Center of all creation, even though that Center is available to us. The remedy for our vanity is to center-down and remember who we are and who God is.

In our on-going moral inventory we need to take stock of whatever it is in which we take pride: our families, our friends; our possessions, our intelligence, our goodness, our sobriety, our whatever. The source of our pride is a path which may lead us back to Vanity Fair where sobriety is threatened and serenity destroyed. We need to constantly remind ourselves that all that we have and all that we are is ours by the grace of God.

THE NEGOTIATION:

Could it be that our greatest source of pride is our greatest enemy?

THE PRAYER:

Forgive us, O Lord, for congratulating ourselves for our achievements and forgetting that we exist by Your grace. Give us grateful and humble hearts that we might be more effective in serving and praising you. Amen.

THE READING: Ecclesiastes 1:1-18

SEPTEMBER 1

GOD IS NOWHERE

THE INSPIRATION:

"God does not die the day when we cease to believe in a personal deity, but we die on the day when our lives cease to be illuminated by the steady radiance, renewed daily, of a wonder, the source of which is beyond all reason." --Dag Hammarskjold

THE MEDITATION:

The God rejected by many atheists is a deity who is "up there" or "out there" beyond human existence who rules by his arbitrary will. The Christian Gospel also rejects this God. The Gospel emphasizes God's immanence as well as his transcendence. God does not act on us from the outside, he acts and reacts from within us so that our lives depend upon his energizing activity. A God "up there" or "out there" is of no help to us in our search for sobriety and serenity.

Because God is thought to be, he is therefore thought to be something and consequently somewhere. But the God of the Christian faith is nowhere. Jesus taught that God is Spirit and Spirit cannot be confined to space or time. Our reason asks, "How can anything be there if it is nowhere?" That is the point: God is not any thing; God is no thing.

God is One, God is Spirit, through whom all things exist. The One Spirit is no thing that can be confined to time or space. He is living, Infinite, Omnipresent, God of eternity. This may seem unreasonable to us. But God is beyond reason. Our reason can stand in the way of our experiencing God. He who is beyond reason stimulates a wonder, a mystery, a presence in us by his radiance. That radiance is renewed daily as we seek him in our devotions and practice his presence. It is not God, but rather we who die when our lives cease to be illuminated by his radiance.

THE NEGOTIATION:

Is our experience of God dependent upon our defining and placing him?

THE PRAYER:

O Lord, we thank You that You who are unknowable have made Yourself known to us in our experience. We praise You for Your transcendence and Your imminence. Help us to know Your presence in this moment. Amen.

THE READING: Psalm 148-1-14

SEPTEMBER 2

ESCAPE

THE INSPIRATION:

>"Wreath the bowl
>With flower of soul,
>The brightest wit can find us;
>We'll take a flight
>Tow'rds heaven to-night,
>And leave dull earth behind us." --Thomas Moore

THE MEDITATION:

We are great escape artists. How often we have taken a bowl of alcohol on a flight to "heaven," desperately trying to leave the dull earth behind us. The flight, however, is soon terminated and we find ourselves once again back on the dull earth. It's not only escape with alcohol at which we become proficient. We looked for other escape hatches. Some of us imagined that if we lived in a different place, or had a different job, or maybe a different spouse, all our troubles would be over. A man who lived in the Midwest, and was having all kinds of problems, decided that if he moved to California everything would be great. He moved. The only problem was that he took himself along. He soon discovered that the problem was not in the Midwest but rather in himself.

Even with the onset of sobriety we do not immediately overcome our will-to-escape. After all, it has probably been years since we have faced our problems and dealt with them. Our re-entry into the land of the living is gradual as, more than likely, was our departure from it. We may find ourselves at times playing "If Only"; "If only I were someplace else." "If only this or that would happen." "If only . . ."

We need to learn what Paul learned: "to find resources in myself whatever the circumstances" (Philippians 4:11). Rather than looking for escape-routes, let us look for resources in ourselves which are available through God's power.

THE NEGOTIATION:

Are we still hanging onto our will-to-escape?

THE PRAYER:

Give us, O Lord, the will to deal realistically with our problems; help us to face them with the resources that You provide and help us to no longer run from them. Amen.

THE READING: Philippians 4:8-13

SEPTEMBER 3

VULNERABILITY

THE INSPIRATION:

"We are no better than pots of earthenware to contain this treasure, and this proves that such transcendent power does not come from us, but it is God's alone. Hard-pressed on every side, we are never hemmed in; bewildered, we are never at our wits' end; hunted, we are never abandoned to our fate; struck down, we are not left to die." –2 Corinthians 4:7-9

THE MEDITATION:

While abusing alcohol we know what it was like to be hemmed in, at our wits' end, abandoned to our fate, and left to die. Now that we have received God's treasure we are able to maintain sobriety and grow in serenity. The treasure is the Gospel, the good news in the life and message of Jesus Christ. The treasure is God's gift to us. Having accepted God's gift does not imply, however, that we will not be hard-pressed with problems. God's treasure gives us the insight to recognize problems, the strength to deal with them, and the courage not to be overcome by them. The serene person is one who has learned to live with problems without being destroyed by them.

As recipients of God's treasure, we need constantly remember that we are no better than pots of earthenware. We are vulnerable to cracking. We are always in danger of the treasure seeping out of us. Because we are aware of our vulnerability we daily fortify ourselves through our devotions and practice of God's presence. As time goes on this practice is not so much motivated by our vulnerability, but rather by the joy we experience when in God's presence. This doesn't mean that we are always thinking about God and nothing else; it means that we are consciously or subconsciously aware of his presence.

THE NEGOTIATION:

Is there a difference between the quality and quantity of our sobriety?

THE PRAYER:

Dear Lord, we thank You for the treasure of the Gospel, which You have given to us without our deserving it. Help us to remember that we are vulnerable earthen vessels who are constantly in need of Your strength and presence. Amen.

THE READING: 2 Corinthians 4:7-15

SEPTEMBER 4

THE QUEST

THE INSPIRATION:

"He comes to us as One unknown, without a name, as of old, by the lakeside he came to those men who knew him not. He speaks to us the same word: 'Follow thou me!' and sets us to the tasks which he has to fulfill for our time. He commands. And to those who obey him, whether they be wise or simple, he will reveal himself in the toils, the conflicts, the sufferings which they shall pass through in his fellowship, and, as an ineffable mystery, they shall learn in their own experience who He is." --Albert Schweitzer

THE MEDITATION:

So Dr. Schweitzer concludes his great work, The Quest of the Historical Jesus. The quest begins with his invitation to "Follow me." Just as Jesus came to Peter, Andrew, James, and John by the lake-side, so he comes to us. Over the centuries and over the miles the invitation, the command has not changed. "Follow me" is directed to us today. And this the quest begins with obedience to his invitation.

But where does he want us to go? That's the rub. We don't know where following him will lead us. It's not so much where he wants us to go perhaps, as it is what he wants us to be. He wants us to be involved in the fulfillment of his tasks in our time and place. The quest begins with a faith that is willing to follow One unknown. Faith means obedience. As we obey him by involvement in the toils, conflicts, and suffering of others, it is there that he makes himself known.

Our other great quest for sobriety and serenity becomes merged with the quest to know him. The quest to know him becomes paramount in our lives, and all other quests, if they are noble become by-products. We discover our central purpose and meaning for life in his life and message.

THE NEGOTIATION:

Can faith and obedience be separated from one another?

THE PRAYER:

Dear Lord, we thank You for the invitation of Your Son to follow him. Give us the faith to respond with obedience that we might find in his life and message the meaning and purpose that You have for us. Amen.

THE READING: Matthew 4:18-25

SEPTEMBER 5

MEANING

THE INSPIRATION:

"The human heart is like a millstone in a mill: when you put wheat under it, it turns and grinds and bruises the wheat to flour; if you put no wheat, it still grinds on, but then 'tis itself it grinds and wears away. So the human heart, unless it be occupied with some employment, leaves space for . . . a whole host of evil thoughts, temptations, and tribulations, which grind out the heart." --Martin Luther

THE MEDITATION:

What is the wheat necessary for the millstone? What is the employment necessary for the human heart? What is "one thing necessary" about which Jesus speaks to Martha (Luke 10:42)? These are questions about life's meaning. Does life have meaning or is it, as Shakespeare ponders, "a tale told by an idiot, full of sound and fury, signifying nothing?"

The trouble with our modern world is that we suffer from "despair over meaninglessness.: This despair is at the heart of alcohol abuse. It follows that the "cure" for alcohol abuse is to be found in terms of meaning—to make some sense out of life. Meaning is at the heart of our religious quest. The most fundamental religious question is "What does it all mean?" We must beware of simplistic answers and pious slogans like the bumper stickers which state: "Christ is the answer." We must first ask, "What is the question?"

"What is the meaning of life?" is the wrong question. Let us rather ask, "How can I make my life meaningful?" Rather than asking, "What is the meaning of my life?", let us ask, "What is God's meaning for me?" Meaning is imposed on us by the choices we make every day. Jesus calls us to choose to turn out lives and wills over to God. He calls us to be sitting, listening Marys and active, serving Marthas.

THE NEGOTIATION:

Are we growing in the serenity of meaning?

THE PRAYER:

Dear Lord, deliver us from meaninglessness, and stimulate us by Your Holy Spirit to seek and find Your meaning for us that we might meaningfully serve You. Amen.

THE READING: Luke 10:38-42

SEPTEMBER 6

PASS IT ON

THE INSPIRATION:

"Have you had a kindness shown?
Pass it on.
'Twas not given for thee alone,
Pass it on;
Let it travel down the years,
Let it wipe one another's tears,
... Pass it on." --Henry Burton

THE MEDITATION:

None of us would have survived without the kindness of others. We are especially cognizant of the kindness of others in regards to our recovery from alcohol abuse. If this kindness means anything at all to us we are compelled to pass it on.

When Jesus sat down with his disciples to eat his Last Supper he said, "I give you a new commandment: love one another; as I have loved you" (John 13:35). In other words, "Pass it on." At first glance we may wonder what's new about this commandment. After all, hasn't the golden rule been around for a long time? But Jesus was not talking about the golden rule: "You shall love your neighbor as . . . yourself" (Leviticus 19:18). Nor was he talking about the bronze rule, "Do unto others as you would have others do unto you." And most certainly, he wasn't talking about the iron rule, "Do unto others before they do it to you."

Jesus' mandate is a "new" commandment. What's new about it? It is not merely to love others as <u>we</u> love ourselves, but rather to love others as <u>he</u> loved us. It is Christ's love that is new. It is his way of loving, giving, forgiving and comforting that he asks us to pass on to others. Having been loved, we love, not according to our standards, but according to his.

THE NEGOTIATION:

Are we passing on Jesus' kind of love?

THE PRAYER:

Dear Lord, You have through Your Son revealed Your love for us as well as the kind of loving You expect from us. Even though we fall short of Your expectations for us, enable us to grow in our willingness and ability to pass Your love on to others. Amen.

THE READING: John 14:15-21

SEPTEMBER 7

FEAR

THE INSPIRATION:

"We promise according to our hopes, and perform according to our fears." --La Rochefoucauld

"The only thing we have to fear is fear itself." --Franklin D. Roosevelt

"Jesus is not so much a savior from sin as a liberator from fear." --Alan Walker

THE MEDITATION:

Someone has calculated that the word "fear" appears in the Scriptures once for each day of the year: 365 times. The Bible is a book which grapples with fear. The words "fear not" are found on Jesus' lips over and over again. Jesus is presented as one who casts out demons, who has dominion over devils, and who brings freedom to people caught in the chains of fear. Jesus is the "liberator from fear" because he is the personification of perfect love. "There is no fear in love; perfect love banishes fear" (1 John 4:18).

As alcohol abusers we know about fear from first hand experience. Perhaps the worst kind of fear is fear of the unknown. If there is a tiger in the room with us we know the source of our fear. We can then do something about it: we can run, jump up on the roof, shut the door, or scare the tiger off with a chair. But if the source of our fear is unknown, we are helpless and hopeless. Alcohol abuse brings on this sourceless fear.

With sobriety we are able to distinguish between fears that are real and fears that are phantoms. There is such a thing as authentic fear. We can legitimately fear alcohol and what it can do to us. It is the destructive, unhealthy, unreal fear that love banishes.

THE NEGOTIATION:

How much of our fear is unreal?

THE PRAYER:

O God our Father, Thou knowest how often we fail because we are afraid. We fear what men will do if we stand for the right; we fear what they will say. We fear that we shall not have the strength to go on even if we begin. Forgive us our weakness. Help us remember our Master Christ, and all that he endured for us, so that we, like him, may never be afraid of men, but only of sinning against Thy love. Amen.

THE READING: Luke 12:4-12

SEPTEMBER 8

COMMUNION OF OUR HEARTS

THE INSPIRATION:

"I cannot pray in the name of Jesus to have my own will; the name of Jesus is not a signature of no importance, but the decisive factor in prayer. The fact that the name of Jesus is invoked does not mean that a prayer really is in the name of Jesus. But it means I must pray in such a manner that I dare name Jesus in my prayer, that is to say, think of him, think of his holy will together with what I am praying." –Soren Kierkegaard

THE MEDITATION:

Prayer is the communion of our hearts with God. It is not necessarily something one says, words; perhaps not even something one does, an activity; and maybe not even something one ponders, thoughts. While each of these can be and is a part of prayer, they are too restrictive for communion of our hearts with God at the level the Scripture presupposes for prayer.

Paul says, "The Spirit comes to the aid of our weakness. We do not even know how we ought to pray, but throughout inarticulate groans the Spirit himself is pleading for us, and God who searches our innermost being knows what the Spirit means, because he pleads for God's own people in God's own way" (Romans 8:26-27). Words and activities and thoughts only get us under way in prayer. Prayer itself represents the deepest, most heartfelt, most agonizing concerns of our inner life.

When we pray, "in Jesus name," we do not merely use the phrase as a superstitious formula or magic axiom. Prayer in Jesus name is living as Jesus lived, in conscious and unconscious communion with God.

THE NEGOTIATION:

Do we recognize these daily devotional periods as preludes to, rather than substitutes for, communion with God throughout the day?

THE PRAYER:

We thank You, dear Lord, for the ever-present opportunity we have for the communion of our hearts with You. Teach us in Jesus' name to grow in our practice of Your presence. Amen.

THE READING: Romans 8:14-27

SEPTEMBER 9

DENOMINATIONALISM

THE INSPIRATION:

"The modern world would listen to Christians much more respectfully if they all spoke with the same voice. But from another point of view, it is a strength; the fact that so many interpretations are possible is the sign that they spring out of genuine personal insights, that theology is not a vast intellectual conspiracy, a pattern of thought imposed on people from outside with no roots in their personal lives. Variety, in other words, may be a sign of life: a sign that God can be found in every human circumstance: a sign that every intellectual statement about him is inadequate." --John Habgood

THE MEDITATION:

While we insist that complete recovery from alcohol abuse must include active involvement in the Church, we never dictate which church. There is, of course, "one Body and one Spirit, as there is also one hope held out in God's call to you; one Lord, one faith, one baptism; one God and Father of all, who is over all and through all and in all" (Ephesians 4:4-6).

Denominationalism is a curse and a blessing to the Church: a curse when it divides Christians, excludes people, and puts us in competition with one another; a blessing when it unifies and provides space for Christian experience of individuals with different backgrounds and characteristics. There are those who, filled with emotion, should, "Alleluia!" There are those who sing "Alleluia" to music written by Bach. Regardless of how it is uttered, Alleluia means "praise the Lord."

Those of us recovering from alcohol abuse need the fellowship of a Christian community. Which community? The one where our roots are, or if that is not feasible (or we have no background in any church), let us shop around until we find one that "feels like home." And let us make sure our home is never exclusive.

THE NEGOTIATION:

What can we do to promote more unity in Christ's church?

THE PRAYER:

Dear Lord, we thank You that You have called us together in fellowship with You and others in the Church. While we service You in a particular community, help us never to lose sight of the truth that Your church is One, Holy, Catholic and Apostolic. Amen.

THE READING: Ephesians 4:1-16

SEPTEMBER 10

EVOLUTION

THE INSPIRATION:

"It is surely quite clear that if anyone studied the world before there was life on it he could never have predicted life; if he had studied vegetation he would never have predicted animal life; if he had studied the animal world he would never have predicted human civilization and the arts; and if he had studied the selfishness of mankind he could never have predicted a life of perfect and selfless love. At each stage (of evolution) we reasonably trace the special activity of the Will whose purpose is the explanation of all things."
--William Temple

THE MEDITATION:

God is absolutely unpredictable! "How unsearchable his judgments, how untraceable his ways! Who knows the minds of the Lord?" (Romans 11:34). The Will behind all existence and all life is unpredictable. Very personally, who would have predicted in days gone by, when we were in the hopeless grasp of alcohol, that we would be where we are now: reading a devotional book, full of excitement about our growing sense of meaning and purpose in life?

The unpredictable and mighty acts of God in the past, both with his whole creation and with our personal lives, can only bring us to ask, "What good things does God have in store for us and his creation in the future?" That question, of course, is unanswerable because God remains unpredictable. If pressed, however, we would have to admit that we really don't want to know the future. If God would offer us a blueprint of the future, we would reject it. It is the unknown that provides much of the zest and excitement we experience in the present. We face that future with hope and trust in the unpredictable God to bring all things to his goal.

THE NEGOTIATION:

Do we recognize God as the Source, Guide, and Goal of all that is?

THE PRAYER:

O great and unpredictable Lord, we know that Your ways are not our ways, and we thank You for this insight. Help us to live in such hope that even when things do not go our way, we may trust in You. Amen.

THE READING: Isaiah 40:9-26

SEPTEMBER 11

TIME

THE INSPIRATION:

"Why wilt thou defer thy good purpose from day to day? Arise and begin in this very instant and say, 'Now is the time to be doing, now is the time to be stirring, now is the time to amend myself.'"
–Thomas A Kempis

THE MEDITATION:

Time has always mystified human beings. Modern science has not solved the mystery but rather added to it. Einstein's relativity theory, in which time and space are regarded as constituting one integrated reality, space-time, has complicated the mystery. Scientists have estimated the earth's age to be from two to five billion years. Taking the two billion figure, G. M. McKinley represents it in one calendar year, with January 1 as the beginning of terrestrial history and December 31 as the present. On this scale a day represents 5,500,000 years of terrestrial history, an hour 200,000 years, a minute 4,000 years, and a second 65 years. According to this representation, on December 31, four hours before midnight, human beings appeared. An hour or so later tentative efforts at social life were made, and not until the last minute of the year is the first civilization organized.

Time baffles the minds. It is as if God gives us life and says, "Here is an indeterminate number of years, months, weeks, days, hours, and minutes for you to use as you wish." When we recognize time as God's gift, how grievous is the memory of hours fritted away with drinking and planning for drinking, and getting over the affects of drinking. Such time fritted is beyond the ability to redeem. Let us, in repentance, ask God's forgiveness, accept God's forgiveness, and arise and begin in this very instant the pursuit of some good and loving purpose God has for us. We don't have to be able to understand time in order to use it.

THE NEGOTIATION:

What good purpose, that we have been putting off, can we do today?

THE PRAYER:

Dear Lord, we thank You for the gift of time. Help us to recognize it as such and use our minutes and hours this day to bring glory to Your name. Amen.

THE READING: Psalm 102:1-16

SEPTEMBER 12

STAGES OF GROWTH

THE INSPIRATION:

"Rejoice in your growth, in which you naturally can take no one with you, and be kind to those who remain behind, and be sure and calm before them and do not torment them with your doubts and do not frighten them with your confidence or joy, which they could not understand." --Rainer Rilke

THE MEDITATION:

Let us rejoice, indeed, in our growth, development, progress, maturity. Many of us have come a long way since we were obsessed with alcohol. Our rejoicing always takes the form of praising God whose power we allowed into our lives. But in our rejoicing and praising, let us never forget that others are not necessarily in the same place we are. Some are ahead of us in sobriety and serenity, some are behind. Let us not scare those behind us off by demanding that they deal with our questions, which they may not yet be asking. Nor should we allow our togetherness, which they cannot comprehend, frighten them off. We are all at different stages in the process of sobriety and serenity. Let us be tolerant toward those ahead of us and those behind us.

The same kind of tolerance is called for, in our growth in the Christian faith, in our relationships with other Christians. The Christian faith is something that by its nature grows. If it stands still it dies. As growing Christians each of us is at a different stage of growth. Paul says, "To the weak I became weak, to win the weak. I have become everything in turn to men of every sort . . . for the sake of the Gospel" (1 Corinthians 9:22-23). As Christians, all of our interpersonal relationships are for the sake of the Gospel.

THE NEGOTIATION:

Can we accept those who are at different stages of growth than we are?

THE PRAYER:

We rejoice, O Lord, for our growth in sobriety, serenity, and faith, and we praise You for Your power that has made this progress possible. Help us to be tolerant toward others at different stages of growth, that we might be inspired by those ahead and inspire those behind. Amen.

THE READING: Colossians 2:9-19

SEPTEMBER 13

DISAPPOINTMENT

THE INSPIRATION:

"Oh! Ever thus from childhood's hour,
I've seen my fondest hopes decay;
I never lov'd a tree or flower,
But 'twas the first to fade away.
I never nurs'd a deep gazelle,
To give me with its soft black eye,
But when it came to know me well,
And love me, it was sure to die." --Thomas Moore

THE MEDITATION:

Life is full of disappointments. Indeed life itself was a disappointment while we were abusing alcohol. One would expect the disappointments to cease when we find sobriety and grow in serenity. "Not so," says life. The disappointments continue, but now we view them differently. Rather than only mourning the loss of that which we loved, we can now thank God for the love we experienced. While life has its disappointments, it is not disappointing. Life is exciting and challenging with its joys and sorrows when we know we live by the grace of God.

Paul's missionary endeavors were constantly interfered with by one disappointment after another. Yet, he pressed on rejoining in God's grace. To keep him from being unduly elated, Paul believed he was given a "thorn in the flesh"—a sharp pain in his body. Paul prayed that God would rid him of it, but the only answer he received was, "My grace is all you need" (2 Corinthians 12:9). In any disappointment we face, God's grace is all we need. There are many things we want that we shall never have, and things we have and want to keep, we lose. And yet we possess all that we need—God's grace.

THE NEGOTIATION:

Do we view disappointments differently that when we were drinking?

THE PRAYER:

O Lord, You know our many disappointments. You also know what we need better than we know ourselves. Fill us with an awareness of Your grace that we may know that is all we need. Amen.

THE READING: 2 Corinthians 21:1-10

SEPTEMBER 14

HOLY CROSS

THE INSPIRATION:

"This doctrine of the cross is sheer folly to those on their way to ruin, but to us who are on the way to salvation it is the power of God." --1 Corinthians 1:18

"I shall draw all men to myself, when I am lifted from the earth." --John 12:32

THE MEDITATION:

The celebration of this day, commemorating the Holy Cross, dates from the dedication, in 335, of the basilica built by Constantine of Jerusalem. Coming as it does in the Pentecost Season, far from the Cross emphasis of Lent, the day reminds us that in the doctrine of the Cross we find God's power throughout the year.

In the Fourth Gospel, Jesus refers to the cross as "being lifted up." Jesus says he "must be lifted up as the serpent was lifted up by Moses in the wilderness, so that everyone who has faith in him may possess eternal life" (John 3:14-15). And again, "When you have lifted up the Son of Man you will know that I am what I am" (John 8:28). The Cross draws people to Jesus, brings life, and gives knowledge of him. In John's theology being "lifted up" refers to Jesus being lifted up to death on the Cross, being lifted up to from the tomb in Resurrection, and being lifted up to heaven in Ascension. We are involved in and affected by that lifting up in our lives from day to day.

There are those who put salvation in the past tense and ask, "Have you been saved?" Salvation, if it is relevant must be a present experience. We are "on the way to salvation." Our day to day growth in serenity and in the practice of God's presence means we are, by God's grace, on the way.

THE NEGOTIATION:

What does the Cross of Christ have to do with our life today?

THE PRAYER:

We thank You, O Lord, that in the lifting up of Your son, we too might be lifted up to new life each day. Give us the strength to take up our cross and follow him today. Amen.

THE READING: John 12:20-33

SEPTEMBER 15

CRISIS

THE INSPIRATION:

"Peter called to him: 'Lord, if it is you, tell me to come to you over the water.' 'Come,' said Jesus. Peter stepped down from the boat, and walked over the water towards Jesus. But when we saw the strength of the gale he was seized with fear; and beginning to sink, he cried. 'Save me Lord.' Jesus at once reached out and caught hold of him . . . " --Matthew 14:28-31

THE MEDITATION:

We can identify with Peter. Wouldn't it be great if we could walk on water? Some of us, while intoxicated, actually tried it. Walking on water, however, is not an issue for most people—the issue is simply keeping one's head above water. While abusing alcohol we do not consider growth or making progress important, our main concern is survival! "Will I make it through this day?" "Can I survive the next hour?" We know the difficulty of facing a single day. We know the terror, desperation, the paralysis, the drowning. The biographer of Janis Joplin says she chose to drown herself in Southern Comfort.

Where Peter is sinking in the raging waters of the Sea of Galilee, he cries out, "Save me, Lord." And what does Jesus do? He doesn't give Peter advice. He doesn't say, "Think positive, Peter, think of your sinking as an external condition, and keep a victorious image." Advice, even good and well meaning, is not much help for Peter or anyone else singing in life's abyss. Jesus responded to Peter's cry, not with advice or simplistic slogans, but with his personal assistance—he reached out his hand and caught hold of him."

We can easily see the many implications of Peter's sinking and Jesus' response in our own experience with alcohol and our reaching out to others still drowning.

THE NEGOTIATION:

Do we keep our "Save me, Lord" prayers for emergencies only?

THE PRAYER:

Dear Lord, we thank You that we have been saved from sinking in alcohol abuse. We are grateful to those who have reached out their hands to us in our helplessness. Use us, O Lord, to be Your helping hands to others still drowning. Amen.

THE READING: Matthew 14:22-34

SEPTEMBER 16

THE SPIRIT

THE INSPIRATION:

"Theology forgets that the wind of the Spirit blows where it wills. The presence and action of the Spirit are the grace of God who is always free, always superior, always giving himself undeservedly and without reservation. But theology . . . supposes it can deal with the Spirit as though it had hired him . . . A foolish theology presupposes the Spirit as the premise of its own declarations . . . But a theology that presumes to have it under control can only be unspiritual." --Karl Barth

THE MEDITATION:

Jesus tells Nicodemus, "The wind blows where it wills; you hear the sound of it, but you do not know where it comes from, or where it is going. So with everyone who is born from spirit" (John 3:8). In the original Greek and same word means both "wind" and "spirit." It is a fascinating play on the word which implies we cannot tie God, who is Spirit, down. The wind cannot be captured in a box, and God cannot be captured in theological formula. There is no such thing, known to human beings, as the essence of God. God's essence is always unknown.

There is something about us alcohol abusers that wants things wrapped up in nice neat packages. We are forever looking for that formula which will unlock the mystery of life. One man, while intoxicated, suddenly announced that he had discovered the mystery of the universe. With many eager ears listening he announced, "It's this: when I stand on my toes, I can reach higher!" In the morning he became aware of the ridiculousness of his solution. Serenity means we live with mystery and yet we keep searching, keep asking questions.

THE NEGOTIATION:

Can we live with unanswered questions and yet keep on asking them?

THE PRAYER:

Forgive us, Oh Lord, for our feeble attempts to confine You in a formula. We thank You, Dear Lord, that we can know You even though You are unknowable. Lead us by Your Spirit to continue the search. Amen.

THE READING: 1 John 4:1-6

SEPTEMBER 17

CONVERSION

THE INSPIRATION:

"Five years ago I came to believe in Christ's teaching, and my life was suddenly changed: I ceased to desire what I had previously desired, and began to desire what I formerly did not want. What had previously seemed good to me seemed evil, and what had seemed evil seemed good. The direction of my life and my desires became different, and good and evil changed places." --Leo Tolstoy

THE MEDITATION:

One of the early pioneers of Alcoholics Anonymous was told by the famous Swiss psychoanalyst, Carl Jung, that nothing but a religious conversion could give him any lasting help. Many of us have discovered the truth of that advice.

We hear a lot about the need to recycle junk from ecologists. There are many people who need recycling. Jesus began the process almost 2000 years ago. He proclaimed the good news of the transforming power of God. Conversion means giving new usefulness to wasted lives. Jesus recycled people who had been junked by everyone else as hopeless. The Gospel shows us God loves us so much he refuses to give up on us. "Christ died for us while we were yet sinners, and that is God's own proof of his love toward us" (Romans 5:8). God's redemptive love is constantly reclaiming and recycling wasted lives.

The Gospel insists that God's power can make us whole. The life and message of Jesus demonstrates that God can restore us his original purpose for creation. We have a share in that purpose. By sharing God's love we bring new love to the earth and thereby share in God's plan for creation. We discover that good and evil change places. Our values and priorities are realigned with God's purpose.

THE NEGOTIATION:

How have we changed in our recycling process?

THE PRAYER:

We thank You, O Lord, that You have never given up on us even when we and others saw ourselves as hopeless. Use us in brining Your transforming power to others and continue to work in us those changes that are necessary for our growth in serenity. Amen.

THE READING: Romans 5:1-11

SEPTEMBER 18

YES

THE INSPIRATION:

"I don't know who—or what—put the question, I don't know when it was put. I don't even remember answering. But at some moment I did answer Yes to Someone—or Something—and from that hour I was certain that existence is meaningful and that, therefore, my life, in self-surrender, had a goal. From that moment I have known what it means 'not to look back,' and 'to take no thought for the morrow.' . . . As I continued along the Way, I learned, step by step, word by word, that behind every saying in the Gospel stands one man and one man's experience." --Dag Hammarskjold

THE MEDITATION:

The one man who stands behind the Gospel is, of course, Jesus. Jesus answered Yes to God in the wilderness at the beginning of his ministry (Matthew 4:1-10). From that moment on his life became a Yes. That Yes was reaffirmed when he decided to go to Jerusalem, and again, in Gethsemane when he prayed, "My Father, if it is possible let this cup pass me by. Yet not as I will, but as thou wilt." (Matthew 26:39). A part of Jesus didn't want to say Yes. Sometimes we forget that. Sometimes we see Jesus as a divine puppet rather than a flesh and blood human being so in tune with God that the Cross was a foregone conclusion. A realistic view of Jesus in the wilderness and in Gethsemane reminds us otherwise.

We too are asked to say Yes to God. It doesn't matter whether or not we can remember when we said Yes. What matters is that somehow that Yes means that life in self-surrender has a goal. Our existence has meaning because our Yes is linked to Jesus' Yes. Our No to alcohol abuse is a prelude to our Yes to God.

THE NEGOTIATION:

Have we found meaning in self-surrender?

THE PRAYER:

Dear Lord, we thank You for the question and for the strength to say Yes. Help us to keep on reaffirming that Yes day by day as our lives find meaning in self-surrender. Amen.

THE READING: Matthew 4:1-10

SEPTEMBER 19

THE GIFT OF REPENTANCE

THE INSPIRATION:

"For thou art Lord Most High, compassionate, patient, and of great mercy . . . For out of Thy great goodness Thou, O God, hast promised repentance and remission to those who sin against Thee, and in Thy boundless mercy Thou hast appointed repentance for sinners as the way to salvation. So Thou, Lord God of the righteous, didst not appoint a sinner, whose sins are more in number than the sand of the sea.
—The Prayer of Manasseh 7-8

THE MEDITATION:

Repentance is a gift from God out of his boundless mercy to us. Repentance is the way of salvation that God has appointed for us. "If we confess our sins, he (God) . . . may be trusted to forgive our sins and cleanse us from every kind of wrong" (1 John 1:9). But, can we accept God's gift of repentance and use it as he intends? Can we trust God to be just and merciful?

Indeed, our sins are more in number than the sands of the sea. As alcohol abusers there are many things that we regret about our past lives. We know the plague of guilt and shame and remorse. But God, in his mercy, tells us we need not be plagued; he offers us his gift of repentance. Repentance is not for God's sake. He knows better than we the depth and number of our sins. Repentance is God's gift to us for our sakes. Through this gift God gives healing, wholeness and health. Let us let God be God and rid us of our guilt.

THE NEGOTIATION:

Can we accept God's acceptance of ourselves?

THE PRAYER:

"O God, our Father, we have sinned against Thee in thought, word, and deed: We have not loved Thee with all our heart; we have not loved our neighbor as ourselves. Have mercy on us, we beseech Thee; cleanse us from our sins, and help us to overcome our faults; through Jesus Christ our Lord. Amen." —1928 Prayer Book

THE READING:

The Prayer of Manasseh 1-15

SEPTEMBER 20

AUTUMN

THE INSPIRATION:

"The melancholy days are come, the saddest of the year, of wailing winds, and naked woods, and meadows brown and sear." --William C. Bryant

THE MEDITATION:

As the days grow shorter and colder we are reminded that autumn is arriving. Flowers fade, leave s fall, birds migrate, and we know the summer is over. But why the melancholy, why the sadness? It is all a part of nature's life cycle. Each season has its unique purpose and particular beauty. It's al a part of the Creator's plan. Let us cherish the beauty and love the uniqueness of each of God's seasons.

We who are new creatures in Christ need not be affected by the myth in our culture which calls one day good and another bad. Our moods need not be determined by the elements. Each day, by the grace of God, is full of opportunities and challenges whether it rains or shines. As our stormy days of alcohol abuse come to an end, every climate and season provides days in which we can rejoice in God's grace. While we may have a preference for a certain climate or type of weather, every day is a "beautiful day" when we practice God's presence.

And so the seasons of life, even though they are no repeated, each has its own beauty and glory. We live in a youth-oriented culture which tell us to "think young" and "act young." It is a disgrace that the greatest compliment that can be given to an older person is that he or she "looks young" or "acts young." As we grow in serenity each season of life, including the "autumn years," is a time of rejoicing in the new life of Christ. Let us now allow the prevalent "ageism" in our culture to rob us of the excitement and glory of living in God's grace.

THE NEGOTIATION:

Do we allow the seasons of nature or life to interfere with our growth in serenity?

THE PRAYER:

Dear Lord, Creator and Sustainer of all Life, we thank You for the beauty and wonder of the days and the seasons. Help us, O Lord, to rejoice in the new life that You, in Your mercy offer to us each day. Enable us to use Your gift of this day to Your glory. Amen.

THE READING: Ecclesiastes 11:7-12:8

SEPTEMBER 21

ST. MATTHEW

THE INSPIRATION:

"As he passed on from there Jesus saw a man named Matthew at his seat in the custom-house; and he said to him, 'Follow me.' And Matthew rose and followed him." --Matthew 9:9

THE MEDITATION:

The name Matthew means "gift from God" in Hebrew. Matthew, the son of Alphaeus, was a tax collector for the Roman government in Capernaum. He is an example of the way that character can be made strongest at its weakest point. If there is any one quality that stands out predominately in Matthew's Gospel, it is his love is Israel. But this love for his people did not come easily. Matthew had betrayed his people: he sold them out to the Romans, he collected exorbitant taxes from his fellow citizens, and be became wealthy by collaborating with the Roman invaders.

One day as Matthew sat collecting the hated taxes, Jesus came along and said, "Follow me." Matthew immediately left the custom-house and followed Jesus. He became a great apostle and evangelist, authoring the first Gospel. By overcoming his weak spot, with God's strength, he became strong; power is made perfect in weakness (2 Corinthians 12:9).

Our weakest point was our dependence on, or addiction to, alcohol. As with Matthew, so with us, power comes to its full strength in weakness. Our character is made strongest at its weakest point. While we regret the misery we endured and the suffering we caused others, we rejoice that in our weakness we became followers of Jesus and experienced God's strength in our lives.

THE NEGOTIATION:

What weak spots do we have, through which, with God's power we might become stronger?

THE PRAYER:

"Almighty God, Your Son our Savior called a despised collector of taxes to become one of his apostles. May we, like Matthew, respond to the transforming call of Your Son, Jesus Christ. Amen." –Collect for St. Matthew

THE READING: Matthew 9:9-13

SEPTEMBER 22

OUR MAIN BUSINESS

THE INSPIRATION:

"I made it my business to be in the Lord's presence just as much throughout the day as I did when I came to my appointed time of prayer . . . In the noise and clutter of my kitchen while several people are, at the same time, calling for different things, I possess God in . . . great tranquility . . . I worshipped him as often as I could, keeping my mind in his holy presence . . . I found no small pain in this exercise, and yet I continued it notwithstanding all the difficulties." --Brother Lawrence

THE MEDITATION:

During these appointed times of devotion, meditation, and prayer we sense that we truly experience God's presence. This we make our business. However, if we are to grow in serenity our business does not conclude with the "Amen" at the close of our devotional period. Our business is to abide in God's presence.

Most of our days are filled with the noise and clutter of our work, our familiar, our recreation. It is difficult for us to perceive that we can possess God in great tranquility during these busy times. However, if we honestly seek to grow in God's presence we soon discover our perception was erroneous. It is not an easy exercise! Even the great Brother Lawrence admits difficulty in his persistence. This is precisely where the practice comes in. As we practice the presence of God we become more proficient at it.

The more we practice this presence of God, not only do we become better at it, we find it more and more necessary. We become addicted to God's presence! We discover that God's presence is not just a nice luxury but an essential part of life—our main business.

THE NEGOTIATION:

Have we discovered God's presence is worth the difficulty of our practice?

THE PRAYER:

"O my God, since Thou art with me, and I must now, in obedience to Thy commands, apply my mind to these outward things, I beseech Thee to grant me the grace to continue in Thy presence; and to this end do Thou prosper me with Thy assistance, receive all my work and possess all my affections." – Brother Lawrence

THE READING: Psalm 41:1-13

SEPTEMBER 23

MATERIALISM

THE INSPIRATION:

"It is imperative to get rid of the tyranny of things . . . The man who for consciousness of well-being depends upon anything but life, the life essential, is a slave; he hangs on what it less than himself . . . Things are given us that through them we may be trained both in independence and true possession of them. We must possess them; they must not possess us . . . But it is not the rich man only who is under the dominion of things; they too are slaves who, having no money, are unhappy from the lack of it . . . If it be things that slay you, what matter whether they are things you have, or things you have not?" -George Macdonald

THE MEDITATION:

Sometimes when alcohol abusers begin to recover, they suddenly become aware of more money at their disposal. This can result in a desperate attempt to make up for lost time and make guilt-payments to their families by accumulating a lot of things. Materialism is our enemy. It is the chief "ism" we have to combat and conquer. The practice of Christian stewardship is extremely important for our sobriety and serenity. The question of bread for all people is a material question; but the question of bread for all people is a religious and spiritual question.

Jesus insists that material things be kept in their place, and if they become too important we lose sight of the distinctive aim of the Christian life, which is to seek to know the will of God and do it. If we have our priorities right and prosperity comes our way it will never stand between us and God. We will know how to use it. Jesus does not discourage planning, insurance, and putting things away for a rainy day. He simply reminds us of the limitations of human planning.

THE NEGOTIATION:

Do we allow material things to stand in the way of spiritual growth?

THE PRAYER:

We thank You, dear Lord, for all of the material things we have. We know that You are the giver of every good and perfect gift. Keep us from allowing these gifts to stand in our way of fellowship with You. Amen.

THE READING: 1 Corinthians 16:1-4

SEPTEMBER 24

THE GREAT WAGER

THE INSPIRATION:

"Let us then examine this point, and say, 'God is, or he is not.' But to which side shall we incline? Reason can decide nothing here . . . According to reason, you can defend neither of the propositions . . . Yes, but you must wager. It is not optional. Which will you choose then? . . . Let us weigh the gain and the loss in wagering that God is. If you gain, you gain all; if you lose, you lose nothing. Wager, then, without hesitation that he is. . . I will tell you that you will thereby gain life, and that you will at last recognize that you have wagered for something certain." --Blaise Pascal

THE MEDITATION:

All human beings have certain wants and needs that are essentially the same. We want our lives to count for something. We need an ultimate concern to which we can give ourselves. We need satisfying relationships. We need to find some meaning in our existence. Whether we call them human needs or spiritual needs, we all have them.

The basic human problem is an unwillingness to wager that God is, and that his promises can be counted on. We want what God promises but we want it on our terms. Ultimately it doesn't matter what we expect from life; what matters is what life expects from us. We are overly concerned about what God can do for us, when the real concern of life is what we can do for God.

There are times when God seems so remote. Times when we live, as we did while we were drinking, as if God was not. At these times we need that God is. To bet our lives on God and live "as if" he is all Jesus revealed him to be.

THE NEGOTIATION:

What have we to lose by wagering on God and his promises?

THE PRAYER:

Dear Lord, it is Your glory always to have mercy. When we in confusion go astray for Your Word, bring us back to You and lead us in faith to receive and hold fast to Your promises. Amen.

THE READING: Hebrews 11:1-40

SEPTEMBER 25

THE DOCTRINE OF FORGIVENESS

THE INSPIRATION:

"Forgiveness is the answer to the child's dream of a miracle by which what is broken is made whole again, what is soiled is made clean. The dream explains why we need to be forgiven, and why we must forgive. In the presence of God, nothing stands between him and us—we are forgiven. But we cannot feel his presence if anything is allowed to stand between ourselves and others." --Dag Hammarskjold

THE MEDITATION:

One of the most therapeutic aspects of the Christian faith, as far as we alcohol abusers are concerned, is the doctrine of forgiveness. The doctrine is the answer to our dream of restoring relationships with ourselves, with others, and with God. God does not wish us to be humiliated by remorse. Shame serves no lasting purpose. God is no sadist who takes pleasure in the agony of the mortification of his children. God's name is Love. He is not against us, but rather One who stands on our side.

We should never be more demanding than God is. If he is willing to mend what is broken, cleanse what is soiled, and give us a clean slate, we must be willing to accept ourselves, live with our past, and learn from our scars. Accepting and forgiving ourselves, because of God's action, means that we can move into the future with new strength and determination.

Being forgiven and consequently forgiving ourselves will have a profound effect upon our relationships with others. We will seek their forgiveness and accept it when it is offered. When others will not forgive us, we will nonetheless forgive them and do all we can to make loving amends. Forgiveness becomes for us more than a doctrine—it is a living experience.

THE NEGOTIATION:

As forgiven sinners, can we confidently enter into God's presence?

THE PRAYER:

"Henceforth I will resound
But praises unto Thee;
Though I was beat and bound,
Thou gav'st me victory. Amen." –Ronald Ross

THE READING: Matthew 9:1-8

SEPTEMBER 26

HABITS

THE INSPIRATION:

"In the acquisition of a new habit, or the leaving off of an old one, we must take care to launch ourselves with as strong and decided an initiative as possible. Accumulate all the possible circumstances which shall re-enforce the right motives; put yourself assiduously in conditions that encourage the new way; make engagements incompatible with the old . . . Never suffer an exception to occur . . . Each lapse is like the letting call of a ball of string which one is carefully winding up; a single slip undoes more than a great many turns will wind again." --William James

THE MEDITATION:

The old habit we must leave off, of course, is alcohol abuse. We come to a point where the miseries of drinking outweigh the rewards. We give up the old habit because we are forced to do so. We look for substitutes, but soon discover there are none. If we are to make progress, how-ever, we begin to look for alternatives. Alcohol had become out god. Sobriety and serenity do not come to us merely by giving up the old god-habit. The acquisition of the new-God habit is necessary.

We give up the alcohol-abusing habit and we take up the practicing-the-presence-of-God habit. We assiduously give ourselves to the task. As Paul advises, we "leave no loophole for the devil" (Ephesians 4:27). Our case against the old habit and for the new habit must be air-tight. At first it may not necessarily be because we want it that way, but rather because we must—it may very well be a question of survival. But as time goes on our diligence begins to pay off. We discover that the new habit becomes a way of life that provides meaning, excitement, and serenity.

THE NEGOTIATION:

Is there any alternative to our old habit other than practicing the presence of God?

THE PRAYER:

We thank You, O Lord, that You brought us to the point where we turned to You. In our powerlessness we have discovered Your power. Strengthen us, O Lord, that we may assiduously seek Your presence and leave no loophole for the devil. Amen.

THE READING: Ephesians 4:17-32

SEPTEMBER 27

THE BODY OF CHRIST

THE INSPIRATION:

"For Christ is like a single body with its many limps and organs, which, many as they are, together make up one body. For indeed we were all brought into one body by baptism in the one Spirit . . . Now you are Christ's body." --1 Corinthians 12:12-13, 27

THE MEDITATION:

Of the many metaphors that the New Testament uses to describe the Church, the one which is probably most meaningful is the body of Christ. As a body has many parts with different functions, so the Church has many members all of which are necessary for the functioning of the whole. The metaphor is not just a body, but rather the body of Christ. When the time came for Jesus to be no longer physically present in the world, he turned his life and message and mission over to his followers who became his body in the world. The Church is not a building on a certain street—that's where the Church worships. The Church is people, God's people, gathered by God's spirit into one body to carry on Jesus' life, message and mission.

The Church came into existence as a result of the life, message, and mission of Jesus of Nazareth, who was crucified under Pontius Pilate sometime between A.D. and A.D. 35. All historians agree with those facts. What is surprising is that one whose life ended on a cross should give birth to a movement that has shaped a world-wide civilization. As followers of Jesus we recognize that the Church has come into existence through the Resurrection. Historians disagree at this point. Our faith tells us that Christ is resurrected in us and that we are his body in the world.

THE NEGOTIATION:

What is our particular function as a part of the body of Christ?

THE PRAYER:

We thank You, Dear Lord, that we have been gathered together through Your Word and Spirit into the body of Your son. Use us, O Lord, to contribute, out of our unique talents and experience, to the functioning of the body of Christ of which we are members by Your grace. Amen.

THE READING: 1 Corinthians 12:12-31

SEPTEMBER 28

CELEBRATION

THE INSPIRATION:

> "This is my Father's world, and let me ne'er forget
> That through the wrong seems oft so strong,
> God is the Ruler yet.
> This is my Father's world; why should my heart be sad?
> The Lord is King, let the heavens ring;
> God reigns, let the earth be glad!" --Maltbie Babcock

THE MEDITATION:

Jesus came proclaiming the Kingdom of God. He often spoke of that Kingdom in parables. He tells us that to live in God's Kingdom means to live a life of celebration, for the Kingdom is like a great feast or banquet (Matthew 22:2). The mood of the Kingdom is joy and celebration, because to live in the Kingdom is to experience the presence and grace of God in our world and in our lives. That is cause to celebrate.

There was a time when we could not, perhaps, conceive of celebrating without imbibing in "spirits". We were always looking for, and finding, some excuse to celebrate. But we have learned, the hard way, that celebration doesn't mean deadening our senses but rather being alive with the Spirit. And even now at times we might find ourselves wondering, "How can we celebrate, when we look at the mess the world's in?" At those times when the wrong seems so strong, we need to remember that God is ruler yet!

In the parables, both the good and the bad are invited to the celebration. We are not invited because we deserve it. The invitation comes by grace. Rather than lamenting over the mess the world's in, let us celebrate the good news by doing something about the mess. It is by our deeds of love and mercy that God's Kingdom comes. Life is not to be put up with, but celebrated with worship and service.

THE NEGOTIATION:

How can we make today a celebration of God's love?

THE PRAYER:

O Lord, let us never forget that You are the Ruler yet. Help us to celebrate Your Kingship by worshipping You and serving others this day. Amen.

THE READING: Matthew 22:1-14

SEPTEMBER 29

ST. MICHAEL AND ALL ANGELS

THE INSPIRATION:

"Angels from the realms of glory,
Wing your flight o'er all the earth,
Ye, who sang creation's story,
Now proclaim Messiah's birth." --James Montgomery

THE MEDITATION:

Michael is a popular archangel in both the Old and New Testaments. According to the vision of James (Revelation 12) Michael led the heavenly army against Lucifer before the creation of the world. The festival had its origin in the fifth century when a small basilica outside of Rome was dedicated in commemoration of Michael. The day, also called Michaelmas, became especially popular in northern Europe and England and was of such importance that it marked the beginning of the last cycle of the Pentecost season. Michael, together with Gabriel and Raphael and all angels are commemorated together on this day.

In the Christian Church we particularly associate angels with the birth of Christ: "The first Noel the angel did say," "Hark! the herald angels sing;" "Angels we have heard on high;" etc. The word "angel" means "a messenger from God." Knowing that God works in mysterious ways his wonders to perform, we cannot rule out any messenger from him whether it be celestial, spiritual, or human. It is the human messengers from God that we can identify with and best understand. Who among us has not known an angel of mercy who has visited us in our deepest need and darkest hour. Without these angels we could never have achieved and maintained sobriety. Having been ministered to by angels, we are called and equipped to be angels to others as we bring God's message to them.

THE NEGOTIATION:

Who are the angels who have brought God's message to us?

THE PRAYER:

"Almighty God, creator of man and angels, in many ways beyond our understanding You make Your will know to us and give us Your protection. May we see Your ways with wonder, accept the messages of Your will, and trust in the loving care you provide. Amen." --Collect for St. Michael and All Angels

THE READING: Revelation 12:7-12

SEPTEMBER 30

QUESTIONS AND ANSWERS

THE INSPIRATION:

> "I keep six honest serving men
> (They taught me all I know):
> Their names are What and Why and When
> And How and Where and Who." --Rudyard Kipling

THE MEDITATION:

A group of people were sitting around drinking one night, and when the conversation dropped off one of them said, "I know what we'll do, I'll give you an answer and you try to guess the question: the answer is, 'From chasing parked cars.'" After several wrong guesses the group was told the right question: 'Why does my dog have a flat nose?' Peter gave an answer one day which was: "God's Messiah" (Luke 9:21). But the answer makes no sense because we don't know the question. Peter's answer is only meaningful when we know it was a response to Jesus' question: "Who do you say I am?"

Jesus asked another question of the disciples that day: "Who do the people say I am?" They answered, "John the Baptist, Elijah, and one of the prophets." It's much easier for us to answer general questions like, "who do people say Jesus is?" or "who does the Church say Jesus is?" It's much harder for us to answer very personal questions like: "Who do you say Jesus is?" It takes a sober mind to deal with that question.

Peter's personal answer was "God's Messiah." Messiah is a Hebrew word which means "the anointed." Jesus was anointed to announce good news (Luke 4:18). John tells us that we also are among the anointed (1 John 2:20). Does that mean we are Messiahs? Yes it does! We are to be Christs in the world. We are anointed to announce the good news. This doesn't weaken our Christology but rather strengthens the importance of our mission. Jesus ushered in the Messianic age in which we are anointed to announce the Gospel.

THE NEGOTIATION:

Do we try to avoid the personal questions that God is asking?

THE PRAYER:

Dear Lord of all truth, help us to hear and respond to the questions You ask of us. As Your anointed people, enable us to proclaim and live the good news You have given us. Amen.

THE READING: Luke 9:18-22

OCTOBER 1

TAKING SIDES

THE INSPIRATION:

> "Into Thy keeping I commit my spirit.
> Thou hast redeemed me, I Lord Thou God of truth . . .
> Lord, I put my trust in Thee;
> I say, 'Thou art my God.' . . .
> Be strong and take courage,
> All you whose hope is in the Lord." --Psalm 31:5,14,24

THE MEDITATION:

When Peter tries to dissuade Jesus from his mission, Jesus tells him he is not on the side of God, but on the side of humans (Mark 8:33). It is a good question to ask ourselves: are we on the side of God or the world? Something in us wants both sides. But we can't walk down the middle. We are either a disciple of Jesus or we are not. But how do we know when we are on God's side? It is not enough to "believe" in God, not enough to pray, "Thy will be done." Do we want God to influence our thoughts, words, and deeds, or is it that we want God on our side to influence his thoughts, words and deeds?

A chicken and a pig decided that they would like to do something for the poor. "I know," said the chicken, "let's give them ham and eggs." "That's easy for you to say," said the pig, "for you to give eggs is a donation, but for me to give ham—that's a total commitment!" If we are to gain sobriety it involves total commitment. If we are to grow in serenity it takes total commitment. Jesus says, "If a man will let himself be lost for my sake and for the Gospel, that man is safe" (Mark 8:35). If we are committed to Jesus we will lose ourselves for the sake of the Gospel: we will find ourselves on the side of peace on earth and good will toward all people. To be on God's side places us in the arena of human need.

THE NEGOTIATION:

Have we lost our lives in commitment to the Gospel?

THE PRAYER:

> Lord, what have I that I may offer Thee?
> Look, Lord, I pray Thee, look and see . . .
> Ah Lord, who lovest me,
> Such as I have now give I Thee. Amen. --Christina Rossetti

THE READING: Mark 8:31-38

RETRIBUTION

THE INSPIRATION:

"A man reaps what he sows." --Galatians 6:7

"Israel sows the wind and reaps the whirlwind." --Romans 8:7

"The man who digs a pit may fall into it, and he who pulls down a wall may be bitten by a snake."
--Ecclesiastes 10:8

THE MEDITATION:

We alcohol abusers know all about retribution. We know from first hand experience that we reap the wild oats we have sown; we know about the whirlwind, the pit, and the snakes. Even after we gain sobriety we sometimes ask, "Will the retribution ever end?" The answer to that question is both an emphatic "Yes" and a probably "No." If the retribution takes the form of a breakdown of health caused by alcohol abuse, it may indeed never end. We may have to learn to live with it, thanking God, that we still have life. If the retribution takes the form of loss of money and possessions, they may or may not be restored. With serenity the importance of the material is replaced by the spiritual. If the retribution takes the form of broken interpersonal relationships, they may or may not be healed. We do all in our power to make amends and get right with our fellow human beings. There may be some individuals, however, who have no forgiveness for us in the hearts. If this be the case, we will have to allow that to be their problem, and not let it interfere with our quest for serenity.

Most of us agree that retribution is just and thank God that it wasn't worse than it was or is. The emphatic "Yes" to the question of our retribution comes in terms of our relationship with God. That broken relationship is restored by his grace, love and forgiveness. He judges us according to the merits of Jesus. We are at-one with him.

THE NEGOTIATION:

Can we accept our retribution with thanksgiving to God?

THE PRAYER:

We thank You, dear Lord, that our retribution was not worse than it was. Above all, we thank You that You accept us in spite of ourselves. May our experience stir us to deeper dedication in Your service. Amen.

THE READING: Galatians 6:1-10

OCTOBER 3

LOVE THAT LETS GO

THE INSPIRATION:

"Modern psychiatry has learned that lovelessness lies behind the disharmony of many a life. Childhood rejection, isolation, loneliness, bitterness, hatred devastates and destroy human personality. Hence recovery of mental and emotional balance depends often on the discovery of love. Love is what the Christian faith is all about. Jesus came into the world to declare, to reveal, the love of God. –Alan Walker

THE MEDITATION:

All our lives we've heard about a love that reaches out, holds on, and will not let go. But there is another side to love—it's the side of love that lets go. Long before Hosea went looking for his wife Gomer, a worthless woman (Hosea 1:3), he let her go. Hosea did not keep Gomer locked up at home; when she decided to go he let her. And so when the Prodigal Son wanted to leave home, his father let him go.

God's love for us is mirrored in Hosea's love for Gomer and the father's love for his son—it is a lone which lets us go. There are two ways of looking at this love. One says it is a casual, uncaring love. The other says that it is a love which takes the relationship so seriously that God will let us go, if we choose, because he respects the freedom he has given us. God loves us so much and respects our freedom to the extent that he let us go to the "distant country" (Luke 15:13) of alcohol abuse. Like the waiting father God stays home, the keeps the lights burning, each day he looks for us down the road that leads home to him. It's the other side of God's love. He is the Waiting Father. His patience is amazing; his forbearance and his compassion never fail. When we return, he welcomes us with open arms. God let us go, but he never gives up on us.

THE NEGOTIATION:

Can we believe in the love of a God who lets us go?

THE PRAYER:

Dear Lord, we thank You for the freedom of will with which You have endowed us. As You respect and honor our freedom, O Lord, we pray that we might be Your responsible children. Amen.

THE READING: Hosea 2:1-3:2

OCTOBER 4

DIGNITY

THE INSPIRATION:

"Deck yourself out, if you can, . . . in dignity."

"No race can prosper till it learns that there is as much dignity in tiling a field, as in writing a poem." --Booker T. Washington

THE MEDITATION:

If there is anything that we lose through alcohol abuse, it is our dignity. There is no such thing as a dignified drunk. Dignity means "of great worth." Who is of great worth? No one, for as Paul says, "all alike have sinned, and are deprived of the divine splendor" (Romans 3:23). There is, therefore, no one of great worth, and alcohol abuse only magnifies our worthlessness.

However, from another point of view, which is God's, all human beings are of great worth—by virtue of our creation we have dignity in God's eyes. Paul continues, "All are justified by God's free grace alone" (Romans 3:24). Accepting God's free gift of grace means that we reserve for ourselves the dignity that God intends for us. By God's grace we are dignified.

The dignity which God grants to us by his grace alone extends to all other human beings. The dignity of every human being is a central Christian principle. The dignity of every person, regardless of sex, race, creed, class, or position, is demanded by the Christian faith.

"Deck yourself out with dignity, if you can." But the rub is, we can't. Dignity is by God's grace alone. Because he loves us we can lift our heads high in self-worth and self-respect.

THE NEGOTIATION:

Can we accept and promote the dignity of every human being?

THE PRAYER:

We thank You, dear Lord, that even in our worthlessness You recognize us as having dignity. Help us to accept the dignity of all Your children and actively be involved in the promotion of their great worth in Your eyes. Amen.

THE READING: Job 40:6-14

OCTOBER 5

AUTONOMY

THE INSPIRATION:

"When Jesus saw him lying there and was aware that he had been ill a long time, he asked him, 'Do you want to recover?' "Sir,' he replied, 'I have no one to put me in the pool.' . . . Jesus answered, 'Rise to your feet, take up your bed and walk.' The man recovered instantly, took up his stretcher, and began to walk." --John 5:6-9

THE MEDITATION:

Autonomy means self-government. An autonomous person is one who governs one's self, makes decisions, takes responsibility for one's life, does bit drift with the crowd, nor play helpless. An Autonomous Christian is one who governs oneself by the Gospel. We are not helpless: we are helped. We can direct our own destinies more than we realize.

The man at the Bethesda Pool couldn't get to the healing water not could he find anyone to help him. As alcohol abusers we know that helpless feeling. We know what it is like to be without autonomy, confused, trapped by our past mistakes, immobile from our dependence on alcohol. Jesus told the man at the pool to get up and stand on his own two feet—and he did. When Zacchaeus was "up a tree," Jesus told him to come down—and he did. (Luke 19:5). It takes an encounter with Jesus to make us autonomous Christians.

When the man at the pool realized it was Jesus who told him to stand up and walk he told others about Jesus. When Zacchaeus was called down from the tree he gave away half of his possessions to the poor. When we encounter the life and message of Jesus, we take responsibility for ourselves and demonstrate our autonomy by telling others about the Gospel and become involved with the alleviation of social injustice.

THE NEGOTIATION:

Can we be autonomous and depend upon God at the same time?

THE PRAYER:

We thank You, O Lord, that You trust us to be responsible for ourselves and to others. As we grow in the autonomy, help us to increase our ability to serve You. Amen.

THE READING: John 5:1-15

OCTOBER 6

ETIOLOGY OF ALCOHOL ABUSE

THE INSPIRATION:

"Some are born great, some achieve greatness, and some have greatness thrust upon 'em." --
Shakespeare

THE MEDITATION:

What Shakespeare says about greatness may be said in reference to alcohol abuse. Some seem
to be born that way, or at least born with tendencies toward alcohol abuse. Some seem to "achieve"
alcohol abuse (not to imply it is an achievement in the ordinary sense of the word). They may gradually
lose control of the use of alcohol over a period of many years of drinking. Some seem to have alcohol
abuse thrust upon them. After years of social and controlled use of alcohol some crisis in their lives
brings on alcohol abuse. And we know too well that we live in a culture which thrusts alcohol upon us.

If there is any human disorder which can be truly said to be of multiple etiology it is alcohol
abuse. There are a combination of factors in the causation of alcohol abuse which include physiological,
psychological, social-cultural, and religious. It is the latter, the religious factors that are often over
looked. Alcohol abuse has to do with our basic needs for transcendence, for meaning, and for
relatedness. These basic needs are religious needs. Alcohol abuse results from our feeble attempts to
satisfy our religious needs by non-religious means: alcohol.

Our religious search is a quest for life. Jesus said he came that we might have life in all its
fullness (John 10:10). In response Paul says, "To me life is Christ" (Philippians 1:21). Christ is the answer
to our religious quest for life, as well as the remedy for our alcohol abuse.

THE NEGOTIATION:

Do we recognize the religious factors in our cause and cure of alcohol abuse?

THE PRAYER:

Dear Lord, You have given us life and the will to live it in all its fullness. As we respond to the
Gospel of Your son, we pray that we might learn serenity through loving service to others. Amen.

THE READING: Philippians 1:15-20

OCTOBER 7

GOALS

THE INSPIRATION:

"Never let success hide its emptiness from you, achievement its nothingness, toil it's desolution. And so keep alive the incentive to push on further, that pain in the soul which drives us beyond ourselves." --Dag Hammarskjold

"God will not look you over for medals, degrees, or diplomas, but for scars." --Elbert Hubbard

THE MEDITATION:

Whether they be unconscious or unarticulated, we all have goals by which we live. We crave and work toward what we define as "success" in life." Our success-goals take two forms: achievement and authenticity.

Our achievement goals are the successes we reach or strive for which bring us honor in the eyes of the world. These achievements include status in our community, a home of our own, cars, boars, being vice president or president, academic degrees, diplomas, medals, etc. It is necessary to have achievement goals which spur us on. These goals, even when reached, do not, however bring us relief from our inner emptiness. We know too many people who have achieved "success" and suddenly wake up one morning in mid-life and ask, "What does it all mean?"

While achievement goals have a place, it is only in authenticity goals that we find meaning. By authenticity goals we mean being real, being the persons we were meant to be, living up to the potential self God meant us to be. Achievements goals bring out rewards; authenticity goals bring inner peace and serenity. Alcohol abuse robs us of being authentic persons. Being freed, by God's grace, from our slavery to alcohol, sets the stage for our discovering and becoming the authentic persons God means us to be.

THE NEGOTIATION:

What are the goals by which we live?

THE PRAYER:

We thank You, O Lord, for the achievements we have reached in life. Help us to discover and strive for those goals of authenticity which bring inner peace and serenity. Amen.

THE READING: Philippians 3:17-4:1

OCTOBER 8

COMFORT

THE INSPIRATION:

"Comfort, comfort my people;
--it is the voice of your God." --Isaiah 40:1

"Thus says the Lord . . .
'Though I have afflicted you,
I will afflict you no more." --Nahum 1:12

THE MEDITATION:

A guest in a home heard his hostess singing one morning, "Nearer my God to Thee." He asked if she always began the day by singing a hymn. "Oh no," she replied, "that's the hymn I boil the eggs by—three verses for soft and give verses for hard." The Gospel has both its soft and hard aspects. It is the soft part of the Gospel which comforts us when we are afflicted. It is the hard part of the Gospel which afflicts us when we are comfortable. Jesus says, "How often I have longed to gather your children, as a hem gathers her brood under her wings" (Luke 13:34). And just when we are cozy and comfortable under his wings, he afflicts us by saying "No one who sets his hand to the plough and then keeps looking back is fit for the Kingdom of God (Luke 9:62). The intensity of commitment he demands is afflicting.

In our history of alcohol abuse we discover the comfort of the Lord as he takes us under his wings of love and power in our powerlessness. But if we are to grow in serenity we will need his afflicting call to self-surrender and service. The Gospel, if fully heard, never allows us to become comfortable and self-complacent. It is by heeding that call to self-denial that we discover a comfort and serenity which goes beyond anything we ever imagined. Thus we experience the full cycle of God's grace: comfort, affliction, comfort. We discover that his yoke is good to bear, and that his load is light (Matthew 11:30).

THE NEGOTIATION:

Have we experienced the hard as well as the soft aspects of the Gospel?

THE PRAYER:

In the comfort which You bestow upon us, O Lord, never let us fail to hear Your call to commitment which demands a response to self-surrender and service. Amen.

THE READING: Psalm 86:1-17

OCTOBER 9

DROPOUTS

THE INSPIRATION:

"Many of his disciples on hearing it exclaimed, 'This is more than we can stomach.' Why listen to such words? . . . From that time on, many of his disciples withdrew and no longer went about with him. So Jesus asked the Twelve, ;D you also want to leave me?' Simon Peter answered him, 'Lord, to whom shall we go? Your words are the words of eternal life.'" --John 6:60, 66-68

THE MEDITATION:

We alcohol abusers know something about dropping out. The more we drank the less responsibility we felt on ourselves and others. The deeper we become hooked on alcohol the less energy we had for the business of living.

The rejection of Jesus is recorded in the Gospels with startling honesty and realism. Why do people drop out from following Jesus? In the first place because of his demands. Jesus demands commitment in terms of self-denial and cross-bearing. He makes us think about the fundamental things of life. He forces us to face ultimate reality. These concerns are not popular. We would rather be concerned with things and situations. The promises of communism and capitalism are preferred to the promises of Jesus.

Secondly, people drop out from following Jesus because of the crowd mentality so rabid in our times. The advertising industry contributed to the crowd mentality by telling us what our needs and wants should be. Our experience with alcohol tells us how difficult it is for us to go against the crowd. Authentic Christian commitment cannot exist in a crowd.

The only positive response to Jesus' question, "Do you also want to leave me?," is to say with Peter, "To whom shall we go? Your words are the words of eternal life."

THE NEGOTIATION:

How much progress have we made in our en-entry into life?

THE PRAYER:

We confess, O Lord, that the call of the Gospel seems too demanding and that we would rather follow the crowd. Help us at these times to rise to the intensity of commitment that You require of us. Amen.

THE READING: John 6:59-71

OCTOBER 10

ESSENTIAL ANXIETY

THE INSPIRATION:

"Man's essential loneliness and seclusion, his insecurity and feeling of strangeness, his temporality and melancholy are qualities which are felt even apart from their transformation by guilt. They are his heritage of finitude." --Paul Tillich

THE MEDITATION:

There are no psychological answers to existential anxiety. There are only religious ways of handling this basic human anxiety. Yet many of us made noble attempts to deal with our basic religious needs by using alcohol. Our existential anxiety was satisfied, temporarily and artificially by the euphoria experienced at certain stages of intoxication. However, this temporary and artificial relief did not bring abundance to living, but on the contrary, increased our anxiety about our existence.

Alcohol helped us to escape from existential questions or to rise to a state of excitement where "everything makes sense." Alcohol allowed us to forget our inner emptiness and painful awareness of our mortality.

With our commitment to sobriety we discovered that our existential anxiety did not disappear. However, we can now seek and find realistic alternatives. Now we are open to the reality of faith which Jesus calls for: "Set your troubled hearts at rest. Trust in God always" (John 14:1). Our heritage of finitude can only be satisfied by the Infinite. The Gospel demonstrates him to be the loving heavenly Father whose children we are. Under his protection and guidance alone we are able to deal with our existential anxiety.

THE NEGOTIATION:

Are we still seeking psychological answers to our existential anxiety?

THE PRAYER:

In our anxiety concerning our existence, come to us, O Lord, with your reassurance of Your love. Enable us to so practice Your presence that we may grow in our trust in You to satisfy all our authentic needs. Amen.

THE READING: Psalm 100:1-5

OCTOBER 11

GOD'S WORK

THE INSPIRATION:

"I am persuaded that religious people do not with sufficient seriousness count on God as an active factor in the affairs of the world. "'Behold, I stand at the door and knock.' But too many well-intentioned people are so preoccupied with the clatter of effort to do something for God that they don't hear him asking that He might do something through them." --Thomas Kelly

THE MEDITATION:

When we ponder, as we ought, what we were like while abusing alcohol, what happened to us, and what we are like now, we become overwhelmed by all that God has done for us. Our immediate response is to pay God back by doing things for him. But with our good intentions we forget that what God does doe us he does by grace. We cannot repay God for his grace. There is nothing we can do for God. But there is much God can do through us.

Jesus says, "My Father has never yet ceased his work" (John 5:17). He enlists us in his work. As Paul says, "We share in God's work" (2 Corinthians 6:1). It is God's work, not ours. And what is the work of God? "From first to last this has been the work of God: he has reconciled us men to himself through Christ, and he has enlisted us in this service of reconciliation" (2 Corinthians 5:18). God's work is reconciliations, and that work he does through us.

We, who have been reconciled to God through Jesus Christ, are enlisted into the ministry of reconciliation. God asks for our cooperation with him in his work of restoring broken relationships. We are instruments of his grace. God doing his work through us makes us extremely important and gives meaning to our lives and purpose in our existence.

THE NEGOTIATION:

How does our experience with alcohol equip us to do God's work?

THE PRAYER:

Dear Lord, we thank You that You have reconciled us to Yourself. Help us to hear and respond to Your call to enlist us in Your work of reconciliation. Use our unique experience and special talents in Your service. Amen.

THE READING: John 3:16-26

OCTOBER 12

ANGER

THE INSPIRATION:

> "I was angry with my friend;
> I told my wrath, my wrath did end.
> I was angry with my foe;
> I told it not, my wrath did grow." --William Blake

THE MEDITATION:

There was a time when we would deal with our anger by drinking. And even though it was ineffective we persisted. How many times did we get drunk "at" our spouse, boss, or someone else, because we were angry with them? Sobriety by no means implies we lose our capacity for anger. Anger is a very natural human emotion. When the people in the synagogue were watching Jesus to see if he would heal a man on the Sabbath so they could bring charges against him, he looked at them with anger (Mark 3:5). When Jesus upset the tables of the money-changers in the temple (Matthew 21:12) he does downright angry.

Too often we tell one another not to be angry. That is says, "Do not feel your natural emotions—do not be human." Paul says, "If you are angry, do not let anger lead you to sin; do not let sunset find you still nursing it" (Ephesians 4:26). Nursing anger and allowing ourselves to be led to sin by it is a negative and destructive response. There can be positive and constructive responses to this very common emotion.

In the first place we need to own our anger. Other people do not make us angry, we allow ourselves to become angry over something they say or do. The anger is ours—we own it. Only then can we positively and constructively deal with it. Being aware of our anger and assuming responsibility for it, we can then express it and decide not to be angry. Anger need not lead us into sin or depression when owned and positively expressed.

THE NEGOTIATION:

Do we allow ourselves and others to express anger?

THE PRAYER:

Help us, O Lord, never to deny the anger we feel, but rather to be aware of it, take responsibility for it, and express it in ways that correspond with Your will for us. Amen.

THE READING: Psalm 4:1-8

OCTOBER 13

THE RIGHT TO DEMAND

THE INSPIRATION:

"If I may proclaim the Christ message in a human way, I would say to all doubters and to all those who yearn in vain to feel his living presence: All right, let everything else go, as long as you hold fast to this one truth: he is a man who has the right to demand your help in the work he began. If you will do this, his glorious presence will come over you and you will become rich, richer, far richer than you can imagine! --Albert Schweitzer

THE MEDITATION:

It is through meditating on the Gospel, the life and message of Jesus, that Christian commitment begins. In the life and message of Jesus we discover the nature of his work: peace, goodwill, love, acceptance, forgiveness, healing, reconciliation. There is an original righteousness within every human being which draws us to this great work. The work of the man draws us to the man himself. So committed was he to his work that he made the ultimate sacrifice: "He had always loved his own who were in the world, and now he has to show the full extent of his love" (John 13:1). His life and message cannot be separated. He believed and lived his message and, therefore, is worthy of the right to demand our help in the work he began.

There are a lot of calls for help ringing in our ears. We hardly know where to begin. Let us begin by asking if these calls are Christ's work, and if so, let us be about it. We cannot respond to all the calls. We may have to be selective and specialize in those areas where we can help the most. Our past experience with alcohol makes us especially equipped for certain kinds of service.

THE NEGOTIATION:

What calls to special service does Jesus have the right to demand of us?

THE PRAYER:

Dear Lord, You have given authority to Your son to Speak for You. His life earned him the right to demand that we follow him. Give us strength and courage to respond to the demand by involving ourselves in the work of the Gospel. Amen.

THE READING: John 12:44-50

OCTOBER 14

THE HARVEST OF THE SPIRIT

THE INSPIRATION:

"Anyone can see the kind of behavior that belongs to the lower nature: fornication, impurity, and indecency; idolatry and sorcery; quarrels, a contentious temper, envy, fits of rage, selfish ambitions, dissensions, party intrigues, and jealousies, drinking bouts, orgies, and the like . . . But the harvest of the Spirit is love, joy, peace, patience, kindness, goodness, fidelity, gentleness, and self-control." --Galatians 5:19-23

THE MEDITATION:

When reading the story of the early Church in the Book of Acts we keep asking what is it that changed these men and women so fundamentally? What gave them the impetus to go out and turn the world upside down (Acts 17:6)? To Paul it was plainly the invasion of the human spirit by the Spirit of God. The power which changed the lower nature of these early Christians and brought them to the new life in Christ, was for Paul another manifestation of the power which God displayed in the Resurrection. The harvest of the Spirit, which Paul lists in Galatians 5, is not the result of fearful effort and tormenting self-denial. They are fruits: they grow naturally, once God's Spirit is allowed to enter our inner being. Jesus puts it quite plainly, "You did not choose men: I choose you. I appointed you to go on and bear fruit, fruit that shall last" (John 15:16).

In Paul's list of the behaviors which belong to the lower nature, the one that jumps out at us is "drinking bouts." A careful study of the list makes us realize that many of the other behaviors were related to, or resulted from, our drinking bouts. What can change, or is changing, our behavior toward Paul's second list? It is the harvest of the Spirit which is ours by God's grace. The fruits of the Spirit all add up to sobriety and serenity, which is God's doing-if we allow it.
THE NEGOTIATION:

THE NEGOTIATION:

How have our natures been changed by God's spirit?

THE PRAYER:

Dear Lord, You have worked and are working wonders in us. May we always be willing to be led by Your Spirit toward a nature which is appropriate to Your children. Amen.

THE READING: John 15:1-17

OCTOBER 15

THE COMPROMISE

THE INSPIRATION:

"One qualification for a useful life is give-and-take, the ability to compromise cheerfully. Compromise comes hard to us 'all or nothing' drunks. Nevertheless, we must never lose sight of the fact that progress is nearly always characterized by a series of improving compromises. Of course, we cannot always compromise. There are circumstances in which it is necessary to stick flat-footed to one's convictions until the issue is resolved. Deciding when to compromise and when not to compromise always calls for the most careful discrimination." --Bill W.

THE MEDITATION:

"All or nothing" indeed describes something close to home in the nature of alcohol abusers. We want things our way. We can't stand being wrong. Until we learn that graceful art of compromise, our sobriety will be threatened and serenity will be impossible. Paul advises us to "steer clear of foolish speculations, genealogies, quarrels, and controversies; . . . they are unprofitable and pointless" (Titus 3:9). Again, he says, "stop disputing about mere words; it does no good, and is the ruin of those who listen. Try hard to show yourself worthy of God's approval" (2 Timothy 2:14-15).

Serenity means learning when to compromise and when not to compromise: learning which controversies are important and which are not. While we will never be worthy of God's approval, we are to try hard to be worthy. In our discrimination over compromise two questions stand out: "What would Jesus do?" and "What would God have me do?" It is by meditating on the life and message of Jesus and practicing the presence of God that we arm ourselves to discern which controversies we should engage ourselves in and whether compromise is called for.

THE NEGOTIATION:

Can we allow ourselves the right to be wrong?

THE PRAYER:

O Lord, we live in a world full on conflict and controversy. Help us by Your presence to become involved in those issues which are worthy of Your children's concern. Amen.

THE READING: 2 Timothy 2:14-26

OCTOBER 16

THE VALUE OF AFFLICTION

THE INSPIRATION:

"We all know there are many different ways of encountering God. Other men have met God along quite different roads—Wordsworth in nature, Haydn in music, Teilhard de Chardin in science, and so on. But here is one of the classic ways—the way of trouble, the way of the wind and the whirlwind. When a man faces the night and the tempest; . . . when the great inexorable questions about the meaning of life and the purpose of it all hits our souls like a tornado—it can be then, in the mercy of providence, that the house of vision comes." —James Stewart

THE MEDITATION:

Our way of meeting God has been through the whirlwind of alcohol abuse. It was in our powerlessness before the alcohol tornado that the house of vision came to us. James writes, "Whenever you have to face trials of many kinds, count yourselves supremely happy, in the knowledge that such testing of your faith breeds fortitude, and if you give fortitude full play you will go on to complete a balanced character that will fall short of nothing" (James 1:2-4). Our vision of God and the fortitude he has given us, through our trials with alcohol, ought to have taught us the value of affliction.

Knowing, then, that we find strength in weakness, we do not pray for easy lives, but rather to be stronger persons. We do not pray for tasks equal to our powers, but for powers equal to the tasks to which God calls us. There is challenge in every problem we face. There is opportunity in every trial. There is joy in hardship. Everyday we wonder at ourselves, at the richness of our life that has come to us by the grace of God.

THE NEGOTIATION:

Do we count ourselves supremely happy when we face trials?

THE PRAYER:

Grant to us, O Lord, the royalty of inward happiness, and the serenity which comes from living close to Thee . . . that . . . we may be diffusers of life, and may meet all ills and cross accidents with gallant and high-hearted happiness, giving Thee thanks always. Amen. —Robert Louis Stevenson

THE READING: James 1:1-18

OCTOBER 17

STRENGTH TO STRENGTH

THE INSPIRATION:

"High hearts are never long without hearing some new call, some distant clarion of God, even in their dreams; and soon they are observed to break up the camp of ease, and start on some fresh march of faithful service. And, looking higher still, we find those who never wait till their moral work accumulates, and who reward resolution with no rest; . . . who do the good only to see the better, who see the better only to achieve it; . . . whose worship is action, and whose action is ceaseless aspiration." --James Martineau

THE MEDITATION:

There are no limits to what we may aspire. God is ever calling us higher. Many of us have come a long way since our days of alcohol abuse. We need not reach a plateau in our spiritual growth and effectiveness of service. Onward and upward is God's call. He still has many great things in store for us. As the Psalmist says, "Happy those whose refuge is in Thee, whose hearts are set on the pilgrim ways" (Psalm 84:5). We are pilgrims in life, not settlers. We are called to go from "strength to strength." We are called to grow physically, emotionally, intellectually, socially, and above all spiritually.

Jesus sees those who follow him as growing people: "First the blade, then the ear, then the full-grown corn" (Mark 4L28). This is what the Kingdom of God is like. In this Kingdom there is no limit to the crops we can produce: "Some of the seed fell onto good soil, where it came up and grew, and bore fruit; and the yield was thirtyfold, sixtyfold, even a hundredfold" (Mark 4:8). God provides the seed which is his Word. As we allow that Word to grow in us we grow from strength to strength.

THE NEGOTIATION:

Considering what God has done for us, can there be any limits to our aspirations?

THE PRAYER:

Dear Lord, we have come a long way, by Your grace. Help us to never cease from hearing and responding to Your call to grow into the persons You mean us to be. Amen.

THE READING: Mark 4:1-34

OCTOBER 18

ST. LUKE

THE INSPIRATION:

"The Author to Theophilus: Many writers have undertaken to draw up an account of the events that have happened among us, following the traditions handed down to us by the original eye-witnesses and servants of the Gospel. And so I in my turn, . . . as one who has gone over the whole course of these events in detail, have decided to write a connected narrative." --Luke 1:1-3

THE MEDITATION:

Luke was a Gentile physician, a follower of Jesus, and a companion of Paul. The most significant contribution that Luke has made to the Christian Church is his two-volume work, the third Gospel, which bears his name, and the Acts of the Apostles. A careful reading of these two volumes tells us a great deal about the man whom we call Luke.

One way to find the stature of a person is to look at that person's indignations. What are the things that made Luke angry? His two volumes show us that he detested pious pretensions, self-righteousness, callousness to human suffering, vindictiveness toward penitent sinners, racial pride, social injustice and greed. Luke saw these attitudes as disease which eats away at people and way raging over the world as epidemic. But that is not all he saw; he also saw their power broken by the healing love of the Great Physician.

A good measure of the spiritual progress we have made is a list of the things that we detest. As we prepare our list, let us beware of projection. If not on top, high on our list will be alcohol abuse and all of the character defects which go with it. As those who are recovering from alcohol abuse, we will be constructively tolerant of those who still suffer. We know the healing love of the Great Physician.

THE NEGOTIATION:

What are our indignations?

THE PRAYER:

Almighty God, You inspired Your servant Luke the physician to reveal in his gospel the love and healing power of Your Son. Give your Church the same love and power to heal, to the glory of Your Name. Amen. –Collect for St. Luke

THE READING: Luke 24:44-53

OCTOBER 19

TODAY IS OURS

THE INSPIRATION:

"Oh, ask not thou, How shall I bear
The burden of to-morrow
Sufficient for to-day, its care,
Its evil and its sorrow;
God imparted by the way
Strength sufficient for the day." --J. E, Saxby

THE MEDITATION:

This is it! Now is the only reality! What kind of a day will it be? Will we enjoy the blessings of this day or sit down on our little handful of thorns? For the most part it's up to us. Let us enjoy the blessings God sends our way, and, if trouble comes, let us patiently and sweetly deal with it. This day is only ours, we are dead to yesterday and not yet born to tomorrow. Evil thoughts and negative thinking will only make this day intolerable and unreasonable. But practicing God's presence can make this day the greatest of our lives.

When asked what he would do if he knew this were the last day of his life, Martin Luther replied, "I'd go out and plant an apple tree." Let us live this day as though it were our last. There are apple trees to be planted. Noble thoughts and deeds wait us. With sobriety and serenity, nothing stands in our way to abundant living today.

Today we are like to God with whom there is no past or future, with whom a day is as a thousand years and a thousand years as one day, when we live and serve in the great present. We therefore walk without fear, full of hope and courage to do this will, experiencing God's endless love which he pours out upon us as fast as we can take it in. Let us go forth with this prayer on our lips, "Satisfy us with Thy love when morning breaks" (Psalm 90:14).

THE NEGOTIATION:

What makes this day different from all the others?

THE PRAYER:

With grateful hearts the past we own;
The future, all to us unknown,
We to Thy guardian care commit,
And peaceful leave before Thy feet. Amen.   --Philip Doddridge

THE READING: Psalm 90:1-17

OCTOBER 20

THE QUIET TIME

THE INSPIRATION:

"As the sun rising each morning is the pledge of light through the day, so the quiet time waiting upon God, to yield ourselves for him to shine on us, will be the pledge of his presence and his power resting on us all the day. See that you be sure that the sun has risen upon your soul." --Andrew Murray

THE MEDITATION:

A man looking over the selections on a juke box in a restaurant asked, "What's number seven?" The waitress answered, "That's three minutes of silence, I push that button when things get too hectic around here." Silence is golden. Silence is next to godliness when used for prayer, contemplation, introspection, and meditation on the life and message of Jesus. Meister Eckhart says, "The very best and utmost attainment in this life is to remain still and let God act and speak in you." Isaiah says, "In stillness and in staying quiet, there lies your strength" (Isaiah 30:15).

God says of Jesus, "This is my Son, my Beloved, listen to him" (Mark 9:7). It is by listening to him in our quiet times that we get to know him. What is his life and message all about? How can we be as he was in the world? What can we do today to carry on his mission?

Such questions inevitably result from listening to Jesus. Our quiet times give us strength for mission. Our utmost attainment in life is listening so that God can act and speak through us. Our daily devotional quiet times are therefore that activity which concerns itself with negotiation with ourselves and God in which he plucks the world out of our hearts and hurls the world into our hearts. As we continue to practice God's presence in the bustling, noisy, hectic world we discover serenity in the midst of all the activity.

THE NEGOTIATION:

Do we allow ourselves enough quiet time to listen to Jesus?

THE PRAYER:

We thank You, O Lord, for these precious moments of quiet time. Help us to listen and be led into deeper involvement in the mission of Your son. Amen.

THE READING: Mark 9:2-13

TAKING OURSELVES TOO SERIOUSLY

THE INSPIRATION:

"All things are in His providence. A little taste of Cosmic Patience, which is Father-heart just have for a wayward world, becomes ours. The world's work is to be done. But it doesn't have to be finished by us. We have taken ourselves too seriously. The life of God overarches all lifetimes. . . Were earthly life to end in this moment, all would be well. For this Here, this Now, is not a mathematical point in the stream of Time; it is swollen with Eternity, it is the dwelling place of God Himself." --Thomas Kelley

THE MEDITATION:

One of the character defects of we alcohol abusers is that we take ourselves too seriously. We sometimes feel that it is up to us to solve all the world's problems. That fantasy, of course, was exaggerated when we were drinking. We thought we could solve the world problems when we couldn't even get ourselves out of bed.

Our personal problems, which we magnify, are not that important to other people. The world will go on without us. Most of us will not be remembered beyond the next two generations. It's not important whether we are remembered a hundred years or more from now. What is important is that the corner of the world in which we live is better and brighter because of our presence.

There is work to be done: God's work. This is important work, even though we will not finish it. We are called to do our best in the work God gives us. Let us take our task seriously, but never take ourselves too seriously. An important element of our serenity is the ability to laugh at ourselves. We are funny people, and perhaps the funniest thing about us is that we sometimes think the universe resolves around us.

THE NEGOTIATION:

Have we cultivated the gracious art of laughing at ourselves?

THE PRAYER:

Dear Lord, You have called us to an important and serious task. As we engage ourselves in that task, help us not to take ourselves too seriously. Help us to laugh at ourselves, O Lord. Amen.

THE READING: Wisdom of Solomon 11:21-12:3

OCTOBER 22

CHARACTER

THE INSPIRATION:

"Reputation is what men and women think of. Character is what God and the angels know of us." -- Thomas Pain

"Fame is what you have taken,
Character's what you give;
When to this truth you waken,
Then you begin to love." -- Bayard Taylor

THE MEDITATION:

We sometimes get the notion that character and reputation are synonymous. Not so. We can indeed fool all the people some of the time and some of the people all the time, but we can never fool God. He knows the stuff of our character better than we know ourselves. Our character is what we give of ourselves.

In one sense of the word no one is without character because it is simply a description of a person's qualities, good or bad, or a mixture of both. We think here, however, of character In terms of one's moral strength. We are concerned with the development of a Christian character. What are the characteristics of a Christian? Paul's list includes "compassion, kindness, humility, gentleness, patience. . . You must forgive as the Lord forgave you. To crown all there must be love, to bind all together and complete the whole" (Colossians 3:12-14). For us, these characteristics are absolutely dependent upon our sobriety and the sum total adds up to serenity. Not only is Christian character what we give, it is also what has been given to us by God, as we allow his Spirit to work in us. Christian character is take – and-give. Character is Christianity in action.

THE NEGOTIATION:

Is our moral strength hindered by what we want people to think of us>?

THE PRAYER:

Dear Lord, forgive us for our many character defects. Strengthen us by Your Spirit toward a moral strength that puts reputation and fame aside. Help us to grow I Christ-likeness. Amen.

THE READING: Ephesians 2:11-22

OCTOBER 23

AMBITION

THE INSPIRATION:

"All our ambitions are lawful except those which climb upward on the miseries of credulities of mankind." --Joseph Conrad

"There are two tragedies in life. One is not to get your heart's desire. The other is to get it." --George Bernard Shaw

THE MEDITATION:

Our ambitions are what we live and work for, and unless circumstances disallow, we achieve. One great ambition which we share is sobriety and, its positive consequence serenity. If our true ambition is sobriety, we will achieve it. External circumstances will not keep us from it. If we fail, the ambition is untrue and we sabotage ourselves along the way,

It is our ambitions that keep us going. We couldn't survive without them. There are, however, different kinds of ambition: those that merely enable us to survive, and those which enable us to live meaningfully. The tragedy of life is that some achieve the former and miss the latter. Our heart's desires it not always good and healthy for us. The Psalmist prays that the Lord would grant us our "heart's desire" (Psalm 20:4). But before we pray that prayer we had better clarify our values to determine just what out ambitions are. He goes on to point out that "Some boast of chariots and horses, but our boast is in the name of the Lord our God" (Psalm 20:7). Our ambitions for chariots and horses, cars and boats, money and positions, degrees and honors, will not, if achieved, bring meaning to our lives.

Our one heart's desire, which comes by way of sobriety and leads to serenity, is the presence of God in our lives. This is the only ambition which gives meaning to life.

THE NEGOTIATION:

Have we taken an inventory of our ambitions lately?

THE PRAYER:

Help us, O Lord, to clarify our ambitions along the lines of Your will for us. Putting first things first, enable us to grow in serenity and in usefulness as citizens in Your Kingdom. Amen.

THE READING: Psalm 20:1-9

OCTOBER 24

OUR BROTHER'S AND SISTER'S KEEPERS

THE INSPIRATION:

"A Christian will not sit in judgment on his neighbor, for he will be only too conscious of his own failings. Since he himself looks for God's forgiveness he will try to see the faults of his fellowmen as God sees them. This of course has no reference to the execution of justice in which the judge acts on behalf of society . . . it is primarily a demand that we exercise charity in our treatment of those who wrong us."
--William Neil

THE MEDITATION:

As alcohol abusers we want to be omnipotent and often demand perfection from ourselves. It follows that we sometimes expect perfection from other people and, when they fail, we are harsh in our judgment of them. If, however, we let God to God and allow ourselves to be his children, we discover that other people need the same acceptance and forgiveness that we cherish.

In our dealing with other people there is a time to "live and let live"—times when there is nothing we can do in our power to help or reach them. There is also a time to become involved in the dilemmas of others. Our involvement ought never be in the spirit of judgment and vengeance but rather with charity and concern.

There is a time to step in and not mind our own business when that business is bringing about the destruction of a human soul. The Christian answer to Cain's question, "Am I my brother's keeper? (Genesis 4:9) is a resounding "Yes". Yes, we are our brother's and sister's keepers, "especially members of the household of faith" (Galatians 6:10) and those with whom we share an experience of alcohol abuse. As the confrontations of others brought us on the road to sobriety, so we have the responsibility to confront those who are drowning in alcohol abuse.

THE NEGOTIATION:

What is our Christian responsibility toward our brothers and sisters?

THE PRAYER:

We thank You, O Lord, that You have so graciously and mercifully dealt with us. Give us the Spirit of Christ that we may forgive and confront our brothers and sisters in their deepest needs. Amen.

THE READING: Genesis 4:1-16

OCTOBER 25

ACCEPTANCE

THE INSPIRATION:

"Sometimes at the moment (of despair), a wave of light breaks into our darkness, and it is as though a voice were saying: 'You are accepted. You are accepted, accepted by that which is greater than you.' . . . Do not try to do anything now. Perhaps later you will do much. Do not seek for anything; do not perform anything; do not intent anything. Simply accept the fact that you are accepted. If that happens to us, we experience grace. After such an experience . . . everything is transformed. In that moment, grace conquers sin, and reconciliation bridges the gulf of estrangement." --Paul Tillich

THE MEDITATION:

Grace is always available to us, however, we are not always susceptible to God's every-present grace. It is when we are in the abyss, in times of crisis, in moments of despair, that we are most susceptible. In our deepest need God comes to us, because then, in our powerlessness, we are open to receive him. For many of us it was in the horrible despair of alcohol abuse that God's grace was most meaningful to us. It was then that we heard God's "You are accepted" ring in our ears and hearts. It was then, perhaps for the first time that we experienced grace.

The experience need not end or taper off. God continually, in all circumstances, declares to us "You are accepted." We can live in a state of acceptance always knowing that his grace is sufficient for us.

Experiencing God's acceptance leads to self-acceptance. Jesus summarized the law by commanding us to love others as we loves ourselves (Matthew 19:19). He didn't tell us to love others only—he included ourselves. Why? Because he knew only too well that, if we did not love and accept ourselves, we have not accepted God's acceptance, and we are incapable of loving and accepting others.

THE NEGOTIATION:

Is accepting the fact that we are accepted too simple for us?

THE PRAYER:

Help us, O Lord, to hear again and again Your voice saying, "You are accepted." In good times and in bad, in sickness and in health, enable us to experience and live Your grace. Amen.

THE READING: 1 Timothy 1:12-17

OCTOBER 26

DISCIPLINE OF TONGUE

THE INSPIRATION:

"If for a tranquil mind you seek,
These things observe with care:
Of whom you speak, to whom you speak
And how and when and where." --Anonymous

THE MEDITATION:

We know from experience that alcohol lubricates the tongue. We regret the many destructive things we said while so lubricated. We don't excuse ourselves, we repent, accept God's forgiveness and seek to make amends to those we may have harmed. That's behind us now, we trust. But, even without the lubrication, we still have our tongues. James says, "What a huge stack of timber can be set ablaze by the tiniest spark! And the tongue is in effect a fire. . . Beasts and birds of every kind . . . can be subdues . . . by mankind; but no man can subdue the tongue" (James 3:5-8). The lack of discipline of our tongue can be destructive and is always irrevocable.

And who is harmed by this lack of discipline? Naturally those who are slandered, but also the slanderers. Again, James says, "A man may think he is religious, but if he has no control over his tongue, he is deceiving himself; that man's religion is futile" (James 1:26). Any unkind word interferes, not only with our relationships with others, but with our relationship with God. A religious person, in the Christian sense, is one who lives in a state of reconciliation with God. We deceive ourselves about our being reconciled if we speak without love to or about others.

"The kind of religion which is without stain or fault," James continues, "is to go to the help of orphans and windows in their distress and keep oneself tarnished by the world" (James 1:27). The authentically religious person not only refrains from doing or speak harm but is full of words of mercy.

THE NEGOTIATION:

Are any of the words we speak ever unrelated to out religion?

THE PRAYER:

Forgive us, Lord, for the unkind and destructive words we have spoken. Help us to practice Your presence that we may be Your spokespersons this day. Amen.

THE READING: James 1:19-27

OCTOBER 27

ENTHUSIASM

THE INSPIRATION:

"When new religious movements are formed, they typically possess spontaneity and enthusiasm, both qualities which attract converts who are disenchanted with the routinized and unexciting older faiths. Spontaneity is an inevitable by-product of the newness of the movement and the absence of established routines. Enthusiasm is also a by-product of the nature of the enterprise, involving as it does the discovery (or rediscovery) of 'truths' about matters of profound importance to humanity." --Gerhard Lenski

THE MEDITATION:

There is sometimes a "honeymoon" period in the process of sobriety. First, we become disenchanted with the routinized problems and suffering of alcohol abuse. Our second discovery is that we can exist without alcohol. The third discovery in the process is that we can live meaningful and productive lives as long as we persist in sobriety. This revelation produces in us a new kind of euphoria which we never dreamed was possible without alcohol. The new way of life produces in us excitement, spontaneity, and enthusiasm. If we continue to live with gratitude in our hearts to God for bringing us through the sobriety process into the serenity process, the "honeymoon" need not end. Like love in marriage, the sobriety-serenity process matures and grows deeper as the years go by.

We cannot, of course, separate our sobriety-serenity development from our Christian faith. The spontaneity and enthusiasm we experience when we discover the power of God's presence in our lives need not lose a position of dominance as time goes by. As we continue to practice the presence of God in our lives, the novelty doesn't only not wear off, but the enthusiasm intensifies.

THE NEGOTIATION:

Have we allowed ourselves to lose some of the original joy of sobriety?

THE PRAYER:

With our hearts full of thanksgiving we praise You, O Lord, for bringing us sobriety and serenity. Let us never lose our enthusiasm for Your gift of Life or the work You have given us to do. Amen.

THE READING: Philippians 2:5-18

OCTOBER 28

ST. SIMON AND ST. JUDE

THE INSPIRATION:

"Judas asked him—the other Judas--, not Iscariot—'Lord, what can have happened, that you mean to disclose yourself to us alone and not to the world?' Jesus replied, 'Anyone who loves me will heed what I say; then my Father will love him, and we will come to him and make our dwelling with him.'" –John 14:22-23

THE MEDITATION:

Simon and Jude, two rather obscure disciples of Jesus, are paired in the apostolic lists (Like 6:14-16 and Acts 1:13). Simon is called a Zealot and Jude, also called Judas, is referred to as the son of James. Beyond that, nothing further is known of them. Why does the Church bother to set a day aside to commemorate two such obscure disciples? Perhaps merely because they completed the list of the original twelve. They are among the innumerable disciples, including ourselves, whom Jesus has called to himself and sent into the world. All who respond to Jesus' call to discipleship, whether notorious or unfamed are important to God.

Anyone, says Jesus, who loves and heeds him is loved by the Father. It is in those persons that God and Christ dwell. Jesus says, "To receive you is to receive me, and to receive me is to receive the One who sent me" (Matthew 10:40). Jesus links us together with himself and God in mission and purpose for the world. That makes us, in all of our obscurity, extremely important. Who would have thought, in our days of alcohol abuse, that we would one day be involved in the Ultimate Concern?

Furthermore Jesus says, "Whoever listens to you listens to me" (Luke 10:16). We are spokespersons for Christ. Being called through the Gospel to live and proclaim that Gospel, we, though obscure to the world like Simon and Jude, have great significance in the Kingdom of God.

THE NEGOTIATION:

Are we fully aware of our importance in God's sight?

THE PRAYER:

Almighty God, You built Your church on the foundation of the apostles and prophets, with Jesus Christ himself the cornerstone. Grant that by their teaching we may be joined together in the unity of the Spirit, so that we may be made a holy temple, acceptable to You. Amen. –Collect for Simon and Jude

THE READING: Luke 10:1-12, 16-20

OCTOBER 29

ADVERSITY

THE INSPIRATION:

"Why art thou troubled, that all things come not to thee as thou willest or desirest? Who is he that hath all things at his own will? There is no man in this world without some manner of tribulation or anguish, though he be king or pope. . . How should thy patience be crowned in heaven if none adversity should befall thee in earth? In thou wilt suffer none adversity, how mayest thou be the friend of Christ? --Thomas A Kempke

THE MEDITATION:

Soon after achieving some degree of sobriety we discovered, that even in this desirable state, we are still confronted with adversity. Now, however, with our new commitment, we are without our old method of anesthesizing ourselves temporarily out of the discomforts of adversity. If sobriety is to be maintained and serenity is to become a reality, we must learn to face adversity in new and constructive ways.

The first thing we have to learn is that adversity is a part of life and accept it as such. We will not have things our own way, nor do we feel we have to. Next, we face the adversity head on and deal with it realistically. Can we or can we not do something about alleviating the adversity? And even when we cannot, we learn from it and are strengthened by it. The adversity help us grow in maturity and patience. We know that God will not allow us to be tested beyond our strength, but when the adversity comes he will at the same time enable us to sustain it (1 Corinthians 10:13).

We no longer need to deny adversity, nor deal with it artificially by drugging ourselves with alcohol. We now accept adversity as a challenge and an opportunity for growth.

THE NEGOTIATION:

Do we feel that we face more adversity than other people?

THE PRAYER:

O Lord, show us Thy favour; we hope in Thee.
Uphold us every morning,
Save us when troubles come. Amen. —Isaiah 33:2

THE READING: Isaiah 33:1-24

OCTOBER 30

GOD AS DEPTH

THE INSPIRATION:

"The name of this infinite and inexhaustible depth and ground of all being is God . . . And if that word has not much meaning for you, translate it, and speak of the depths of your life, of the source of your being, of your ultimate concern, of what you take seriously without and reservation. Perhaps . . . you must forget everything traditional that you have learned without God, perhaps even that word itself. For if you know that God means depth, you know much about him . . . He who knows about depth knows about God." --Paul Tillich

THE MEDITATION:

"Infinite and Inexhaustible Depth," "Ground of All Being," "Ultimate Concern:" these are untraditional names for God which have been helpful to a lot of Twentieth century people. They may or may not be helpful to us. We may prefer the more traditional names: "Father," "Shepherd," "Love," "Ultimate Concern" may make more sense to us in defining "god." There was a time when our ultimate concern was alcohol. It was alcohol that we took seriously without any reservation. It was alcohol to which we responded unconditionally. Alcohol was our god.

If, however, we speak of alcohol in terms of depth, we have difficulty squeezing out a definition of god. Depth, which is infinite and inexhaustible and ground of all being, can only be related to God and never god. Our god (alcohol) is replaced by the God of depth. He is the Source, Guide and Goal of all that is (Romans 11:36). The god, alcohol on detracts from depth and contributes to the shallowness and meaninglessness of life. Through the Spirit we can know and experience God as depth. As Paul says, "The Spirit explores everything, even the depths of God's own nature" (1 Corinthians 2:10).

THE NEGOTIATION:

Do we need to forget some things we have learned about God?

THE PRAYER:

Give us, O Lord, the mind of Christ, that we may know and experience You as the infinite and inexhaustible depth and ground of all being. Amen.

THE READING: 1 Corinthians 2:1-16

OCTOBER 31

REFORMATION

THE INSPIRATION:

"A mighty fortress is our God, a bulwark never failing;
Our helper he amid the flood of mortal ills prevailing:
For still our ancient foe doth seek to work us woe . . .
Did we in our own strength confide our striving would be
losing; were not the right Man on our side, the Man of God's
own choosing. Dost ask who that may be? Christ Jesus, it is he." —Martin Luther

THE MEDITATION:

On the anniversary of the beginning of the sixteenth century reformation we do not celebrate the divisions of the Church, but rather contemplate God's continuous call for the renewal of the Church. The festival of reformation belongs to all Christians. The whole Church is called to its evangelical origins. We recall the revolutionary, cleansing Word of God which constantly renews and reforms the Church of Jesus Christ. Reformation is not a historical event, but rather the permanent state of the Church.

Jesus says, "If you dwell within the revelation I have brought, you are indeed my disciples; you shall know the truth, and the truth shall set you free" (John 8:31-32). This was revolutionary news for Jesus' day, Luther's Day, and our day. Dwelling in the revelation of Jesus is always the source of renewal for individuals and the Church. Jesus' revelation is the Good News of peace and love and righteousness which comes from God as free gifts. God treats us unworthy people as if we were worthy. It is not a question of our righteousness before God, but the righteousness of God given freely to us. Having set us free from working out our own righteousness, God frees us for his service.

THE NEGOTIATION:

What can we do to help renew the Church today?

THE PRAYER:

God our Father, we praise you for the men and women you have sent to call the church to her tasks and renew her life. Raise up in our own day teachers and prophets inspired by your Spirit, whose voices will give strength to your church and speak to all men the reality of your kingdom. Amen. — Collect for Renewers of the Church

THE READING: Jeremiah 26:1-16

NOVEMBER 1

ALL SAINTS

THE INSPIRATION:

"Paul... to the saints and faithful brethren in Christ... Grace to You and peace from our Father. We always thank God, the Father of our Lord Jesus Christ, when we pray for you, because we have heard of your faith in Christ Jesus and of the love which you have for all the saints." Colossians 1:1-4 (RSV)

THE MEDITATION:

Paul begins his letter to the Church at Colossae in his customary way by addressing the congregation as saints. In the broadest New Testament usage the saints are simply God's people—as the New English Bible translates the term. All Christians, in this sense, are saints by virtue of being "incorporate in Christ Jesus" (Philippians 1:1). Saints are simply forgiven sinners. That means that even we alcohol abusers are numbered among God's Saints.

Historians have a way of preserving the records of the world's greatest people and forgetting the ordinary, common people like most of us. Even the Church remembers the outstanding leaders, theologians, and missionaries, but there is little memory of the untold millions who loved God and sought to live a life of conformity to his will. And so, as if to do penance for this memory lapse, the Church sets aside one day of the year to remember with thanksgiving that unknown host of common men, women, and children who loved God and served him in his Church. Today is that day—we call it All Saint's Day.

All Saint's Day dates back to 609AD when all saints, known and unknown, were commemorated when the Roman Pantheon was rededicated as a Christian Church. This is our day. We are reminded that God, through his grace, bestows sainthood upon us. And with the title, of course, comes responsibility.

THE NEGOTIATION:

How seriously do we accept the sainthood God gives us?

THE PRAYER:

Almighty God, whose people are knit together in one holy Church, the body of Christ our Lord, grant us grace to follow Your saints of old in lives of faith and commitment, and to know the inexpressible joys You have prepared for those who love you. Amen. —Collect for All Saints

THE READING: Psalm 34:1-22

NOVEMBER 2

ANONYMITY

THE INSPIRATION:

"Moved by the spirit of anonymity, we try to give up our natural desires for personal distinction as A.A. members, both among fellow alcoholics and before the general public. As we lay aside these very human aspirations, we believe that each of us takes part in the weaving of a protective mantle which covers our whole Society and under which we may grow and work in unity." --Bill W

THE MEDITATION:

The anonymity component of Alcoholics Anonymous is taken very seriously for very good reasons. First, for the protection of its members, especially newcomers who fear the public stigma. Secondly, because service rendered in A.A. is done in the name of the Society and not for the personal recognition of its individual members. "Do not let your left hand know what the right hand is doing" (Matthew 6:3), is the principle which guides A.A. service. When friends wanted to erect a monument honoring the dying Dr. Bob, he said to his A.A. co-founder Bill W., "God bless 'em. They mean well. But let's you and me get buried just like the other folks." And thirdly, those who break their anonymity and then return to drinking give A.A. a bad name.

As we gain confidence in our own commitment to sobriety we lose the fear of the stigma which our culture has for alcohol abusers. As we grow I serenity we care less and less about who finds out about our past. A good rule of thumb for us is this: if breaking our anonymity can do some good or bring some understanding to others, by all means let's do it. Let us keep in mind, however, that there are some, unfortunately, who will not accept us if they know of our past. Breaking our anonymity may interfere with our ministry to them. In any event we should criticize neither those who wish to remain silent, nor those who publicly witness to what God has done for them.

THE NEGOTIATION:

Have we developed a policy concerning our own personal anonymity?

THE PRAYER:

Give us guidance, O Lord, in the dilemma we face concerning our anonymity. In all things may our lives give glory only to You. Amen.

THE READING: John 5:31-47

NOVEMBER 3

ETERNAL LIFE

THE INSPIRATION:

"To many moderns this (belief in life everlasting) sounds almost unbearably naïve—as does any idea of reward of punishment in a future life. We must do good, we are told, for the sake of doing good. Similarly, we must not hurt others because it is a bad thing to do . . . I believe that by cutting out the whole realm of (future life) . . . we are robbing ourselves of more than we know. Instead of being sons of God with unlimited potentialities, . . . we are merely decent humanists with a possible tinge of Christian piety." —J. B. Phillips

THE MEDITATION:

In the Apostles' Creed we profess, "I believe in . . . the life everlasting," and in the Nicene Creed: "I believe in . . . the Life of the world to come." The Church has always believed in and witnessed to the immortality of the human soul as taught by Jesus. "God loved the world so much that he gave his only Son, that everyone who has faith in him may not die but have eternal life" (John 3:16).

At times the Church has overemphasized the future life at the exclusion of the present. The purpose of the Christian faith and life is not only to prepare us for life after death but also to enable us to live and serve in life after birth. "This is eternal life: to know thee who alone art truly God, and Jesus Christ whom thou hast sent" (John 17:3). The present tense, "is" needs to be emphasized, but not to the exclusion of our faith and hope in life everlasting. A balanced accentuation on present and future life is necessary for us.

In order to gain sobriety and serenity we have to learn the importance of living life in the now. At the same time, we life as "aliens in a foreign land" (1 Peter 2:11) with our eyes fixed on the "place" Christ has prepared for us (John 14:2). Ours is the best of two worlds: abundant life now and the glorious life everlasting.

THE NEGOTIATION:

Have we overemphasized either the present or future life?

THE PRAYER:

Dear Lord, we thank You for the gift of life. Help us to use this gift abundantly in the present as we long for eternal life with You in heaven. Amen.

THE READING: 1 John 5:13-21

NOVEMBER 4

THIRST

THE INSPIRATION:

"God keeps no man waiting, he is love. Like a stream of water which keeps the same temperature summer and winter—so is God's love. But a spring sometimes runs dry—no, no, how shall I praise him, there is no other praise than the expression which perfectly fits him whom we speak of, 'God be praised!'—and so, God be praised, God's love is not of such a kind. His love is a spring which never runs dry." --Soren Kierkegaard

THE MEDITATION:

We know what it is like to be thirsty. Most of us, in our drinking days, did a lot of rationalizing about out insatiable desire for liquid refreshment.   We know now that it was not physical thirst with which we were plagued, but rather a craving to alter our minds, find relief from emotional pain, or escape from mundaneness. Of all people we alcohol abusers understand that third is far more than a physical need.

God's love is like a spring of water which never runs dry. We may shut ourselves off from that water, but the spring never ceases to flow. Even when we find ourselves in the drought of depression and the desert of despair, "water springs up in the wilderness" (Isaiah 35:6). God's love is always available to us, therefore, "let the wilderness and the thirsty land be glad, let the desert rejoice and burst into flower" (Isaiah 35:1).

Jesus told the Samaritan women at Jacob's well, "Whoever drinks the water that I shall give him will never suffer thirst any more" John 4:14). The women interpreted this on the physical level and speculated on how nice it would be not to have to make the trip to the well any more. But Jesus is talking about the love of God which is an inner spring always welling up for eternal life. This ever available spring satisfies all our thirsts—including the one for alcohol

THE NEGOTIATION:

Do we sometimes ignore the inner spring?

THE PRAYER:

We are thirsty people, O Lord. Help us to thirst for righteousness, and always be ready to drink from the inner spring of living water that You provide. Amen.

THE READING: Isaiah 35:1-10

NOVEMBER 5

ENOUGH

THE INSPIRATION:

"Troll King: What's the difference between a troll and a man?

Peer Gynt: No different, so far as I can see.

Troll King: . . . There is a difference down at the root. I'll tell you what it is. Outside, among men, under the shining sky, they say: 'Man, to yourself be true!' While here, under our mountain roof we say: 'Troll, to yourself be—enough!'" -- Henrik Ibsen

THE MEDITATION:

Being authentic human being means being who God meant us to be, which means being true to ourselves and enough to ourselves. It means being satisfied with who we are and not trying to be someone else. It means wearing no masks to disguise our true identity. One of the great lessons we must learn in order to achieve sobriety and serenity is to be true to ourselves and enough to ourselves.

"Original sin" as emphasized in Christian theology does not mean that we have no choice: that we are not responsible for our sins. We also have "original righteousness" as a part of our human make up. Beneath all of the garbage that we accumulate—all the pride, hate, jealousy, and lust—there lay a core of goodness. When we are our most authentic selves we express that core of goodness. That's the image of God being mirrored through us.

Saul of Tarsus was a middle-aged failure, an unauthentic person. He was well educated, came from a prosperous family, and achieves great success in his "religious" profession. But when Saul encountered the living Christ he found a new identity, a new authenticity. He became Paul, true to himself and enough to himself, who testifies, "When anyone is united in Christ, there is a new act of creation" (2 Corinthians 5:17). Being who God meant us to be is enough.

THE NEGOTIATION:

Are we enough for ourselves?

THE PRAYER:

Help us, O Lord, to grow into the persons You created us to be; and as we are true to ourselves, give us the peace and satisfaction to knowing that is enough. Amen.

THE READING: 2 Corinthians 6:11-7:4

NOVEMBER 6

SURRENDER AND SUBMISSION

THE INSPIRATION:

"One fact must be kept in mind, namely, the need to distinguish between submission and surrender. In submission, an individual accepts reality consciously but not unconsciously. He accepts as a practical fact that he cannot at that moment conquer reality, but lurking in his unconscious is the feeling, "there'll come a day'—which implies no real acceptance and demonstrates conclusively that the struggle is still going on. With submission, which at best is a superficial yielding, tension continues." -- Harry Tiebout

THE MEDITATION:

In our struggle again alcohol abuse we discover, hopefully, that there is a great difference between submitting to something and surrendering to God: which means turning our lives and wills over to him. Surrender means not "giving in" to the power of alcohol, but "giving up" to the power of God and it is then that there is no residual battle and serenity ensues. It is surrender that Jesus calls for when he says, "By gaining his life a man will lose it; by losing his life for my sake, he will gain it" (Matthew 10:39). Surrender means we take "a leap of faith" toward the power of God's grace. As Paul says, "In baptism you were buried with him (Christ), in baptism also you were raised to life with him through your faith in the active power of God who raised him from the dead" (Colossians 2:12).

To be raised to life with Christ means to be "born over again" (John 3:4). Birth, whether physical or spiritual is God's doing. Those who consider themselves "born again Christians" know that God is the source of their birth. They also know, hopefully, that birth is not an equivalent of maturity. Birth is the beginning of a never ending and maturing process in the new life in Christ.

THE NEGOTIATION:

Do we know the difference between surrender and submission in our rebirth?

THE PRAYER:

O Lord of all Life, we thank You for the gift of life: both physical and spiritual. Help us to always gain life more fully by surrendering our lives to You. Amen.

THE READING: Matthew 10:32-39

NOVEMBER 7

THE CENTRALITY OF THE GOSPEL

THE INSPIRATION:

"One thing and one thing only is necessary for Christian life, righteousness and liberty. That one thing is the most hold Word of God, the Gospel of Christ." --Martin Luther

THE MEDITATION:

By now it has been demonstrated that there is a wide range of literature that can prove helpful in inspiring our daily meditations and devotions. Behind all inspiration, for the Christian, is the Gospel—the life and message of Jesus Christ. The main source of the Gospel is, of course, the Bible. While all parts of the Bible do not equally convey the Gospel to us, the basic devotional tool of the Christian Church is, nonetheless, the Holy Scriptures. Historically, the New Testament came out of the life and traditions of the community that followed Jesus of Nazareth and called itself by the name of Christ. That community in turn was nurtured and constituted by the biblical witness to the Christ-event. There would have been no New Testament without the community, and no enduring community without the Gospel inspiration and witness.

Whenever in the Scriptures, Old or New Testaments, the love and grace of God, and peace and goodwill among people, is proclaimed, there is the Gospel. Nor is the Gospel confined to the Bible. Whenever the life and message of Jesus Christ is acknowledged, proclaimed, and lived, there is the Gospel. Creeds and doctrinal statements are interpretations of the Gospel. They have their justifications as such, but they do not have the power to stand on their own apart from the Gospel's foundation. The Gospel is central to our faith. It is the power of the living Gospel that enables us to maintain sobriety and grow in serenity.

THE NEGOTIATION:

Is the Gospel the message which motivates our lives?

THE PRAYER:

We thank You, O Lord, for Your Church built upon the foundation laid by the apostles and prophets, and Christ Jesus himself the foundation—stone. Help us to find, in the life and message of Christ, motivation for living, and serving. Amen.

THE READING: 1 Timothy 1:3-11

NOVEMBER 8

OUR PLACE

THE INSPIRATION:

"Nora: I believe that before all else I am a reasonable human being, just as you are—or, at all events, that I must try to become one . . . I can no longer content myself with what most people say . . . I must think over things for myself and get to understand them.

Helmer: Can you not understand your place in your own home?. . . Have you no religion?

Nora: I am afraid I do not exactly know what religion is."
                         --Henrik Ibsen

THE MEDITATION:

We live in a pigeonholing culture. People are always telling other people where their place is. Sometimes me buy into the classifying myths and believe that because we are of a certain sex, race, creed, or social class, we do belong in a certain place. How tragic it is to limit our potential by being content "with what most people say." Men and women are expected to stay in their respective places. People of other distinctions are expected to stay in their proper places. Alcohol abusers are expected to abuse alcohol. The human tragedy is when we live up to these crazy expectations. Could it be that Nora, who didn't understand exactly what religion is, was embarking on a religious journey by deciding to try to be a reasonable human being? The religiou9s quest is nothing more than being human, living up to our human potential, being humans.

The dignity and sacredness and great value of every human being is at the heart of the Gospel. "This belief in the essential sacredness of everyone," says William James, "expressed itself today in all sorts of humane customs and reformatory institutions." As we grow in humanness and work to make our institutions more humane, we are practicing religion in the Gospel sense.

THE NEGOTIATION:

Do we allow other people to determine our place?

THE PRAYER:

We thank You, O Lord, that in Your entire creation You have reserved a place for us as Your human children. Keep us from being put, or putting others, in places below the sacredness You reserve for those created in Your image. Amen.

THE READING: Isaiah 54:1-17

NOVEMBER 9

SUBJECTIVE THEOLOGY

THE INSPIRATION:

"NO matter how much Christians may stress the objective historical aspects of their faith, and claim that their faith is the faith of an historical community, there remains a large personal element in it. Theology gives us a programme for personal action. To know 'God' is not to add an extra card labeled 'God' to our mental card index; it is to become a changed person." --John Habgood

THE MEDITATION:

In the final analysis the Christian Faith is very personal, very subjective. Christianity is the opposite of any one, cubby-holed experience. If we are not Christian in the way we eat or drink, or have sex, or deal with our families, friends, and all others, or work, or play, or read, or think, the fact that we accept all the theology ever written does not make us so. As Paul says, "Whether you eat or drink, or whatever you are doing, do all for the honour of God" (1 Corinthians 10:31).

At the same time, we need a program for personal action—theology gives us such a program. Theology is the intellectual expression of our experience of knowing God. The church needs theology; each of us needs a theology of our own. If all we have is a theology, we are on an intellectual head-trip. If all we have is a religious feeling, we are on an emotional heart-trip. Jesus said, "Love the Lord your God with all your heart, with all your soul, with all your mind" (Matthew 22:37). No head or heart or soul trip here—no cubby holed experience—but rather a total expression of the love of God. This total expression can only result in changed persons.

THE NEGOTIATION:

Does our theology affect what and how we drink?

THE PRAYER:

Dear Lord, we thank You for raising up great theologians in Your church. We pray that they might inspire us as we formulate a program of personal action, that we might do all things for Your honour. Amen.

THE READING: Deuteronomy 6:1-9

NOVEMBER 10

EXPECTING GOODNESS

THE INSPIRATION:

Aesop, the storyteller, was one day walking from Athens, when he met a man from Argus going to the city he had left. As they talked, the man from Argus said, "You came from Athens. Tell me, what sort of people are they there?" "Tell me first," replied Aesop, "what the people of Argus are like." "Oh, very disagreeable," said the man, "mean and selfish and quarrelsome." "I am sorry to tell you," said Aesop, "that you will find the people of Athens just the same."

Later, he met another man also coming from Argus, who asked him the same question about what the people of Athens were like. "Tell me first," said Aesop again, "what the people of Argus are like." They are very pleasant people, "said the second man, "kind and friendly and good neighbors." "I'm happy to tell you," said Aesop, "that you will find the people of Athens just the same."

THE MEDITATION:

We generally find what we are looking for in other people. This is true of the Church as well as those outside the Church. It's true of alcohol abusers and non abusers; it's true of former and active alcohol abusers. If we anticipate goodness, kindness, and love, we generally find it. If we play "blemish" we will discover all kinds of imperfections. Our expectations play an important part in our interpersonal relationships.

And, lest we forget, God has high expectations for us. Jesus says, "You must be all goodness, just as your heavenly Father is all good" (Matthew 5:48). It is a cop-out to make light of this passage by saying, "All goodness is impossible, after all we're only human." We are expected to be all goodness, and when we fail in that expectation, God, nonetheless by his grace, accepts us as all goodness, which is our motivation for goodness.

THE NEGOTIATION:

Are we challenged or demoralized by those who have low expectations for us?

THE PRAYER:

Dear Lord of all goodness, forgive us for our lack of goodness, help us to look for and demonstrate goodness in our relationships with others. Amen.

THE READING: Leviticus 19:1-18

NOVEMBER 11

BLINDNESS

THE INSPIRATION:

"Jesus asked (the blind man), 'What do you want me to do for you?' "Sir, I want my sight back,' he answered. Jesus said to him, 'Have back your sight; your faith has cured you.' He recovered his sight instantly; and he followed Jesus, praising God. And all the people gave praise to God for what they had seen." --Luke 18:41-43

THE MEDITATION:

When the tenacious blind man was told Jesus was passing by, he shouted out for pity. The people told him to hold his tongue and stay in his place, but he persisted until Jesus heard him. Displaying such relentlessness, it is little wonder Jesus told him, "Your faith has cured you."

Our faith too, will cure our blindness if that's what we really want. We know now how blind we were while abusing alcohol. There is much beauty we see now that we could never see through the haze of alcohol. But have we been totally cured? Do we still have blind spots of which we are unaware? If we relentlessly pursue greater vision with a persistent faith, God will open our eyes to unthinkable sights.

God will open your eyes to the world and we will see a beauty and glory in his creation beyond imagination. God will open our eyes to other people. We will no longer see them as faces in a crowd, or cogs in the machinery of civilization, or factors in social problems: but everyone a brother and sister for whom Christ died and rose. God will open our eyes to ourselves. This can be a humbling experience, yet it can also be a door to penitence, pardon, and peace. God will open our eyes to himself. We will no longer see God as Someone we read about, or hear preachers tell about, or argue about in theological discussions, but the living Center of our lives. Through faith God will do this—if we want.

THE NEGOTIATION:

Do we really want to see more than we do now?

THE PRAYER:

Dear Lord, give us the courage and strength and faith to want to see more. Open up our eyes to the beauty and ugliness in the world, and help us to respond to these sights in accordance with Your will. Amen.

THE READING: Luke 18:31-43

NOVEMBER 12

LAUGHTER

THE INSPIRATION:

"When God had finished the stars and whirl of coloured suns,
He turned his mind from big things, to fashion little ones.
Beautiful tine things like daisies, he made, and then
He made the comical ones, in the case the minds of men
Should stiffen and become
Dull, humourless and glum,
And so forgetful of their Makers be
As to take even themselves—quite seriously.
Caterpillars and cats are lively and excellent puns;
All God's jokes are good, even the practical ones!
And as for the duck, I think God must have smiled a bit
Seeing those bright eyes blink on the day he fashioned it.
And he's probably laughing still at the sound that came out
of it's bill." --F.W. Harvey

THE MEDITATION:

On two occasions, according to the New Testament, Jesus wept (Luke 19:41 and John 11:35). Most certainly, Jesus wept at other times i.e. in Gethsemane; and just as surely, he often laughed. Between the lines and through the translations we hear the humor of Jesus when he used metaphors like "the log in your eye" (Matthew 7:5) and "a scorpion for an egg" (Luke 11:13).

To believe in God means, among other things, to have a sense of humor. Atheists, agnostics, skeptics, and materialists take themselves seriously because they have no spiritual vantage point from which they can look at themselves and see how laughable they are. The only cause for laughter for them stems from the belief that life is a meaningless farce.

We have every reason to rejoice and laugh—God has given us life and sobriety. It is only those who are not yet sure of God who are afraid to laugh in his presence. "Look towards him and shine with joy" (Psalm 34:5).

THE NEGOTIATION:

Can a sober Christian be without a sense of humor?

THE PRAYER:

O Lord of all joy, help us to rejoice in all things. Enable us to laugh at ourselves and with others, while doing them no harm. Thank You, O Lord, for Your gift of laughter. Amen.

THE READING: Proverbs 17:1-22

NOVEMBER 13

RECOLLECTION

THE INSPIRATION:

"Recollection makes me present to myself by bring together two aspects, or activities, of my being as if they were two lens of a telescope. One lens if the basic semblance of my spiritual being, the inward soul, the deep will, the spiritual intelligence. The other is my outward soul, the practical intelligence, the will engaged in the activities of life . . . When the outward soul knows only itself, then it is absent from its true self . . . It never acts in accordance with the need and measure of its own true personality, which exists where my spirit is wedded with the silent presence of the Lord's Spirit." -- Thomas Merton

THE MEDITATION:

Recollection or practicing the presence of God is an infallible road to sobriety, serenity and integration. It is when we practice the silence presence of God that we are our real selves –our own true personality. It is getting our two selves together. Too often when people speak of "getting it together," they refer only to the outward soul—their practical intelligence. True integration comes only by looking at ourselves, others, life, and God through both lenses with which we are equipped.

Recollection is an action in which we engage in our daily devotional periods, but it doesn't stop there. Our devotions are springboards for recollection during our daily activities. Our activities need not be extraordinary or spectacular, but, as in most cases, common or even mundane. The sacred is in the ordinary, in our daily life, in our neighbors, friends, and family, in our own back yard. The love of God can be found in "taking a straw from the ground" or in celebrating the Sacrament of the Altar. To be looking elsewhere for miracles is a sure sign that everything is miraculous. All of God's creation is sacred of has the potential of sacredness when utilized with love: "Where we and he carry it in infinitely tender love."

THE NEGOTIATION:

Will we be guided by recollection this day?

THE PRAYER:

Keep us from getting lost in the perplexities and duties of life, O Lord; and enable us to practice recollection that we might be the integrated and true selves You mean us to be. Amen.

THE READING: Acts 17:24-31

NOVEMBER 14

HYMN TO ALCOHOL

THE INSPIRATION:

"Why, liquor of life, do I love you so,
When in all our encounters you bring me low?
You're my soul and my treasure, without and within,
My sister, my cousin, and all my kin!

O Usquebagh! I love its kiss—
My guardian spirit I think it is;
Had my christening bowl been filled with this,
I had swallowed it, were it a fountain?

Many's the quondam fight we've had,
And many a time you've made me mad,
But while I've a heart it never can be sad
When you smile at me, full on the table . . .
Oh! I'll stand by you, while I am able." --Turlogh O'Carolgn

THE MEDITATION:

It does not surprise us that sooner or later someone would write a hymn to alcohol. All worshippers sing praises to their god. Why shouldn't the god alcohol have hymns written and sung to its praise? To most people a hymn to alcohol would seem sacrilegious—and indeed it is! But as much as a hymn to alcohol violates the sacred, we can nonetheless understand its existence. There was a time when our lives constituted a hymn to alcohol. In many ways we sang praises to our god.

We human being are basically religious in that we search for transcendence, meaning, and relatedness. The god alcohol gave us temporary and artificial satisfaction for our needs—until it let us down. We stood by our god as long as we were able. It was then in our powerlessness that we turned to the power of Almighty God. The further we get from the old god, the closer we get to the living Lord and the deeper we feel the need for his perpetual presence.

THE NEGOTIATION:

Are our lives hymns of praise sung to the Lord?

THE PRAYER:

We thank You, O Lord, for delivering us out of the hands of the god who had betrayed us. May our lives be hymns of praise to the glory of Your name. Amen.

THE READING: Acts 16:25-34

NOVEMBER 15

THE TWO DIMENSIONS OF PEACE

THE INSPIRATION:

"If we open the shutters in the morning the light will pour in. We do not need to beseech it to pour in. It will pour in if we let it. If we open the sluice in flood-time the water will flow through. We do not plead with it to flow. It will flow if we will let it. It is so with the peace of God. It will rule in our hearts if only we let it." --Amy Carmichael

THE MEDITATION:

Two artists each painted a picture of their respective conception of peace. The first painting depicted a quiet scene with a lone lack among far-off mountains. The second showed a thundering waterfall, with a fragile birch tree bending over the roaring water; at the fork of the branch, almost wet with the spray, a robin sat on her nest. The first painting was only stagnation; the second was peace. There are always two dimensions of peace: tranquility and energy, silence and turbulence, fearlessness and fearfulness.

It is this kind of two-dimensional peace that Jesus knew and proclaimed. We who have suffered with alcohol abuse know the turbulence of being at war with ourselves and others. In our recovery process we have discovered the peace which the Prince of Peace brings. Our practice of the presence of God brings us a peace which does beyond human understanding.

It is this inner peace which disturbs us about the absence of peace in the world: quarreling, fighting, social injustice, prejudice, the plight of our cities, crime, wars and rumors of wars among nations. Of the city of Jerusalem Jesus said, "If only you had known, on this great day, the way that leads to peace" (Luke 19:42). If we think we have inner peace without being disturbed by the turbulence about us, we are fooling ourselves. Being disturbed, however, is not enough. Jesus calls us to join him in working for external peace in the world. This work, in turn, brings inner peace.

THE NEGOTIATION:

Have we found peace in the struggle against violence?

THE PRAYER:

Give us the peace, O Lord, which comes from surrendering our lives and wills to You; and use us as instruments of Your peace in the turbulence of the world about us. Amen

THE READING: Micah 4:1-4

NOVEMBER 16

LEARNING AND DOING

THE INSPIRATION:

"No man is a true Christian who does not think constantly of how he can lift his brother, how he can assist his friend, how we can make virtue the rule of conduct in the circle in which he lives." – Woodrow Wilson

THE MEDITATION:

For the Christian the Word of God is living and active. It is not merely something which is learned and memorized, but, above all, lived out in action. Long ago Moses said, "The commandment that I lay on you this day is not too difficult for you, it is not too remote. It is not in heaven . . . nor is it beyond the sea . . . It is a thing very near you, upon your lips, and in your heart ready to be kept" (Deuteronomy 30:11-14). God's word is not inaccessible, not mysteriously unknowable, but rather in use ready to be demonstrated in loving action on our neighbor's behalf.

On one occasion a lawyer put a test question to Jesus about what he must do to inherit eternal life (Luke 10:25). Jesus asked him what the Bible said and the lawyer answered, "Love God with all your heart, soul, strength and mind; and your neighbor as yourself." Jesus said he answered right and challenged him to it. The lawyer, wanting to vindicate himself, asked who his neighbor was. Jesus responded by telling the Parable of the Good Samaritan. For Jesus the Word of God goes beyond the written word, even if it is well memorized, and is translated into loving action like that of the Samaritan. Jesus concludes the story by saying, "Go and do as he did" (Luke 10:37).

We can likewise learn all there is to know about alcohol abuse. We can learn all about its history, its chemistry (C_2H_5OH), it's physiology, and its psychological effects, and still not put sobriety and serenity into action. Blessed are those who learn the word of God and act upon it (Luke 6:47). Sober and serene are those who learn about alcohol abuse and do something about it.

THE NEGOTIATION:

Do we over-intellectualize our faith and our sobriety?

THE PRAYER:

O Lord, Your call to learning and action rings in our ears. Enable us to respond by study and loving action. Amen.

THE READING: Deuteronomy 30:11-20

NOVEMBER 17

THE PRAYER OF SILENCE

THE INSPIRATION:

"In the prayer of Silence the child ceases to chatter, and waits for the Father to speak, and thus staying quietly in His presence, at once gains an intimacy and trustfulness." --Evelyn Underhill

THE MEDITATION:

In prayer the ear is more important than the tongue. Paul says that "faith is awakened by the message, and the message that awakens it comes through the word of Christ" (Romans 10:17). We cannot hear the message if we are always chattering. Jesus quite bluntly tells us, "In your prayers do not go babbling on like the heathen, who imagine that the more they say the more likely they are to be heard" (Matthew 6:7). It's like the chattering and babbling that we used to engage in when lubricated with alcohol: raising our voices with verbose repetitions to which no one was listening. In prayer we have the tendency to dominate the conversation. We would like to reverse the words of Scripture from "Speak, Lord; thy servant hears" (1 Samuel 3:9) to "Listen, Lord; thy servant speaks." Our communication with God is two-way; we sometimes forget we have a receiver as well as a speaker.

Communication is the key word for our prayers, meditations, and devotions. Intimacy is out goal. The best of all communication of intimacy is non-verbal. The simplest analogy, and the most profound, for communion with God is that of loving, intimate, trustful intercourse between friend and Friend. There is "a time for silence and a time for speech" (Ecclesiastes 3:7). The deepest intercourse between friends is without words. The prayer of Silence extends beyond our devotional periods. As we become more proficient in the practice of the presence of God, we learn to listen to him and experience an intimacy with him, even while engages in our day's activities and in conversations with others.

THE NEGOTIATION:

Are we making progress in our practice of presence of God?

THE PRAYER:

Dear Lord, enable us to hear Your voice with us, not only during this quiet time with You, but throughout this entire day as we seek to praise You in thought, word, and deed. Amen.

THE READING: Psalm 62:1-12

NOVEMBER 18

PSYCHOLOGY

THE INSPIRATION:

"The Christian scale of values . . . by no means denies the importance of these ideas advanced by psychology. It contains them, and goes beyond them. To experience the 'new birth' of which our Lord speaks, is to become the 'new man' of which St. Paul speaks, is indeed to become adult, to attain to the fullness of humanity ordained by God; but it is much more than that. It is to recover, through the redemption of Christ, fellowship with God and dependence of him." --Paul Tournier

THE MEDITATION:

Alcohol abuse is a total affliction which affect the whole of a person: psychologically, physiologically, socially, and spiritually. Even though we see it as basically a spiritual problem which needs a spiritual solution, we must never deny the other aspects of alcohol abuse either in their etiology or solution. Modern psychology has learned a lot from Scriptures and has reinterpreted many of these truths in secular terms. Religion can in turn learn something from the insights of psychology.

Many different psychological approaches have been used in treating alcohol abusers. We can and should take advantage of the help these therapists have to offer. The best therapeutic method is the one that works for the individual. We can learn something and gain insight from each of them—but none is them are utopian. We must never insist that our particular psychological solution is the best for everyone.

Our concern is, however, with far more than sobriety—we are concerned with serenity, which for us comes through fellowship with and dependence on God. As Paul says, "You must be new in mind and spirit, and put on the new nature of God's creating, which shows itself in the just and devout life called for by the truth" (Ephesians 4:24).

THE NEGOTIATION:

Is fellowship with God and dependence on him our main concern?

THE PRAYER:

We thank You, O Lord, for the insights into ourselves that we gain from psychology. Above all, we thank You for the experience of Your abiding presence. Amen.

THE READING: Psalm 113:1-9

NOVEMBER 19

BENEVOLENCE

THE INSPIRATION:

"Christian perfection, that people have a sort of dread of from the idea that it imposes gloom and constraint, is not perfection, but inasmuch as it increases benevolence. We do not consider it constraint to do those things which we love to do. We find a pleasure in sacrificing ourselves to anyone that we truly love. Thus, the more we advance in perfection, the more willing we are to follow its author." --Francois Fenelon

THE MEDITATION:

We can speak of perfection in terms of physiological sobriety. That simply means refraining from alcohol abuse. However, in terms of serenity perfection is not so easily attained. Paul said, "I have not yet reached perfection, but I press on, hoping to take hold of that for which Christ once took hold of me" (Philippians 3:12). It is the pressing on, not achieving, that is our concern so far as perfection in serenity is concerned. We press on toward peace with God, with ourselves, with all other human beings.

Serenity means not only peace with God and ourselves, but also with all others. As we grow in serenity we increase in benevolence. If we truly want to grow toward perfection in serenity, we will. For the most part, we do those things we want to do. We indeed find pleasure in giving of ourselves to those whom we love. But what about those whom we do not love? There is our growing edge! It works both ways: we show benevolence toward those whom we love, and we learn to love those to whom we are benevolent. If we perform some benevolent deed, some giving of ourselves, for someone we dislike that dislike will turn into love. It is here, on this growing edge, that we press on toward perfection and take hold of that love with which Christ once took hold of us.

THE NEGOTIATION:

What benevolent deed will enable us to press on today?

THE PRAYER:

Dear Lord, You are the author of all perfection. Give us, we pray, the courage to reach out to others with benevolent deeds that we might grow toward the perfect love to which You call us. Amen.

THE READING: Proverbs 25:1-12

ACTIVISM

THE INSPIRATION:

"Set me free from the laziness that goes about disguised as activity when activity is useless, and from the cowardice that does what is not demanded, in order to escape sacrifice." –Thomas Martin

THE MEDITATION:

"Keep busy," is often the advice that is given to those who are recovering from alcohol abuse. To keep active is good advice when it keeps us from sulking over our dispirited condition. But it is bad advice when that activity means business or mere motion. Useless activity is time consuming and saps energy from us. Physical exercise, of course, when engaged in with prudence is constructive activity which will be of benefit to all of us. But the kind of activity in which we run from one place to another meaninglessly is destructive. In can indeed be a cover-up for our history of procrastination. It can keep us from doing what is demanded for our sobriety and serenity.

Is the activity God's work? Is a good question to repeatedly ask ourselves. God's work is best done away from the periphery and close to the center. When Judas led a detachment of soldiers to Gethesmane to arrest Jesus, Peter drew his sword and struck at the High Priest's servant, cutting off his ear. But Jesus said to Peter, "Sheathe your sword. This is the cup my Father has given me; shall I not drink it? (John 18:11). All who take to the sword died by the sword" (Matthew 26:52). We do not need activism like Peter's, which neglects the quiet task of watching and praying, in favor of swinging swords because our enemies swing them. Jesus calls for activity which is constructive, loving, healing, and forgiving. The way to serenity if activity which does God's will, and avoids activities which grows out of selfishness, laziness and cowardice.

THE NEGOTIATION:

What can we do to avoid destructive and meaningless activism?

THE PRAYER:

Lord, help us to actively pursue Your presence at all times, that we, overcoming our laziness and cowardice, might be actively involved in Your service. Amen.

THE READING: John 18:1-11

NOVEMBER 21

THE WAY OF OBEDIENCE

THE INSPIRATION:

"Jesus is alive for all those who let themselves be guided by him in things both great and small, as though he were still walking in our midst. He says to them, 'Do this,' or 'Do that.' And they answer, 'Yes,' and go quietly and do as they were bidden. . . The fact that the Lord makes demands on us in our own day is proof to me, the only proof, that he is not a ghost or dead. He is alive." --Albert Schweitzer

THE MEDITATION:

Obedience is a word we have been reluctant to use. With our great emphasis on freedom in our political realm, the idea of obedience leaves us with a bad taste in our mouths as if it were a stale fragment left over from the age of feudalism. But as far as our Christian faith is concerned we are free to obey. Obedience goes ahead in hand with faith: it's the other side of the same coin. Our faith is based on the promises of God. Faith is strengthened by obedience and negated by disobedience. It is through obedience that faith comes alive, and life becomes abundant and meaningful.

Jesus says, "Not everyone who calls me 'Lord, Lord' will enter the Kingdom of Heaven, but only those who do the will of my heavenly father" (Matthew 7:21). As trees are judged by the fruit they produce, so faith is judged by obedience. We are to live life on Jesus' terms: to be fruitful, productive, and obedient. With faith and obedience our possibilities for abundant and meaningful living are unlimited.

What obedience does Jesus demand of us? Obviously he asks that we not abuse alcohol, and that we pursue serenity. But serenity comes only by obedience. As we meditate on the life, message and mission of Jesus, his demands become quite clear. The proof of his being alive in us is found in out obedience to him.

THE NEGOTIATION:

Do we take Jesus' demands seriously?

THE PRAYER:

Dear Lord, help us to know and do what You demand of us. And by being obedient to Your heavenly vision, we pray that we might live abundantly and meaningfully. Amen.

THE READING: Matthew 7:21-29

NOVEMBER 22

THE DIVINE MILIEU

THE INSPIRATION:

"The perception of the divine omnipresence is essentially a seeing, a taste, that is to say a sort of intuition bearing upon certain higher qualities in things. It cannot, therefore, be attained by any process of reasoning or any human artifice. It is a gift, like life itself, of which it is undoubtedly the supreme experiential perfection . . . to experience the attraction of God, to be sensible of the beauty, the consistence and the final unity of being, is the highest and at the same time the most complete of our 'passivities of growth.' God tends by the logic of his creative effort, to make himself sought and perceived by us; . . . he made men that they might grope their way towards him." --Pierre Teilhard de Chardin

THE MEDITATION:

There is something in us which, against our inclination, our self-interest and even our social conditioning, makes us grope our way towards God. Perhaps, rather than in us, it is an external power outside of ourselves. This outside influence is that theologians have traditionally called "grace." It is a free gift, like life itself. It is this enabling power which enables us to be and do what we could not by our own effort.

In order to deflate our egos and keep us humble we must always remember that our sobriety and growth in serenity is by the grace of God. La Rochefoucauld said, "When our vices leave us, we flatter ourselves with credit of having left them." If we are honest we can only say with Paul, "By God's grace I am what I am" (1 Corinthians 15:10). It is by the grace of God that we are what we are: sober and on the road to serenity. By experiencing the attraction of God, nothing that he wants for us is beyond our grasp.

THE NEGOTIATION:

Do we sometimes live as though God's grace has been given to us in vain?

THE PRAYER:

We thank You, O Lord, for Your grace, which draws us to You and enables us to do Your will. Help us always to accept Your free gift and live to the glory of Your name. Amen.

THE READING: 1 Corinthians 15:1-11

NOVEMBER 23

SLIPS

THE INSPIRATION:

"A fall is not a signal to lie wallowing, but to rise." --Christina Rossetti

"Refuse to pander to a morbid interest in your own misdeeds. Pick yourself up, be sorry, shake yourself, and go on again." --Evelyn Underhill

"We are what we are now, not an hour ago, and what we are planning, not what we are vainly trying to forget." --Frank Laubach

THE MEDITATION:

A slip is when an alcohol abuser, who is committed to sobriety, returns for a short duration to alcohol abuse. If the abuse continues it is more than a slip and constitutes a return to the former condition. In general, there are two things about slips which we must always keep in mind: one, they are not necessary or inevitable, and secondly, we are always vulnerable to them.

When slips do occur, the advice in the inspirations needs to be reinforced: not to morbidly lie wallowing, but to rise, go on again, and live in the now. A slip does not have to be the end of the world, but if we don't take it seriously, it very well could be. It was to Joshua the Lord said, "Stand up; why lie prostrate on your face?" (Joshua 7:10). And Micah says, "I will wait for God my savior; my God will hear me . . . I have fallen, but shall rise again" (Micah 7:7-8). When we slip God says, "Get up," and gives us the power to do it.

If we allow ourselves to slip, the important thing is what we can learn from it and how we can be strengthened from it. Slips require some deep soul-searching. They lead us to question the authenticity of our commitment: was it only an intellectual thing? We need to examine what happened prior to the slip and how did we allow ourselves to get into such a frame of mind. Undoubtedly, we were not practicing the presence of God.

THE NEGOTIATION:

What is our defense against slips?

THE PRAYER:

O Lord, help us with the grace of courage, that we be none of us cast down when we sit lamenting amid the ruins of our happiness of our integrity: touch us with fire from the altar, and we may be up and doing to rebuild out city. Amen. --Robert Louis Stevenson

THE READING: Micah 7:1-20

NOVEMBER 24

THANKSGIVING

THE INSPIRATION:

"When you have plenty to eat and live in fine houses of your own building, when your . . . silver and gold and all your possessions increase, . . . do not become proud or forget the Lord your God who brought you out of . . . the land of slavery." --Deuteronomy 8:12-14

THE MEDITATION:

At this time of the year the President of the United States usually signs a proclamation officially calling for a day of Thanksgiving. With or without any official proclamation, our hearts turn at this time to Thanksgiving. Thanksgiving means, of course, many things to many people. It can mean simply a date in red on the calendar, it can men commemorating an event, it can mean turkey, reunion with family and friends, football, a four-day weekend, etc.

For us, Christian alcohol abusers, however, Thanksgiving may mean all of these things, but always much, much more. Above all, for us, Thanksgiving means thanks-giving. We give thanks to God for food, family, friends, homes, and all the material possessions we enjoy. But above all, we thank God for life through Jesus Christ which is abundant and everlasting. And we thank God for bringing us out of the land of slavery to alcohol. We are, therefore, never proud of the possessions we accumulate—they are at most symbols of God's grace. It is our deliverance from sin, death, and alcohol abuse, and for sobriety, life, and serenity, which dominates our spirit of Thanksgiving.

While it is a good thing to have a special day set aside annually for a Thanksgiving observance, as far as we are concerned, every day is Thanksgiving Day. Our unique advantage is that we know we must always live with a spirit of thanksgiving in our hearts.

THE NEGOTIATION:

Is Thanksgiving for us a way of life?

THE PRAYER:

Dear Lord, You have given us so much and done so much for us, we ask nothing more, but grateful hearts. Amen.

THE READING: Luke 17:11-19

NOVEMBER 25

WAITING

THE INSPIRATION:

"Vladimir: That passed the time.
Estragon: It would have passed in any case.
Vladimir: Yes, but not so rapidly.
Estragon: What do we do now?
Vladimir: I don't know.
Estragon: Let's go.
Vladimir: We can't.
Estragon: Why not?
Vladimir: We're waiting for Godot.
Estragon: (despairingly), Ah!"

            – Samuel Beckett

THE MEDITATION:

Who is Godot? The dramatist himself doesn't know. We must decide for ourselves who our Godot is. Our Godot is that for which we wait: our ship to come in, our compulsion for alcohol to cease, reconciliation with those whom we alienated, a promotion on the job, retirement, and so on. As in the play, Godot is not as important as the waiting itself. My waiting for something to happen that will give ultimate meaning to life, we rob ourselves from the meaning, which is realizable in the present. We can be distracted from our waiting by sideshows that are meaningless. Bring absorbed with future goals prevents us from living in spontaneity and abundance.

Meaning is beyond time. The Resurrection of Jesus Christ has eternal significance, but only if it brings new life to us in the present does it have meaning. The meaning of life is not disclosed by our reasoning or by our waiting for some new revelation. Meaning is revealed in a moment of existence. We live by grace, we are held by faith, and the meaning in the moment surprises us. While we hope for, and have faith in, the life of the world to come, we do not look for things to do to "ass the time;" we live eternally while waiting.

THE NEGOTIATION:

Have we learned the difference between passing time and living?

THE PRAYER:

Help us, O Lord, to make the most of our time, using the present opportunity to the full, for we know "the days are evil." Amen.

THE READING: Psalm 130:1-8

NOVEMBER 26

OUR NEGATIVE VALUE

THE INSPIRATION:

"A man may be if value to another man, not because he wishes to be important, not because he possesses some inner wealth of soul, no because of something he is, but because of what he is—not. His importance may consist in his poverty, in his hopes and fears, in his waiting and hurrying, in the direction of his whole being towards what lies beyond his horizon and beyond his power. The importance of an apostle is negative rather than positive. In him a void becomes visible. And for this reason he is something to others: he is able to share grace with them . . . The Spirit gives grace through him." --Karl Barth

THE MEDITATION:

Our experience with abusing alcohol makes us vulnerable to other people, not because of our strength but because of our weakness. It is not our wealth, but our poverty, which makes us important to others. It is through being wounded that we become effective healers. The fact that we have fallen gives us accessibility and ability to help others rise. Our recovery from alcohol abuse is not only for our own enjoyment, but for the enhancement of the quality of others' lives. Our experience becomes our calling.

We are called and sent to heal, reconcile, buildup, and service others. An apostle is literally one who is sent. Through the negative history God sent us to share his grace with others. We are especially equipped to identify with the minister to other alcohol abusers. But our ministry does not stop there. While alcohol abuse focuses on certain character defects and exaggerates certain human needs, all people have identical basic needs: i.e., transcendence, meaning, relatedness. Our past, as negative as it may have been, equips us with a special humanness and humaneness through which God's Spirit gives grace to others.

THE NEGOTIATION:

How valuable is our negative experience to others?

THE PRAYER:

You are always ready, O Lord, to bring good out of evil. We pray that our negative experience may prove to be a blessing not only to ourselves but to others. Amen.

THE READING: Romans 4:13-25

NOVEMBER 27

ADVENT

THE INSPIRATION:

"Remember how critical the moment is. It is time for you to wake out of sleep, for deliverance is nearer to us now than it was when first we believed. It is far on in the night; day is near. Let us therefore throw off the deeds of darkness and put on our armour as soldiers of the light. Let us behave with decency as befits the day: no reveling or drunkenness, no debauchery or vice, no quarrels or jealousies! Let Christ Jesus himself be the armour that you wear; give no more thought to satisfying the bodily appetites.
—Romans 13:11-14.

THE MEDITATION:

The First Sunday in Advent, New Year's Day in the Church Year, comes on the last Sunday in November or the first Sunday in December—or, more accurately, on the Sunday nearest to St. Andrew's Day, which is November 30th. These four Sundays anticipate Christmas and help us to prepare for its celebration. Advent is preparation for Christ's coming; its mood is joy, anticipation, and excitement.

This is a busy time for most people. There is much preparation that goes into the secular observance of Christmas. We need especially, therefore, the spirit and mood which Advent provides. We need to "remember how critical the moment is." Advent calls us to prepare our hearts for Christ's three-fold coming: his coming in the past in history at Bethlehem, his coming in the future in an eschatological sense, and his coming in the present through Word and Sacrament. This time is ripe! There is no time for "reveling or drunkenness," only time for sobriety and serenity, "for deliverance is nearer to us than it was when we first believes." Christ's coming demands preparation. Christmas without Advent is a farce.

THE NEGOTIATION:

Are we ready to get ready for Christ's coming?

THE PRAYER:

Excite our hearts, Lord, to prepare the way for Your only Son. By his coming give us strength in our conflicts and throw light on the paths we travel in our broken, fear-filled world. Amen. —Collect for Advent

THE READING: Isaiah 2:1-5

NOVEMBER 28

INVISIBILITY

THE INSPIRATION:

"I am an invisible man. No, I am not a spook like those who haunted Edgar Allen Poe . . . I am a man of substance, of flesh and bone, fiber and liquids—and I might even be said to possess a mind. I am invisible, understand, simply because people refuse to see me. . . When they approach me they see only my surroundings, themselves, or figments of their imagination—indeed, everything and anything except me." --Ralph Ellison

THE MEDITATION:

We may be invisible to other people. There are two reasons for this. The first is that these others are blind to us. They do not see us as human beings with needs and wants, sorrows and joys. There was a time perhaps when we were recognized only as nuisances, drunks, objects that cause vexation. Even now we are not always seen as true, struggling human beings that we are. Secondly, we may be invisible to other people because we fail to reveal ourselves to them. Others fail to see us because we fear taking the risk of showing them our true human identity. If we wear masks to cover our weakness and try only to show our strengths, we remain invisible, unrecognized as human persons. We have a deep need to be seen.

We also have a deep need to see other people. We need to remove our blinders and recognize all others as human beings with the same hurts and pleasures we experience. Of relevance to us is the old question, "Is it of no concern to you who pass by? If only you would look and see: is there any agony . . ." (Lamentations 1:12). We pass by many people every day who are invisible to us because we will not take the time or trouble and see if there is any human agony. When we exaggerate our hurts and pains, other people become invisible to us.

THE NEGOTIATION:

What can we do to improve our visibility and the visibility of others?

THE PRAYER:

Dear Lord, give us the courage to reveal ourselves to others and help us to see and respond to the needs of others whom we pass by in our daily lives. Amen.

THE READING: 1 Peter 3:8-18

NOVEMBER 29

WILLPOWER

THE INSPIRATION:

"The strength of the will is enormous. There is no such thing as a weak will. A man often says his will is weak because he cannot resist temptations. Or a man is accused of lack of willpower because he does not follow through the work to which he sets his hand. On the contrary, he has such colossal willpower that he follows his own inclinations, irrespective of the demands of the situation." --Paul Campbell and Peter Howard

THE MEDITATION:

How many times, during the days of alcohol abuse, were we told, "If only you would use a little willpower, you could lick your drinking problem?" In some cases the advice may have been quite accurate. However, when dealing with a psychological dependence and physical addiction, much more than willpower is required. We then need a program which will enable us to revamp our entire selves. In any event, as far as a drinking problem is concerned, what we need more than willpower is won't power.

Once the dependence and addiction is broken, however, willpower plays an enormous role in our sobriety and serenity. As soon as we learn that we can exist without alcohol, our wills take over our lives. Victor Hugo said, "People do not lack strength, they lack will." We use "lack of willpower" as a cop-out to do and not to do a lot of things. Most often we hear ourselves saying, "I can't," when what we really mean is, "I won't."

Jesus said, "I have come . . . not to do my own will, but the will of him who sent me" (John 6:38). He asks us to join him in doing God's will. When we turn our lives and wills over to God, we learn what serenity is. Turning over our self will is the most difficult, important, and rewarding thing in life.

THE NEGOTIATION:

Can our will and God's will be one and the same?

THE PRAYER:

Not mine, not mine the choice
In things or great or small;
Be Thou my Guide, my Strength,
My Wisdom and my All. Amen. –Horatius Bonar

THE READING: John 4:31-42

NOVEMBER 30

ST. ANDREW

THE INSPIRATION:

"One of the two who followed Jesus . . . was Andrew, Simon Peter's brother. The first thing he did was to find his brother Simon. He said to him, 'We have found the Messiah' (which is the Hebrew for 'Christ'). He brought Simon to Jesus . . ." --John 1:40-42

THE MEDITATION:

Andrew was born in Bethsaida in Galilee. He was a fisherman by trade, the brother of Simon Peter, and the first apostle to follow Jesus. Tradition claims that he was martyred at Patras in Achaia on November 30th. He has been commemorated by the Church on this day since the fourth century.

If anyone ever had reason to develop a "little brother complex," it would be Andrew. He was completely over-shadowed by his "big brother" Peter. Andrew is constantly identified in the New Testament as the brother of Peter—outside of that fact practically nothing is known of him. However, Andrew was the first to follow Jesus; and the first, and maybe most important thing he ever did, was to go and tell Peter. "We have found the Messiah." Andrew's greatest deed may have been his first—bringing Peter to Jesus. Andrew, from then on, remained in the background, while Peter became the first great leader of the Early Church.

We never know how important little deeds may turn out to be. Little acts of kindness, little remembrances of love, little displays of concern may change people's lives and, indeed, the course of history. There may have been little deeds of kindness done for us, which were considered insignificant at the time, which brought us to the road of sobriety and serenity. Without Andrew, perhaps the Church would have no Peter, without Barnabus, no Paul.

THE NEGOTIATION:

What little deed of kindness can we do for someone today?

THE PRAYER:

Almighty God, as the apostle Andrew readily obeyed the call of Christ and followed him without delay, grant that we, called by Your holy Word, may offer ourselves in glad obedience to Your service. Amen. –Collect for St. Andrew

THE READING: John 1:35-42

DECEMBER 1

THE CHURCH YEAR

THE INSPIRATION:

"The heart of the Christian message is God's revelation of himself, in time in the person of Jesus Christ, his Son. God's salvation is revealed in the stream of human history. The manger at Bethlehem, the Virgin Mary, the disciples, the cross on Calvary, the empty tomb in the garden, we all 'in time,' and were transfigured by the eternal presence of God in Christ. Christian faith is rooted in the belief that God has acted in Christ in human history. It was a unique action. . . God chose the time for time and eternity to meet, and time can never be the same again. –Edward Horn

THE MEDITATION:

In Advent as we begin a new Church Year we are reminded that just as we have a civil calendar with its months and seasons, so the Church has a liturgical calendar—the Church Year. The Church Year seeks to relate all time to the redemptive purposes of God. The major events of the life of Jesus pass in review perennially. While we understand that no system of periscopes or calendar is enjoined by God, the need for some order and plan must be conceded if the whole counsel of God for our salvation is to be presented. The Church Year is a proven and time-honored system of this presentation.

By observing the Church Year we walk with Jesus: we anticipate his coming in Advent, we celebrate the Incarnation at Christmas, his manifestation of himself to the world in Epiphany, his passion in Lent, his Resurrection on Eastern and its season, his Ascension, his gift of the Holy Spirit on Pentecost, and his teachings during the "growing" season of Pentecost.

Just as we need a system to follow in our daily devotions to help us practice the presence of God, so we need a system to guide our public worship. It is this practice which enables us to maintain sobriety and grow in serenity.

THE NEGOTIATION:

Have we discovered the advantages of living by the Church Year?

THE PRAYER:

We thank You for the revelation of Yourself in the person and message of Jesus Christ. Help us to walk with Your Son through the year that we may experience in our lives Your unique action in history. Amen.

THE READING: 1 Thessalonians 5:1-11

DECEMBER 2

THE HERD

THE INSPIRATION:

"Daisy: Let things just take their course. What can we do about it?
Berenger: They've all gone mad. The world is sick. They're all sick.
Daisy: We shan't be the ones to cure them.
Berenger: How can we live in the same house with them?
Daisy: We must be sensible. We must adapt ourselves and try and get on with them.
Berenger: They can't understand us.
Daisy: They must. There's no other way.
Berenger: Do you understand them?
Daisy: Not yet. But we must try to understand the way their minds work, and learn
                their language."
                                        −Eugene Ionesco

THE MEDITATION:

There may be times when we feel the whole world has gone mad. And perhaps we're right. We live in a world that believes in violence, believes in alcohol and drugs, believes in money, believes that bigger means better, and believes that the majority is right. When feeling out of step with that world, we better check out feelings—with the Gospel. Is this or that way of the world in line with the life and message of Jesus Christ? And if the world is out of line, what can we do about it? Can we curse them? Can we live with them? Can they understand us? Can we understand them? Can we learn their language? How far can we go without compromising ourselves and our faith in the Gospel?

Daisy went too far. She began thinking that rhinoceroses were real people. She saw how "happy" they were. Finally she exclaims, "They're like gods." It is not long after that the slips away from Berenger and joins the herd—she becomes a rhinoceros!

It takes courage, faith, and grace to stand up for our conviction when the herd is going in a different direction. God's ways are not the ways of the herd. We need constantly to pray, "Teach me Thy way, O Lord" (Psalm 27:11). Learning and following God's way is the only way to serenity.

THE NEGOTIATION:

Are there ways in which we have joined the herd?

THE PRAYER:

Teach us Your ways, O Lord, and give us the courage, faith, and strength to reject the herd, never compromising the mission to which You have called us. Amen.

THE READING: Psalm 27:1-14

DECEMBER 3

THE MEANING FACTOR

THE INSPIRATION:

"Drink! For you know now whence you came, nor why;
Drink! For you know not why you go, nor where." --Omar Khayyam

"O God, that men should put an enemy in their mouths to steal way their brains! That we
should, with joy, pleasance, revel, and applause, transform ourselves into beasts!" --Shakespeare

THE MEDITATION:

If we don't know where we come from, nor why, nor where we're going, we may as well steal
away our brains and turn ourselves into beasts. It is this very lack of meaning that played an important
part in the etiology of our alcohol abuse. Sooner or later we learn that this "meaning factor" which
caused the abuse is also necessary in curing and preventing it.

We will however, of course, fully comprehend the mystery of life. Our lives are, as Eugene
O'Neill suggests, "strange dark interludes in the electrical display of God the Father." While the meaning
factor" evades us, we nonetheless "make sense" out of life by knowing God as the Source, Guide, and
Goal in all that is. This knowing is our faith which gives meaning to life.

Our problem, as John Knox says, "is not out ignorance, or even our weakness, but out
homesickness." What we need most is not answers to the ultimate questions about our existence,
others, and God, which will enable us to hear the unanswered and unanswerable questions. The
questions will either destroy us, driving us to cynicism, despair, or alcohol abuse, or lead us to God in
whose presence alone we can face the unknown meaning of our existence through faith in him as
Source, Guide, and Goal of all that is. And then we can find peace and joy knowing that the ultimate
issues of life are not in our hands or subject to our control.

THE NEGOTIATION:

Are we doing business with the "meaning factor"?

THE PRAYER:

O Lord, of all wisdom and knowledge, may our homesickness for You, lead us into Your presence
where we can find peace and joy in living out Your purpose and meaning for us. Amen.

THE READING: Psalm 73:1-28

DECEMBER 4

FEAR IS FOR WORMS

THE INSPIRATION:

"Do not look forward to the changes and chances of this life in fear; rather look to them with hope that, as they arise, God, whose you are, will deliver you out of them. He has kept you hitherto,--do you but hold fast to his dear hand, and he will lead you safely through all things . . . The same everlasting Father who cares for you today, will take care of you tomorrow, and every day. Either he will shield you from suffering, or he will give you unfailing strength to bear it. Be at peace then, and put aside all anxious thoughts and imaginations." --Francis de Sales

THE MEDITATION:

Our society, which seems to be "in-between cultures," has been properly called "the age of anxiety." Not knowing what the emerging culture will be like, the only thing we can count on is the inevitability of change. It is not enough for us to tell one another, "Don't be anxious." We need to point one another to the Father who says, "For I, the Lord your God, take you by the right hand; I say to you, Do not fear; it is I who help you, fear not, Jacob you worm. . . . It is I who help you, says the Lord" (Isaiah 41:13-14).

Jacob is called a worm. A worm has every reason to fear. A worm does underground to avoid the threats of change and the issues that face our times. Worms cannot stand up and face life with courage and faith and hope. As worms we submerged ourselves into the darkness of alcohol abuse. But we have been called into the light. A transformation is taking place in us. We are growing legs and arms and hands. We can now stand erect and grasp the hand of the Father which he extends to us. We are no longer worms—we are children of the heavenly Father. With our hand held by his we need not d=fear not be anxious what change tomorrow may bring.

THE NEGOTIATION:

Do we avoid the issues that face our times because of fear?

THE PRAYER:

With our hand in Yours, O Lord, may we find peace and security. Use us as Your instruments to bring about this changes that will make our world a more living place. Amen.

THE READING: Isaiah 41:11-29

DECEMBER 5

CONSECRATED CHICKEN SOUP

THE INSPIRATION:

"If it's the religious life you want, you ought to know right now that you're missing out on every single . . . religious action that's going on around this house. You don't even have sense enough to drink when someone brings you a cup of consecrates chicken soup—which is the only kind of chicken soup Bessie every brings to anyone." --J. D. Salinger

THE MEDITATION:

Thus Zooey speaks to Franny who had repeatedly refused Bessie's offer of a bowl of hot chicken soup. It was Bessie's way of demonstrating her love and concern for Franny who has depressed and all mixed up about life and religion. Notice, it was "consecrated" chicken soup. Bessie's deed constitutes a religious action. Any gift given or deed performed out of love and compassion is consecrated and religious. It's what Jesus is talking about when he speaks of giving a cup of cold water in his name (Matthew 10:43).

In the pre-Christmas season of Advent, when we are so often reminded of the dangers of materialism, perhaps a word in its defense is in order. Material things are consecrated when taken up in the hands of love: a basin of water, a towel, a cup, a loaf of bread—a bowl of chicken soup.

Gifts, of course, may be given because custom demands or as guilt offerings or in order to evade involvement, but when given with love and compassion they are consecrated. Consecrated gifts and deeds have contributed to our recovery from alcohol abuse. A cup of cold water, a bowl of chicken soup, a band-aid, a cup of coffee, a warm hand shake, a pat on the back—do we recognize them as consecrated gifts and deeds?

THE NEGOTIATION:

What consecrated actions can we engage in today?

THE PRAYER:

We thank you, O Lord, for material things. Help us to use them in love and compassion. And enable us to recognize them as consecrated when offered to us. Amen.

THE READING: Genesis 1:31 and Luke 21:1-4

DECEMBER 6

CURES FOR LONELINESS

THE INSPIRATION:

"Immortal drunkenness! What tribute can we ever pay, what song can we sing, what swelling praise can be sufficient to express the joy, the gratefulness and the love which we, who have known youth and hunger . . . have owed to alcohol? We are so lost, so lonely, so forsaken: . . . immense and savage skies bend over us, and we have no door!" --Thomas Wolfe

THE MEDITATION:

In the mood of a psalmist the results of alcohol abuse are praised and lamented. And why not when alcohol is used to attempt to satisfy our universal and religious need for relatedness? One of our "reasons" for turning to alcohol was to ease the pain of broken relationships. Before we realized it, a new relationship was established—with alcohol. But sooner or later we became aware that the relationship with alcohol only put more strain on our other relationships. We drank to "cure" our loneliness, but out drinking only brought deeper loneliness.
"All the world is sad and dreary, Everywhere I roam."
These words reflect the pathos of loneliness of an alcohol abusers inner world. Their author died in the alcoholic ward of New York's Bellevue Hospital at the age of thirty-eight. By the grace of God we have discovered another way to deal with our relatedness needs. In our powerlessness we opened ourselves to God's power. Broken relationships with God and others are mended. Reconciliation becomes the theme of our lives. Now, when we experience loneliness, we know to whom we can turn. We no longer need to be like a lonely bird "that flutters on the roof-top" (Psalm 102:7).

THE NEGOTIATION:

Is it possible that the cure for loneliness is solitude?

THE PRAYER:

You know, O Lord, the pain of loneliness in our inner world. Help us to respond to Your perpetual offer of Your presence that we might experience reconciliation and intimacy with You and others. Amen.

THE READING: Mark 1:35-39

DECEMBER 7

GOD'S LANGUAGES

THE INSPIRATION:

"God speaks to you in a language all his own, and it is not always the same language. Sometimes it is in the language of conscience, and the voice is the stern voice of duty. Sometimes he speaks in the language of beauty, the most visual of all languages, but lost of many an eye that has been blinded by vulgarity and ugliness. To some who are able to understand, he speaks in the language of suffering, the most universal of all languages, the most easily misunderstood, and the one capable of saying things that none of the others can say." --Theodore Parker Ferris

THE MEDITATION:

The list is not complete. Each of us could extend the number of languages that God speaks from our own experience. The main point is that God speaks in many ways and it is up to us to be open to hear, and translate if necessary, his languages in our own experience. God's most intimate language is not spoken about us or at us or above us but within us. God speaks within our conscience not only telling us the difference between right and wrong, but also gives us guidance concerning what to do when two or more things are good. He helps us distinguish between that which is right and that which is good.

God speaks most intimately within us through the language of suffering: and, in our case, the suffering involved with alcohol abuse. It is here, if we will listen and understand, that he communicates our need for his abiding presence and the values and priorities which give meaning to our existence.

THE NEGOTIATION:

What are the languages which God speaks within us?

THE PRAYER:

I was wandering like a lost sheep, searching outside of myself for that which was within. I ran through all the streets and squares of this great city, the world, searching for Thee, O God, and I found Thee not, because I sought Thee wrongly. Thou wert within me, and I sought Thee without. Amen. -- Augustine

THE READING: Acts 2:5-13

DECEMBER 8

BE ALERT

THE INSPIRATION:

"Be alert, be wakeful. You do not know when the moment comes. It is like a man away from home; he has left his house and put his servants in charge, each with his own work to do and he has ordered the door-keeper to stay awake. Keep awake, then, for you do not know when the master of the house is coming." --Mark 13:33-35

THE MEDITATION:

The theme of Advent is preparation and anticipation of Christ's coming. Jesus and his disciples are engaged in an eschatological discussion: the second coming is the topic of their conversation. Jesus doesn't emphasize the questions dealing with when or where, but rather the manner of waiting: "Be alert," he says. Let us not get involved with playing Bible games and try to figure out when the second coming will take place. The Bible is more of a compass than it is a road map or blueprint dealing with the future.

Jesus is concerned that we stay alert and keep busy at the work he has given us to do. The second coming, the end of this age will come in God's time. It may come collectively tomorrow, next month, or in many years, or it may come individually at anytime when we die. The important thing for us is to be ready at all times. Our readiness is determined by our being involved in our Master's work.

There is a great element of urgency here. For Jesus the hour is now! Anticipation means being alert each moment. To have faith simply means to be faithful at each moment. Through our alcohol abuse we became accustomed to living in the past and for the future. Serenity means a reorientation for us toward living the moment. The urgency of this makes Advent a symbol of our total life-style, not merely a mood ("the Christmas spirit") we experience each December.

THE NEGOTIATION:

Are we alert to Christ's coming to us each moment?

THE PRAYER:

Stir up Your power, Lord, and come. Remove the hindrance of our sins and make us ready for the season of celebration, to receive You in joy and service You forever. Amen. –Collect for the Fourth Sunday in Advent

THE READING: Mark 13:3-37

DECEMBER 9

THE WAY, THE TRUTH, AND THE LIFE

THE INSPIRATION:

"He is the way.
Follow him through the Land of Unlikeness;
You will see rare beasts, and have unique adventures.

He is the truth.
Seek him in the Kingdom of Anxiety;
You will come to a great city that has expected your return for years.

He is the Life.
Love him in the World of the Flesh;
And at your marriage all its occasions shall dance for Joy."
                                                    --W. H. Auden

THE MEDITATION:

The definite article "the" implies that there is only one Way, only one Truth, and only one Life. And yet we have tried another way: the way of alcohol which led to destruction, another truth: the truth of alcohol which turned out to be a lie, and another life: the life of alcohol which leads to death. We are, therefore extremely sensitive to "the" Way, "the" Truth, and "the" Life that Jesus offers (John 14:6).

"I am the way." Jesus does not merely point the way, he is the Way. Union with Jesus and his way of living is the one sure way to God. It is this concept that gave rise to the earliest name by which Christians were known: people of the Way (Acts 24:14). "I am the truth." Jesus does not just point to truth, he is the Truth. The Truth is God's ultimate reality which is the goal of all thought and effort. "I am the life." Not the way to life, but the Life. Authentic, abundant, and external living are perceived in the life of Christ and extended to us. As we live in the Land of Unlikeness, the Kingdom of Anxiety, and the World of the Flesh, Christ is our Way, our Truth, and our Life.

THE NEGOTIATION:

Will we allow the Way, Truth, and Life to be outs today?

THE PRAYER:

O Lord, open up our hearts and minds to the possibilities of living authentically, abundantly, and eternally this day. Unite us with Christ that his way, truth, and life may be ours. Amen.

THE READING: John 14:6-14

DECEMBER 10

SEEDS

THE INSPIRATION:

"Willy Loman: Oh, I'd better hurry. I've got to get some seeds. I've got to get some seeds, right away. Nothing's planted. I don't have a thing in the ground." --Arthur Miller

"Remember: sparse sowing, sparse reaping; sow bountifully, and you will reap bountifully." --2 Corinthians 9:6

THE MEDITATION:

For Willy Loman, in "Death of a Salesman," time was running out. He had no seeds in the ground. Life had lost its meaning. For Willy, it was too late; for soon he was to take his own life. If only he knew that it is in giving of one's self that life has purpose. While we were abusing alcohol we were too tied up with ourselves. But, by the grace of God, time did not run out on us. We were given a second chance, a new birth. With sobriety we became increasingly aware that the meaning and purpose of life is to be found in planting seeds: giving of ourselves.

Serenity begins to take hold when we give of ourselves cheerfully. We begin to discover the truth of what Paul talks about: "God loves a cheerful giver" (2 Corinthians 9:7). All that we have and all that we are is provided by God. And so Paul continues, "He who provides seed for sowing and bread for food will provide the seed for you to sow." There is, therefore, meaning and purpose for all that we have and are. We have achieved sobriety and are on the road to serenity for a good purpose – God's purpose. He has provided us seed to sow. Our sowing can only, therefore, be done in the spirit of thanksgiving. Sobriety and serenity are gifts from God that must be given in order to be retained. The more we give of ourselves, the richer we become.

THE NEGOTIATION:

What seed will we cheerfully and gratefully sow this day?

THE PRAYER:

Dear Lord, You have so richly provided us with good gifts; help us to find Your meaning and purpose for these gifts as we learn to give of ourselves cheerfully and with thanksgiving to You. Amen.

THE READING: 2 Corinthians 9:6-15

DECEMBER 11

TEMPORARITY

THE INSPIRATION:

"We all live temporary lives . . . We think that just for now things are going badly, that we have to adapt just for now, and even humiliate ourselves, but that all this is temporary. Real life will start someday. We prepare to die with the complaint that we've never really lived . . . You live only once, and for this one time you live a temporary life, in the vain hope that one day real life will begin. That's how we exist . . . No one thinks that what he does everyday is anything but temporary. No one is in a position to say, 'From now on . . . my life has really started.'"

THE MEDITATION:

The notion of the temporarity of life is appealed to by one of our leading beer manufacturers: "You only go around one in your life." Therefore live it with "gusto". The implication is: since life is only temporary, let us live it with the zest which alcohol provides. Long ago Isaiah warned against those whose philosophy of life is "Let us eat and drink; for tomorrow we die: (Isaiah 22:13). The "Wine, Women (Men) and Song" philosophy of life is for those who have no way to deal with the reality of death and cannot perceive life beyond its physical dimension.

The Gospel proclaims that life is not temporary, but rather linked to the eternal purposes of God "who has shown us such love, and in his grace has given us such unfailing encouragement and such bright hopes" (2 Thessalonians 2:16). The Gospel deals with the "victory" and "sting" of death (1 Corinthians 15:55). The Gospel sees through life's physical dimension: "Though our outward humanity is in decay, yet day by day we are inwardly renewed. Our troubles are slight and short lives; and their outcomes an external glory which outweighs them far" (2 Corinthians 4:16-17).

THE NEGOTIATION:

What eternal significance will today have for us?

THE PRAYER:

Dear Lord, we thank You that day-by-day we are inwardly renewed by Your eternal Spirit. Help us, who are physically temporary, to perceive the eternal significance of our daily lives. Amen.

THE READING: 2 Thessalonians 2:13-3:5

DECEMBER 12

IN WHOSE IMAGE?

THE INSPIRATION:

"Julian: I . . . I lost my faith. In God . . . I . . . declined . . . I . . . shriveled into myself; a glass dome . . . descended, and it seemed I was out of reach, unreachable, finally reaching, in this . . . paralysis, of sorts. I . . . put myself in a mental home . . . I could not reconcile myself to the chasm between the nature of God and the use to which men put . . . God." --Edward Albee

THE MEDITATION:

Thus Julian in "Tiny Alice" describes a period in his past. At another point he says, "It is God the mover, not God the puppet; God the creator, not the God created by man. . . Men create a false God in their own image, it is easier for them!" In "Inherit the Wind" Lawrence and Lee have Bertram Cates say virtually the same: "God created Man in his own image—and Man, being a gentleman, returned the compliment." The entire Biblical history of the failure of humanity can be properly summarized in these terms: "Human beings try to create God in their image."

When we were in the grips of alcohol abuse we were great ones to try to create God in our image, to make a puppet of him, to use him for our purposes. Perhaps our sobriety, and certainly our serenity, commenced when we were willing to let God be God and began looking for the uses to which he could put us. Every now and then we may still find ourselves reverting back to our almost innate desire to have a God in our own image. It's easier for us to have a God like ourselves who will condone our violence, revenge, resentments, procrastinations, and all the evil done and the good left undone. But as we practice God's presence and meditate on the life, message, and mission of Jesus, we can only know the God of love who never condones our lack of love. Try as we may to create God in our image, God remains who he is: Love.

THE NEGOTIATION:

What are some of the ways we try to create God in our image?

THE PRAYER:

Dear Lord, forgive our foolish ways. Help us always to acknowledge You as Love, and enable us to reflect your image in our lives that we may be used by You. Amen.

THE READING: Colossians 1:13-27

DECEMBER 13

ASPIRATORY PRAYER

THE INSPIRATION:

"There is . . . one kind of prayer which all . . . types and levels of spirituality can use and make their own: and which is unequalled in psychological and religious effectiveness. This is the so-called 'prayer of aspirations': the frequent and attentive use of little phrases of love and worship which may help us, as it were, to keep our minds pointing the right way, and never lose their power of forming and maintaining in us an adoring temper of soul . . . The habit as aspiration is difficult to form, but once acquired exerts a growing influence over the soul's life . . . The most important thing in prayer is never what we say or ask for, but our attitude towards God." --Evelyn Underhill

THE MEDITATION:

Aspiratory prayer can plan an important role in our sobriety and serenity. The Psalms, the "Confession" of St. Augustine, the "Imitation of Christ," and other devotional classics, are full of such aspiratory prayers. They stretch and re-stretch our spiritual muscles; and, even in the stuffiest surroundings, can help us take deep breaths of spiritual refreshment. In any situation and under any conceivable circumstances aspiratory prayer is in order. These brief phrases of love and worship enable us to maintain the presence of God.

In the early stage of sobriety such aspirations as "Be merciful to me, O Lord," or "Keep me, O God," may prove helpful. As time goes by our aspirations will become less "us" and more "God" centered. "I will exalt thee, O Lord," "Praise be to God," and "I love Thee, O Lord," are examples of aspirations that we may repeatedly utter in our hearts throughout the day. The habit is difficult to acquire, but the results are worth the effort.

THE NEGOTIATION:

What will be our prayer of aspiration for this day?

THE PRAYER:

Be merciful to us, O Lord. Keep us, O God. We exalt in You, O Lord. Praise be to You, O God. We love You, O Lord. Be with us, O God. Bless Your name, O Lord. Amen.

THE READING: Psalm 30:1-12

DECEMBER 14

DARK NIGHT OF THE SOUL

THE INSPIRATION:

"It is most fitting and necessary, if the soul is to pass on to great things, that the dark night of contemplation should first of all annihilate and undo it in its meanness, bringing it into darkness, aridity, affliction and emptiness . . . (The soul must be) brought into emptiness and poverty and purged of all help, consolation and natural apprehension with respect to all things, both above and below. In this way, being empty, it is able indeed to be poor in spirit and freed from the old (Nature), in order to live that new and blessed life which is attained by means of this dark night, which is the state of union with God." --St. John of the Cross

THE MEDITATION:

Sobriety and serenity demand discipline. An important part of that discipline are these daily devotion periods when we negotiate with ourselves and God who plucks the world out of our hearts and hurls the world into our hearts. This enables us to continue through the day with prayers of aspiration and the practice of the presence of God. Another important discipline for us is our weekly corporate worship with the fellowship of Christ's Church. The discipline takes other forms: our reading and studying, Bible studies, prayer groups, theological discussions with friends—any activities which inspire and equip us for service to God.

Some of us feel the need occasionally for an extended period of spiritual refreshment: a retreat, the dark night of contemplation. By getting away by ourselves for a day or more in meditation, we discover new meaning and zest to live that new and blessed life which is ours in Christ. By taking the time and effort to empty ourselves in God's presence we gain a fresh perspective of ourselves, our God, and our world. Union with God grows out of the dark night of contemplation.

THE NEGOTIATION:

Is the dark night of contemplation a priority for us?

THE PRAYER:

We thank You, O Lord, for the new life, which is ours by Your grace. We pray that You would give us the motivation to strengthen our union with You and our love for all Your children. Amen.

THE READING: Ephesians 1:3-10

DECEMBER 15

THE HOUND OF HEAVEN

THE INSPIRATION:

"I fled Him, down the nights and down the days;
I fled Him, down the arches of the years;
I fled Him, down the labyrinthine ways
Of my own mind; and in the midst of tears
I hid from Him, and under running laughter." --Francis Thompson

THE MEDITATION:

Could it be that when we feel we are desperately searching for God, we are actually fleeing from him? This was certainly true for us down the nights and down the days of alcohol abuse. While under the impression we were looking for God, we were indeed running away from him. A part of our problem is that we search for a God of our own making. But God refuses to be created in our image. It isn't that he evades us, but rather the labyrinthine ways of our own minds lead us away from him.

In the final analysis we can never find God—it is always God who finds us. We are the pursued. He bounds us. He relentlessly keeps after us. He reveals himself to us through his Word, through Christ and the Gospel, through nature, through history, through the witness and writings of other people. Try as we may to hide from him, the Hound of Heaven never gives up his pursuit,

Adam was the first to try to hide from God—he hid behind a tree in the Garden of Eden (Genesis 3:8). Ever since, we humans have attempted the same ridiculous game. When we play hide-and-go-seek with God we always lose. Sooner or later, in our time or his, he is going to find us and take hold of us. We may as well surrender ourselves to him now, and let him be the God of love and righteousness that he reveals himself to be.

THE NEGOTIATION:

In what ways do we still try to hide from God?

THE PRAYER:

We thank You, O Lord, that you relentlessly pursue us. Keep us from running away from You. Give us the strength to surrender to You and live under You in Your Kingdom. Amen.

THE READING: Genesis 3:1-13

DECEMBER 16

MILK AND SOLID FOOD

THE INSPIRATION:

"Larry: All I know is I'm sick of life! I'm through! I've forgotten myself! I'm drowned and contented on the bottom of a bottle. Honor, or dishonor, faith or treachery are nothing to me but the opposite of the same stupidity, which is ruler, and King of life, and in the end they rot into dust in the same grave. All things are the same meaningless joke to me, for they grin at me from the one skull of death." --Eugene O'Neill

THE MEDITATION:

The relationship between alcohol abuse and religious quest to deal with meaninglessness is a frequent theme in literature. We know what Larry is talking about: "All things are the same meaningless joke." We know too, that the contentment on the bottom of a bottle is not in finding meaning but rather in temporarily removing the pain of meaninglessness.

Now then can we make sense out of life? How can we deal with the innate will-to-meaning with which we are plagued? Is there a key to the mystery of life? Is there some simple clue or slogan that will clear away the fog that distresses us? Simple answers appeal to us, and they may bring relief for a time, but they will not bring lasting satisfaction because we are created with the painful ability to think.

The closest we can come to a simple key which opens up the meaning of life is, "Put love first" (1 Corinthians 14:11), and again the words of Jesus, "Set your mind on God's Kingdom and his justice before everything else, and all the rest will come to you as well" (Matthew 6:33). Simple? perhaps, but at the same time, extremely profound. We begin with simple answers and simple questions but as we grow in grace our diet must change from milk to solid foods (Hebrew 5:15-16). As we grow, "all the rest" that Jesus talks about, will come to us.

THE NEGOTIATION:

Have we become stuck on a milk diet?

THE PRAYER:

In our need to be fed in our search for meaning, O Lord, we thank You for the food You provide. Help us never to be satisfied with milk when You offer us solid food. Amen.

THE READING: Hebrews 5:11-6:9

DECEMBER 17

DAY BY DAY PREPARATION

THE INSPIRATION:

"Day by day, Day by Day,
Oh, dear Lord, three things I pray
To see Thee more clearly, love Thee more dearly,
Follow Thee more nearly day by day, day by day." --Stephen Schwartz

THE MEDITATION:

One of the productions of the musical "Godspell" begins with John the Baptist wearing a sweatshirt with the word, "Prepare ye the way of the Lord." The Gospel story begins with John proclaiming the message: "Prepare a way for the Lord, clear a straight path for him" (Mark 1:3). John the Baptist is a prominent character during the Advent Season because his life and message dealt with preparing the way for the coming of Christ. The Advent spirit echoes those words of long ago, "Prepare a road for the Lord through the wilderness, clear a highway across the desert for our God" (Isaiah 40:3). In ancient days when word was received that a King or some important person was to visit a city, the people would go out and repair the road, remove the rocks, fill in the holes, straighten out the detours caused by washouts, and everything possible to make it smooth and safe.

The road we are to prepare is our heart. Advent bids us to build in our hearts a superhighway for the Lord. We need to bulldoze off the mountains of pride and prejudice, to fill in the valleys of neglect with deeds of love. This preparation is not completed at one time, but rather needs attention day by day.

We get involved with a lot of preparation for Christmas Day, let us not forget to prepare our hearts for Christ. Let us make sure it is the right road we are preparing, for Christ comes when and where we least expect. He comes not in the brightness of day but while shepherds watch their flocks by night. He comes not to proud Jerusalem but to humble Bethlehem. He comes not to the beautiful temple but to the smelly stable. The purpose of Advent is to bring us to Christ's incarnation on our knees, in awe, wonder and gratitude day by day.

THE NEGOTIATION:

Are we preparing the right road for Christ's coming?

THE PRAYER:

We thank You, O Lord, that You have laid Your son at the doorstep of our hearts. We pray that we may be prepared to receive him. Amen.

THE READING: Luke 3:1-17

DECEMBER 18

CLIMAX OF THE GOSPEL

THE INSPIRATION:

"Jesus said, . . . 'Happy are they who never saw me and yet have found faith.' There were indeed many other signs that Jesus performed in the presence of his disciples, which are not recorded in this book. Those here written have been recorded in order that you may hold the faith that Jesus is the Christ, the Son of God, and that through this faith you may possess eternal life by his name." --John 20:29-31

THE MEDITATION:

With these words John intended to conclude his Gospel. He related to us his over-all purpose for relating his account of Jesus' life and message—that we, through faith may possess eternal life. That is the purpose of the Gospel—it is for us and for all people. Eternal life may be a possession of ours, now. We need not wait, all of the fullness of God's grace is outs at this moment. "This is eternal life: to know Thee who alone art truly God, and Jesus Christ whom Thou hast sent" (John 17:3).

Just prior to stating the purpose of the Gospel, John brings it to its climax: Happy are they who never saw me and yet have found faith. The "they" of whom Jesus speaks are us. We, who have never seen Jesus physically, are the "happy" ones. We sometimes wish that we could have been contemporaries of Jesus so we could physically touch him. Thomas had that opportunity, but Jesus makes it clear that we, who have not seen him, have the real advantage.

Our serenity, and to some extent our sobriety, is dependent upon faith, not physical proof. It is with the eyes, ears, and hands of faith that we see, hear, and touch Jesus. Our faith makes Jesus just as real to us as he was to Thomas. And Jesus adds, "Happy" are we. The entire Gospel of John builds up to this happy climax.

THE NEGOTIATION:

Are we fully aware and appreciative of the advantage that is ours?

THE PRAYER:

We thank You, O Lord, for Your gracious Gospel through which we possess eternal life. We pray that we might grow in faith that we might experience more and more happiness and serenity in Your presence. Amen.

THE READING: John 20:24-31

DECEMBER 19

FRUITS OF DEVOTION

THE INSPIRATION:

"God commands all Christians . . . to bring forth the fruits of devotion, each according to his vocation and station in life. The practice of devotion ought to be adopted to the strength, the employments, and obligations of each individual . . . True devotion not only does no injury to any vocation or employment, but, on the contrary, adorns and beautified it . . . by devotion, the care of the family is rendered more peaceable, the love the husband and wife more sincere . . . and every employment more pleasant and agreeable." --Francis de Sales

THE MEDITATION:

Devotion is to be understood as the total framework of one's existence as a Christian: one's point of view, one's center of circumference, one's spirit, and one's work. It is not a description of something one does, but of what one is and how it informs every dimension of one's life. Our daily devotional periods are a part of our devotion.

The pragmatic results of devotional periods have been shown in a study by Harvard psychologists: 1) decreased oxygen consumption, heart rate, and metabolic rates; 2) increased electrical resistance of the skin; 3) heightened intensity of alpha brain waves; and 4) reduced production of lactic acid. Together these phenomena signify relaxation of tension and reduction of anxiety. Most of us are not very concerned about our lactic acid and the like. We look for, and often find, mystic experience, a sense of transcendence, a feeling of wholeness, being at home in one's inner sanctuary, being at peace with oneself, God, and others, with reconciliation, harmony, forgiveness, contentment, serenity, and commitment. The practice of devotion has two main objectives: to find, or be found by, God, and to be transformed into the pattern of Christ, and to be thus enabled to lead the active Christian life more effectively, which can only be when action is taken up in the name of Christ.

THE NEGOTIATION:

Has our motivation for devotion gone beyond our desire to stay sober?

THE PRAYER:

We thank You, O Lord, for the fruits of devotion. We pray that our devotion may be motivated by the sole desire to equip us for greater service to You. Amen.

THE READING: Hebrews 13:18-21

DECEMBER 20

WINTER

THE INSPIRATION:

"In the bleak mid-winter, Frosty wind made moan,
Earth stood hard as iron, Water like a stone;
Snow had fallen, snow on snow, snow on snow,
In the bleak mid-winter, Long ago.
Heaven cannot hold him, Nor earth sustain;
Heaven and earth shall flee away, When he comes to reign;
In the bleak mid-winter, A stable place sufficed
The Lord God Almighty, Jesus Christ." --Christiana Rossetti

THE MEDITATION:

The days are very short now and the nights cold. Over much of our land snow has fallen. Must of nature is dormant. Some allow the bleakness of the season to effect their spirits adversely, others are warmed in their hearts by the bare beauty of the season. Whether winter has a negative or positive effect on us, is up to us. We are responsible for our reactions to the environment. If we look for beauty we will find it; if we look for cheerlessness we will find it.

Overhanging these winter days in our culture is the spirit of Christmas. That spirit means many things to many people. For some it is a depressing time: a time when childhood memories of Christmas are gone, never to return; a time when something within us says that Christmas should be more than it is. It is to drown that "something," more than to celebrate nothing which makes this a time of such heavy drinking. While we were abusing alcohol perhaps there were Christmases that we can't remember, and others that we wish we could forget.

With sobriety, Christmas, like everything else, takes on new meaning. We are now open to the real spirit of Christmas which is the Spirit of Christ. It is a most exciting and beautiful time for us as we make room in our hearts for Christ to be born anew.

THE NEGOTIATION:

Are we ready to celebrate Christ being born anew in our hearts?

THE PRAYER:

Dear Lord, you have come and continue to come to us as we open our hearts to You. Hear our prayers and bring the warmth and light of Your Son into the dark and cold places in our hearts. Amen.

THE READING: Hebrews 10:5-10

DECEMBER 21

ST. THOMAS

THE INSPIRATION:

"Then Jesus spoke out plainly: 'Lazarus is dead. I am glad not to have been there; it will be for your good and for the good of your faith. But let us go to him.' Thomas, called 'the Twin,' said to his fellow disciples, 'Let us also go, that we may die with him.'" --John 11:14-16

THE MEDITATION:

Some liturgical calendars have wisely moved St. Thomas' Day to July 3rd to get it out of Advent. Thomas is the Aramaic form of the Greek "Didymus" which means "twin." While Thomas is referred to only four times in the New Testament, the biographical information presents him as slow to believe. The phrase "doubting Thomas" has survived through the centuries. Thomas doubted that Jesus could do anything for Lazarus. Thomas doubted where Jesus was going (John 14:5). Thomas doubted Jesus' Resurrection (John 20:25).

But before we are too harsh on Thomas, let us remember that his were honest doubts. It is through our honest doubts that we are led to deeper faith. Doubt is not the opposite of faith, but more often its prerequisite. We must never allow others to belittle us because of our doubts. If we honestly admit and deal with our doubts they become thresholds for spiritual growth. If we recall how dishonest we were without doubts while abusing alcohol, we begin to grasp this truth.

Let us remember too, that it was Thomas who made the great profession of faith: "My Lord and my God!" (John 20:28). And furthermore, tradition tells us that Thomas brought the Christian Gospel to India where he became a martyr for his faith at Madras. Thomas' doubting brought him to a faith that was willing to make the ultimate sacrifice. Perhaps he is mislabeled, and we should refer to him as "Faithful Thomas" rather than "doubting Thomas."

THE NEGOTIATION:

Do we have enough faith to thank God for our doubts?

THE PRAYER:

Almighty and ever-living God, You have given great and precious promises to those who believe. Grant us the perfect faith which overcomes all doubts. Amen. –Collect for St. Thomas

THE READING: John 11:1-16

DECEMBER 22

WHAT'S THE HURRY?

THE INSPIRATION:

"There is a way of life so hid with Christ in God that in the midst of the day's business one is inwardly lifting brief prayers, short ejaculations of praise, subdued whispers of adoration and of tender love to the Beyond that is within. No one need know about it . . . One can live in a well-nigh continuous state of unworded prayer, directed toward God, directed toward people and enterprises we have on our heart. There is no hurry about it all, it is a life unspeakable and full of glory, an inner world of splendor within which we, unworthy, may live. Some of you may wistfully long for it; it can be yours." --Thomas Kelly

THE MEDITATION:

It would be difficult to find a more eloquent, beautiful, and meaningful description of the practice of the presence of God than this inspiration. The phrase that jumps out at us during the Christmas "rush" is, "There is no hurry about it all." How much we need this inner world of splendor during these days when there is so much to be done: shopping, wrapping, decorating, cooking, etc. We often get so involved in all the external preparations that we forget "how silently the wondrous gift was given."

If only we would let Advent be Advent and Christmas, Christmas, we could concentrate of the Beyond that is within. Tied up with the Christmas "rush" there are, of course, the parties and the drinking that goes with them in our culture. In all of external business and rush there is available to us a life unspeakable and full of glory. It can be ours—if we truly want it. There is no need to hurry.

THE NEGOTIATION:

Will we allow the inner world of splendor to be ours?

THE PRAYER:

Slow us down, Lord. In all of our external preparations for Christmas, let us not miss the splendor of Christ's rebirth within us. Amen.

THE READING: Isaiah 9:2-7

DECEMBER 23

SEEING OTHERS

THE INSPIRATION:

"Emily: I can't go on. It goes so fast. We don't have time to look at one another. . . I didn't realize. So all that was going on and we never noticed . . . Oh, earth, you're too wonderful for anybody to realize you . . . Do human beings ever realize life while they live it?—every every minute? --Thornton Wilder

THE MEDITATION:

In "Our Town" Emily is given the opportunity to revisit her family after her death. Emily wanted her family and friends to "see" her, to express their love for her. But they were too busy making plans for the day. Emily felt like an object—a thing. She could not stand it. The failure of living p0eople to see her drove Emily back to the grave.

The Bible tells us that we are to love our neighbors as ourselves. This doesn't mean to have warm, sentimental feelings about our neighbors but to "see" them as individuals: individuals, indeed, for whom God sent his son into the world. It is the failure to be aware of the infinite moment and the living individuals that produces inhumanity, domestic conflict, and even war in the world. Do we really "see" the poor, minorities, alcohol abusers, drug addicts, bewildered adolescents, senile aged, and all who suffer from physical and social disease, as individuals loved by God? By failing to "see" them, we drive them to revolt and violence.

To realize life while we live it means to "see" others through the eyes of Jesus. The Christian Gospel, emphasizing, as it does, God's love for every human individual, bids us to take time to see one another. We, whose eyes have been opened from the blindness of alcohol abuse, are called to "see" one another this Advent-Christmas Season.

THE NEGOTIATION:

Will we "see" those with whom we come into contact this Christmas?

THE PRAYER:

Dear Lord, You have so loved the entire world that You sent Your Son. Help us to realize this Gift by seeing all your children as individuals whom You love. Amen.

THE READING: Titus: 2:11-14

DECEMBER 24

CHRISTMAS EVE

THE INSPIRATION:

"Joseph went up to . . . Bethlehem . . . and with him went Mary who was betrothed to him. She was pregnant, and while they were there the time came for her child to be born, and she gave birth to a son, her first-born. She wrapped him round, and laid him in a manger, because there was no room for them to lodge." --Luke 2:4-7

THE MEDITATION:

One of the things about Christmas Eve which strikes us alcohol abusers, is the number of Christmases we have been sober. Is this our first, fifth, tenth, twentieth? Whatever the number, we have every reason to rejoice and praise God for his mercy. In addition to reminiscing over our anniversaries of sobriety, we are overwhelmed with God's outpouring of love for all people which we celebrate.

And yet, within the Christmas Gospel itself, we are faced with the stark reality that the Christ Child was laid in a manger because there was no room for him in the inn. If we have no room for the Christ Child Christmas will be a disaster rather than a blessing. Charles Schultz in a comic strip has Charley Brown say, "Everything I do turns to disaster." Linus says, "You're the only person in the world who can take a wonderful thing like Christmas and turn it into a problem." Linus is wrong; Charley Brown is not the only one, we all have that option. But Linus goes on to read Luke 2:1-20, and Charley says, "Nothing is going to take my Christmas away from me." As we worship this Christmas let us hear the old, old story and sing the old carols with a new zest and freshness. Christ will be reborn in our hearts if we make room for him.

THE NEGOTIATION:

Will we let this Christmas be the most meaningful ever?

THE PRAYER:

Ah, dearest Jesus, Hold Child,
Make thee a bed, soft undefiled,
Within my heart, that it may be
A quiet chamber kept for thee. Amen. --Martin Luther

THE READING: Luke 2:1-20

DECEMBER 25

CHRISTMAS

THE INSPIRATION:

"So the world became flesh, he came to dwell among us, and we saw his glory, such glory as befits the Father's only Son, full of grace and truth." --John 1:14

THE MEDITATION:

The power of words has been so emphasized that we are tempted to think that language is all important in communication. In recent years, however, psychologists have demonstrated that non-verbal communication can and often does modify and override the literal meaning of our words. We sometimes think God's communication is primarily verbal. This is to misunderstand the Incarnation. That concept comes from the Latin word meaning "taking flesh." Incarnation means God's Word, Logos, Idea, taking flesh; more particularly, the communication of God in the human life of Jesus. Incarnation is the theological term for the historical event which took place in Bethlehem.

Christmas is a demonstration of God's non-verbal communication: God's body language. The verbal word, the Bible, tells of the mighty acts of God: Incarnation, Resurrection, the Outpouring of his Spirit. Through God's body language his Word is made flesh so that we can experience his love. Jesus not only spoke the Word of God—he is the Word of God. Our knowledge of God is incarnational. God is hidden in flesh,, in human form. God's spirit is in people.

An incarnational approach to life affects how we live, our life-style, our relationships, our drinking, how we perceive the world, how we determine our values and priorities; it is our response to God's communication as we seek to make our worship, our learning, our socializing, our serving become the flesh, bones, and blood of the Gospel in our world.

THE NEGOTIATION:

Will this Christmas bring us an Incarnational approach to life?

THE PRAYER:

Almighty God, You sent Your only Son as the Word of Life for our eyes to see and our ears to hear. Help us to believe with joy what the Scriptures proclaim. Amen.

THE READING: John 1:1-18

DECEMBER 26

ST. STEPHEN

THE INSPIRATION:

"Not only do we at the feast of Christmas celebrate at once Our Lord's Birth and his Death: but on the next day we celebrate the martyrdom of his first martyr, the blessed Stephen. Is it an accident, do you think, that the day of the first martyr follows immediately the day of the Birth of Christ? By no means. Just as we rejoice and mourn at once, in the Birth and in the Passion of Our Lord; so also, in a smaller figure, we both rejoice and mourn in the death of martyrs." --T. S. Elliot

THE MEDITATION:

Stephen was one of the seven deacons (Acts 6:5) appointed by the apostles, and the first Christian to die for his faith. In his death he closely imitated the death of Jesus, praying for his executioners and commending his spirit to the hands of God: "Receive my Spirit . . . Lord, do not hold this sin against them" (Acts 7:59-60).

The commemoration of the first Christian martyr on the day after Christmas may serve as an antidote for the sentimentality about Jesus which too easily marks that festival. We do, indeed, praise God that "away in a manger, no crib for his bed, the little Lord Jesus laid down his sweet head." But we must also remember that the little Lord Jesus grew up and commissioned us to carry on his mission in the world by taking up our crosses and following him. As that Christ Child is born in our hearts anew our commitment to his service is intensified. Without a renewed and deepened commitment, our celebration of Christmas is merely a sentimental birthday party for Jesus. Our growing serenity comes through commitment and service, not through a sentimental journey.

THE NEGOTIATION:

In retrospect, what has this Christmas meant to me?

THE PRAYER:

Grant us grace, O Lord, that like Stephen we may learn to love even our enemies and seek forgiveness for those who desire our hurt. Amen. —Collect for St. Stephen

THE READING: Acts 6:8-7:2a, 51-60

DECEMBER 27

ST. JOHN

THE INSPIRATION:

"Peter looked round, and saw the disciple whom Jesus loved following . . . 'Lord, what will happen to him?' Jesus said, 'If it should be my will that he wait until I come, what is it to you? Follow me.'"
—John 21:20-22

THE MEDITATION:

John the Divine, or the theologian, together with his brother James and Peter, formed the inner circle of Jesus' disciples. It is probably from a school of John that came the Fourth Gospel, the three epistles that bear his name, and the Book of Revelations. John has been traditionally assumed to be the "beloved disciple" of the Fourth Gospel. Tradition teaches that John went to Ephesus after Pentecost and there died a natural death in old age. John is the only one of Jesus' disciples not to die a martyr's death.

Commemorating St. John on the Second Day of Christmas reminds us of the continuing Incarnation of God's love in the world. God's love incarnate in us means not only sobriety and serenity, but also our being "christs" in the world. Having been saved by God's grace from a humiliating and painful death of alcohol abuse, we rejoice in anticipation for what God has in store for us. Long life or short life, the death of martyrs or from natural causes, whatever our future holds, we realize now how precious are the days and moments. We meditate on the life and message of Jesus, we practice the presence of God, we turn our lives and wills over to him, we equip ourselves for the task before us. With the Christmas bells ringing in our ears, the Christmas light shining in our eyes, the Christmas Gospel burning in our hearts, we go forth with peace, joy, and love as "christs" in God's world.

THE NEGOTIATION:

Is not the quality of our lives more important than their quantities?

THE PRAYER:

Merciful Lord, shine the brightness of Your light on us church so that all of us, instructed by the teachings of the apostles and evangelists, may walk in the light of Your truth and attain eternal life. Amen.

THE READING: John 21:20-25

DECEMBER 28

HOLY INNOCENTS

THE INSPIRATION:

"An angel of the Lord appeared to Joseph in a dream, and said to him, 'Rise up, take the child and his mother and escape with them to Egypt, and stay there until I tell you; for Herod is going to search for the child to do away with him . . . When Herod saw how the astrologer had tricked him he fell into a passion, and gave order for the massacre of all the children in Bethlehem . . ." --Matthew 2:13-16

THE MEDITATION:

The Holy Innocents were the children of Bethlehem, two years old and under, killed by King Herod's soldiers in his attempt to do away with the infant Jesus. Since they were killed for the sake of Jesus, the Church very early commemorated these Jewish babies as "the buds of the martyrs" killed soon after they appeared by "the frost of hate." Medieval commentators suggest that the three days following Christmas reveal the three faces of martyrdom: Stephen, the martyr in deed and in will; John, the martyr in will but not in deed; the Innocents, martyrs in deed but not in will.

On the Third Day of Christmas we mourn the slaughter of innocents throughout history: in Bethlehem, Wounded Knee, Auschwitz, London, Berlin, Hiroshima, Seoul, Mylai, Saigon, etc. This mourning can only drive us to deeper commitment to work for peace on earth and good will toward all people.

We also recall with remorse the suffering of the innocents that we brought on by our alcohol abuse: the anguish of our children, spouses, parents, and friends. We remember but we do not wallow in guilt; we seek to make amends, we seek forgiveness, we become reconciled with God, and we rise to deeper commitment to sobriety, serenity, and service.

THE NEGOTIATION:

Can we forgive ourselves for the innocent suffering we have brought to others?

THE PRAYER:

O God, Your innocent martyrs bore witness not by words but by their death. Grant that our way of life may give witness to the faith in You, which our words profess. Amen. --Collect for Holy Innocents

THE READING: Matthew 2:13-18

DECEMBER 29

CONFORMITY

THE INSPIRATION:

"It takes plenty of courage to live according to one's convictions. That is why it is always so difficult to break away from social conformity, to act differently from everyone else. And it is because everybody conforms to the "done thing" that it becomes so hard to depart from it. Thus society becomes a game of personages. 'Dare to detach yourself from the herd,' . . . As soon as a man obeys his inner call, he upsets the game and brings to light around him the persons buried beneath the personages." --Paul Tournier

THE MEDITATION:

As alcohol abusers, we have done enough conforming to our drinking culture. When we made a commitment to sobriety we became aware of the courage which is necessary not to conform to the whims of those who would "push" alcohol on us. We soon learn that to survive in a drinking culture with its many "pushers," we cannot conform to the "done thing".

Paul says, "Adapt yourselves no longer to the pattern of this world, but let your minds be remade and your whole nature thus transformed" (Romans 12:2). Our experience with conformity to and from drinking, helps us understand what Paul is talking about. Serenity enters the picture as we allow ourselves to be transformed by the power of God at work in us.

We are not personages; we are persons—persons with an inner call. It is this inner call which gives us the courage to detach ourselves from the herd and be the persons God means us to be. As we become more and more persons and less and less personages we discover that there is a contagious factor in our transformation. Not only do those around us display more personhood, but we see the personness in each individual we meet.

THE NEGOTIATION:

Are we winning the battle against conformity?

THE PRAYER:

O Lord, You have sent us into the world with the Gospel of Your Son. As we go forth into this world, we pray that we may not be of the world. Give us the courage to live according to our inner call. Amen.

THE READING: 1 Peter 1:13-25

DECEMBER 30

RESOLUTION

THE INSPIRATION:

"The only influence that can really upset the injustices and iniquity of men is the power that breathes in Christian tradition, renewing our participation in the Life that is the Life of men." --Thomas Merton

THE MEDITATION:

As the civil year draws to a close, our minds often turn toward the making of resolutions for the year ahead. As we take stock of the ending year, and a moral inventory of ourselves, we become aware of the fact that things and ourselves could be better. And so we make resolutions. AT the same time, we are painfully aware of our broken resolutions in the past. How many times did we resolve to stop abusing alcohol before that resolution became a reality for us? And what made the resolution we kept different from all the rest? Was it not that our successful resolution was not an item in and of itself, but rather the beginning of a process? The best word for that process is surrender. We do not surrender once and for all, but rather we begin surrendering our lives in participation in the Life that is the Light of the world.

Participation is the key word for successful resolutions. We participate in the world and we participate with God. We become involved with God in the struggle for the alleviation of injustice and iniquity. Resolution means surrender and surrender means participation in life with God.

All of our New Year's Resolutions for self improvement, if they are to be meaningful, must be supported by a foundation of surrender and participation in the Life of Christ. Let us resolve to keep the process of sobriety and serenity going through the practice of the presence of God.

THE NEGOTIATION:

What are our resolutions for the New Year?

THE PRAYER:

We thank You, O Lord, for the blessings of this year now drawing to a close. Keep us mindful of the injustice and iniquity in our world and our own shortcomings, and help us to participate in life with You. Amen.

THE READING: Revelation 21:1-7

DECEMBER 31

NEW YEAR's DAY

THE INSPIRATION:

"Listen with devotion to the Word of God, whether you have it in familiar conversation, with your spiritual friends, or in a sermon. Make all the profit of it you possibly can, and suffer it not to fall to the ground, but receive it into your heart as a precious balm . . . Always have at hand some book of devotion . . . and read a little in it every day, as if you were reading a letter sent to you from the saints in heaven to show you the way and encourage you to come thither." --Francis de Sales

THE MEDITATION:

We who have participated during the year in these daily devotions—inspirations, meditations, negotiations, and prayer—know by now their value for us. We have discovered that these daily periods of spiritual exercise have value not only in and of themselves, but pour over throughout each day as we have developed in the practice of the presence of God. We have discovered that the God who "plucks the world out of our hearts, hurls the world into our hearts where we and he together carry it in infinitely tender love. " We have contemplated the uniqueness of our calling as alcohol abusers. We have learned to look for and hear the Gospel in many places and situations. We have developed in our ability to live the life, message, and mission of Jesus Christ. Our commitment to sobriety and growth in serenity has deepened. We have experienced the glory of living the new life in the moment.

It has been a good year. We praise God for all his blessings. We look forward in joyful anticipation to the year ahead. There is much to be done in our world and in us. We go forth facing the challenges with hope, devotion, sobriety, and serenity.

THE NEGOTIATION:

Where have our daily devotions led us this year?

THE PRAYER:

We thank and praise You, O Lord, for your guiding presence during this year. Continue to bless us as we rededicate our lives to You in the year that lies before us. Amen.

THE READING: Psalm 98:1-9

46/P